Scribners

Swanbrooke Down

For Frank and Annie Holland

SWANBROOKE DOWN

A Century of Change in an English Village

◆

ROSAMOND RICHARDSON

With Illustrations
by Peter Firmin

Scribners

A Scribners Book

First published in Great Britain in 1990 by Scribners
a Division of Macdonald & Co (Publishers) Ltd
London & Sydney

Typeset by Leaper & Gard Limited, Bristol
Printed and bound in Great Britain by
Butler & Tanner Ltd, Frome and London

British Library Cataloguing in Publication Data
Richardson, Rosamond *1945–*
Swanbrooke Down : a century of change in an English village.
1. East Anglia. Social life, history
I. Title
942.6

ISBN 0 356 19070 6

Scribners
A Division of
Macdonald & Co (Publishers) Ltd
Orbit House
1 New Fetter Lane
London EC4A 1AR

A member of Maxwell Macmillan Pergamon Publishing Corporation

ACKNOWLEDGEMENTS

I am grateful to Rosemary Cheetham who put me on the trail of the idea for this book.

Thank you to all the 'voices', to the people who talked to me so willingly and openly, and without whom this book could never have happened. Particular thanks to Frank and Annie Holland, for their interest, encouragement and help over the years of writing; and to Win Bailey for her memorabilia. I owe a debt of gratitude, sadly posthumous but acknowledged to him before he died, to David Appleby, for all his help with background material, for detailed work with me on 'A Younger Generation', and for many fascinating discussions.

I am grateful to Sheila McIllwraith for her skillful editing. And my thanks to Alan Samson for his wholehearted support and enthusiasm, and for all his expert editorial help.

I am indebted to the authors of the following books for source material and inspiration while researching *Swanbrooke Down*:

Ronald Blythe: *Akenfield: Portrait of an English Village* (Penguin, 1969)

Emmanuel le Roy Ladurie: *Montaillou* (Penguin, 1978)

Spike Mays: *Reuben's Corner* (Robin Clark, 1981)

Howard Newby: *Country Life* (Wiedenfeld & Nicolson, 1987)
A Green and Pleasant Land? Century Hutchinson, 1979)

R.E. Pahl: *Patterns of Urban Life* (Longman, 1970)

Miss Read: *Affairs at Thrush Green* (Penguin, 1983)
At Home in Thrush Green (Penguin, 1985)
Return to Thrush Green (Penguin, 1978)

Flora Thompson: *Lark Rise to Candleford* (Century Hutchinson, 1989)

G.M. Trevelyan: *English Social History* (Pelican, 1964)

W.M. Williams: *The Sociology of an English Village: Gosforth* (Routledge and Kegan Paul, 1956)

One year in a village somewhere in East Anglia in the 1980s. The seasons turn from a mild autumn to a bitterly cold winter; from winter to spring, from spring to a fine summer. The villagers were interviewed through one such year, and their contributions make an unique document. This picture of village life is captured, like a photograph, in a moment of time; for even uniqueness is ephemeral.

Swanbrooke Down is a mirror of life anywhere in a small community, reflecting changes, never still, in essence as organic and as elusive as the stream that flows through Swanbrooke Down.

Contents

Swanbrooke Down

SWANBROOKE DOWN

Men make their homes where water is. Swanbrooke Down is no exception. Winter Water, as it is called by the locals, rises in Dickling Wood, a stretch of ancient forest beyond the neighbouring village of Elmshaw. It runs through the village, a narrow stream that swells after rain and reduces to a trickle in dry weather. The houses stand behind the stream on one side of the only road through the village, reached by little bridges with crisply-painted white palings. Picturesque indeed; dreadfully inconvenient if you are moving house or installing a new wardrobe. Wonderfully convenient if you are playing Poohsticks.

The banks are thick with long grasses, willowherb, vervain and rushes. The villagers have planted spring bulbs along the verges, so that at blossom time the street is like a picture postcard of the

English countryside at its most idyllic. The sound of running water, whether trickling or rushing, makes incessant music in the stillness; for this is a quiet place, as yet denied the horrors of heavy traffic, rush hours, aeroplanes and other noisy paraphernalia of urban England in the late twentieth century.

Things have changed, of course. Things change all the time, even in a quiet village. The face of the village has altered unrecognisably since its recording in the Domesday book. Its fortunes have ebbed and flowed; generations have been good or wicked, generous or acquisitive, churning a rhythmical pattern unchanging in its essence. Like the water, never still, impelled by its own energy, going who knows where and who knows why.

Houses stand where houses have stood since the eleventh century; they harbour ghosts, mostly good, friendly ghosts who faintly mock the strivings and posings of the present occupants; they have seen it all before. Today's dwellers do not stop to think that nothing is new; it seems to them unique and unprecedented. The ghosts know better. There are one or two bad ghosts though, looming suddenly to frighten, wishing harm – restless, troubled souls who walk where dogs, hair rigid on their backs, will not pass, and where horses shy and canter away terrified.

In spite of its prettiness Swanbrooke Down is no rural idyll preserved in a time capsule. Nowadays it is partly a commuter village, with a contingent of folk who work locally, and a residue of retired old-timers who have lived there all their lives and who remember the First World War and how they lived then: without radio, electricity or the motor car, with no sanitation or running water, just as people had lived for centuries before under feudal lords. They remember the last Lord of the Manor, they recall the horse-drawn harvest carts, gleaning in the fields for corn to feed the chickens, the pig-killing in the yard, the blacksmith at the forge, the local fairs. Arguably they have seen more changes in three-quarters of a century than any of their ancestors.

Possibly Swanbrooke Down is a 'typical' English village with its church, post office, pub and chapel, its parish council, its WI and its bi-monthly *Village News.* It is prettier than average, peaceful, friendly, not too remote – on the surface many people's idea of a perfect place to live. Scratch that surface though, and you find a diversity of human experience too complex to be called typical.

Apparently, however, life goes on here as 'normal' for a village in the 1980s. The postmistress, Pauline the Post as we call her, delivers the mail, starting out at about 7.30 a.m. on her walk around the hundred or so houses, whatever the weather. A few pale commuters yawn their way to their cars; children are bundled on to the school bus by bleary mothers. The village begins to stir, but not in a rush. You seldom see anyone running in Swanbrooke Down. Just the occasional follower of fashion jogging.

So starts the average day, if there is such a thing. All life is here, so it seems, with its predictable and universal energy. The surface changes, styles of life may change, but the underlying humanness we call human nature appears not to, much. Yet for all the sameness and banality, it has a fascination and uniqueness; in all its detail it seems out of the ordinary. And so it is, and so it is not.

SWANBROOKE DOWN AND ITS SURROUNDINGS

The village of Swanbrooke Down nestles in a small valley on the westerly borders of East Anglia, about forty miles from London. The soil is clay on chalk, ideal for wheat and barley so long as it remains well-fertilised – although after several decades of intensive cereal cropping bald patches are appearing and the chalk is showing through. Where the land is left to itself, in rare pockets of spinney or disused quarry, wild flowers of the chalk flourish – purple milk-vetch, sainfoin, rock rose and mist-blue scabious. But these are sanctuaries in an area largely taken over by agribusiness.

The countryside is a gently rolling landscape of large fields, occasional hedgerows and groups of trees, under wide skies. In spring, fields of brilliant yellow rape radiate their colour between young barley and wheat. Edged ethereally with white cow-parsley, and under a blue May sky, the road to the neighbouring market town of Kings Tarrant is a pleasant one. The narrow lanes wind hedgerow-linked up out of the valley past the village church, down a long, steep hill towards the railway station. At certain times of day these lanes are busy – the morning and evening rush hours, the school runs, the cyclists' rallies on Sundays. Otherwise they are quiet, for Kings Tarrant is an undemanding place where life has a measured pace and people still smile at you from behind the shop counter. For centuries the town has been a stronghold of Quakerism, and something of this permeates its atmosphere, in spite of the magnificent Anglican church. It is one of East Anglia's finest 'wool' churches, made extra prosperous by the saffron trade of the sixteenth and seventeenth centuries. It is set on a hill overlooking the high street, with an elegant spire and tall slim leaded windows of clear glass.

Tuesdays and Saturdays are market days; the streets are crowded with people, giving it an almost festive feeling. The market square is closed to vehicles so that traders can put up their stalls, covered with brightly-covered striped awnings, around the memorial cross where usually cars are parked. The library, the DIY and the chemist are set for busy days on Tuesdays and Saturdays, the supermarket queues are longer than usual. People stop to chat; clearly this is a local market town where folk are familiar with each other.

Returning to Swanbrooke Down by another route, we leave the main road and pass under a motorway bridge – both road and rail link to London. The road begins to twist and narrow as we approach the crest of the hill; on a sharp bend at the very top is a wild patch where, in high summer, briar roses festoon the hedges and bee-orchids are to be found in the waving grasses. Slowing as we descend the curling hill, we enter the village of Little Bendysh, passing the pub and the Hall and a row of council houses, before turning off to Swanbrooke Down.

Here the road narrows dramatically; trees hang over the road until they almost meet in the middle. At the other end of this green tunnel the fields unfold either side of the lane, low-lying land once meadow and pasture, now ploughed to its boundary hedges and sown with beans sometimes, sometimes potatoes, more often with wheat and barley.

The road straightens as we approach the village, Poor Street it was called in days long forgotten. It leads past Sparrows Farm and its cottage, now desirable thatched residences, and the interlinking modern houses built over the past twenty or thirty years. Neat flower-gardens, hedge-lined, trim and pretty. We come to a T-junction and here we pause at the ivy-clad bridge where Winter Water runs under the road.

To the left the road is signposted to Haverley, Swanbrooke Down's closest neighbour, now a large and rambling village with a cricket team and a modern, efficiently-run supermarket. But Swanbrooke Down still has only three hundred inhabitants, no shop, no cricket team nor even a green to play it on – that was gobbled up by builders long ago. The village seems to slumber now, at mid-morning; it harbours a blessed peace wherein, behind cottage doors, all sorts of useful activity may be going on, undisturbed by traffic, noise, or crowds.

From the T-junction you can get a pretty clear idea of the layout of the village. Up towards Haverley lies the manor house, Domesday-listed, with its outlying farm cottages. No longer does a squire grace this fine estate, but a property-developer who has sold off the land and built a jaccuzi and a hangar for his helicopter. Along to the right is what might be called the main street, as it boasts the pub, the post office and most of the cottages.

At the end of this street the road divides: to the left it meanders past Cold Spring Farm, to Grinchells Manor and on to the hamlet of Elmshaw. Just beyond the secret garden of Grinchells a tiny lane, a no-through road, leads up Mouse Hill past a couple of houses to Foulmire End. Buried up an overgrown lane, in the shelter of the dense woods, stands an almost derelict cottage. The thatch is balding, the walls are damp and beginning to crumble. Yet once it was a beautiful house – too large to call a cottage – looking out beyond its now overgrown garden to meadows, sheltered by woodland at the back. Wildlife abounds here – the green lane is a sanctuary for wild flowers, insects and birds.

The place in not uninhabited. A man lives here alone, who used to be the village blacksmith. The yard which once was teeming with life, raging furnace and the sound of iron upon iron, is still now. There are only echoes of suntanned muscled days. Now he tinkers in what remains of the forge, inventing strange machines, with the birds as his companions.

The gate at the end of the path running up to the front door is rotting on its hinges, and inside the house it is bitterly cold all year round. There is no running hot water, only cold, and the toilet consists of a hole in the ground in a smelly privy several yards from the back door. Mice run amok in the rafters. Yet the blacksmith is not a poor man. He has chosen solitude and simplicity as his way of life.

Back in Swanbrooke Down the villagers – albeit most of them now urbanites – have chosen to adapt their conception of the rural idyll to a modern, relatively affluent, convenience-laden lifestyle. The signpost where the street divides tells all, for it gives the station as two miles distant. A hundred years ago everyone who lived in the village worked in the village; nowadays many hop into their cars and onto the train, gasp through their working day in the polluted air of the city, and return relieved to slow sanity and clean air.

The signpost points over a bridge built for the village by the last lord of the manor in the 1920s, towards the road that rises steeply past the church. Around the corner it continues up to Hawthorn Hill's council estate, a semi-circle of fifties houses set on the crest looking down over wheat fields into the nestling village.

THE VILLAGE IN THE PAST

FROM DOMESDAY TO THE LAST OF THE LORDS OF THE MANOR

The date is 1066. Swanbrooke Down lies cradled in its valley, the land around far more densely wooded than it is today. The stream runs the same course, but there are no roads, no bridges, no cottages along its banks. There is a small church with a round tower, and a Norman font which still stands at the west end of the nave. But St Michael's will not be completed until 1371. A landmark now, but in 1066 just a tiny chapel on a rise between two of the five manors that made up the village of Swanbrooke Down.

William of Normandy's men were acquisitioning land throughout the country, persuading Saxons with established rights to manorial farms to surrender their land and swear allegiance to the conquering king. The chief of these lords in Swanbrooke Down was Aelfric Wand, who held the most important farm, now called Mumford Hall. Aelfric was to confront a Norman nobleman called Eudo Dapifer.

The archives tell us that 'this Eudo Dapifer was son of Hubert de Rie, a noble Norman in great request with William the Conqueror. He was steward of this house, founder of the Abbey of St John the Baptist at Colchester; and there lyes interred 1120. He left issue one sole daughter and heir named Margaret that became wife of William de Mandervill by whom he had Geffrey de Mandeville first. By this match a vast estate was brought in to the family.'

So Aelfric was forced to capitulate. But he turned defeat to some advantage, unlike other Saxons who forfeited all their possessions along with their livelihoods: he is soon to be found working for William his conqueror in Suffolk, as reeve in charge of a number of Crown manors.

His fellow-landowners in Swanbrooke Down, possibly less

enterprising men, were ousted by the Norman lords. Ulmar, Aelfric's nearest neighbour at Eineswarda (now Cold Spring Farm), surrendered his lands to a certain William de Warren. His neighbours Goduin Sech at Bledstowes, and Grinchel at Mynchens, were taken over by Robert de Gernon. The great manor of Wyggefosse, held at the time by Boso, 'a free man', capitulated to Geffrey de Magnaville, and Peverells – now Pebblegate Farm, next to the church – held by Leofwin, was forfeited to Roger de Arburville.

The Domesday book gives us a clear idea of how manors in Swanbrooke Down – Swaynbroka to the Normans – were managed. Here are the entries for Mumford Hall and Grinchells Manor:

> Eudo holds SWAYNBROKA in lordship, which Aelfric Wand held as a manor, for 2 hides less 15 acres.
> Always 2 villagers; 7 smallholders, 2 slaves.
> Then and later 2 ploughs in lordship, now 1.
> Always 2 men's ploughs.
> Woodland, 20 pigs; meadow, 10 acres.
> Value 100s.
>
> GRINKELS
> Picot holds SWAYNBROKA from Robert, which Grinkel held as a manor, for 1 hide less 8 acres. Robert has it by exchange.
> Now 4 smallholders. Always 2 slaves. 1 plough.
> Meadow, 6 acres. Now 2 cattle. Always 12 pigs; 32 sheep. Now 2 beehives.
> Value 20s.

The Domesday book goes on to mention Plash Wood: people in Swanbrooke Down today, who call it Splash Wood, remember the ancient woodland with a mound in the centre surrounded by a moat – probably the remains of a medieval motte and bailey. The wood was bulldozed in the 1960s to make space for more wheat, and not a trace remains. But a legend endures: local folk say there was a tunnel down from the wood to the oldest pub in the village, the Green Man, although nobody is quite clear why. There was a landlord once who was involved in smuggling, it would seem;

hundreds of stone bottles were found sealed up in a cellar at the tunnel entrance. When opened, the wine effervesced to the ceiling. A local woman's version of this tunnel is that it ran to Little Bendysh and that the future King Charles II used it as a hideout.

In the eleventh century, Swanbrooke Down's five manors were in the hands of Norman lords. Mumford Hall passed through numerous families, seldom for more than two or three generations. Other halls sprang up in medieval times, now lost without trace: Frogs Hall where Bledstowes used to be – on what are now windswept arable fields; High Hall, on Mouse Hill, overlooked Foulmire End for a couple of centuries; now it's just a memory. The names changed with their owners – Wyggefosse became Stocks Farm after Humfrey de Stokella in the fourteenth century, and still bears that name. Sparrows Farm, to which one Richard gave his name in 1325, is still known as such.

Grinchells Manor, still named after its owner in Edward the Confessor's time, became part of the endowment of a Suffolk nunnery, and was attached to the abbey at Kings Tarrant in the fourteenth century. Like Wyggefosse, it had its own chapel and said its own masses. After the dissolution of the monasteries in 1538 the manor was granted to a favourite nobleman of King Henry VIII and passed by marriage to the Duke of Norfolk. He eventually sold it to the then owner of Mumford Hall, and Grinchells settled to its old existence of farmhouse and dairy.

Many medieval manor houses had their own private chapels in which to say mass, and although remains of a small Norman church were discovered in the nineteenth century during reconstruction work, St Michael's church was not granted patronage until 1371. The nave and chancel are thirteenth century, and during the reign of Henry VIII the north aisle was built by one Thomas Alderton, fishmonger, of London; he also founded a chantry and bequeathed a peal of six bells. Up until the dissolution of the monasteries the patrons of St Michael's were the Abbot and Convent of Kings Tarrant, but under the Catholic reign of Mary Tudor the vicar of Swanbrooke Down was deprived of his benefice.

Patronage was restored to the lord of the manor in 1572 – this was Francis Gilbert, who owned Mumford Hall and Grinchells.

In 1632 patronage passed to the king, Charles I, because Gilbert's son was a minor, but it reverted to the family in 1662. The parish register dates from 1690. In 1721 the patrons were still local men, and this remained the tradition right up until the death of the last of the lords of the manor, Robert Stockbridge, in 1925. The patronage was eventually made over to the Warden and Fellows of an Oxford college.

One of the most eye-catching things in the church is a huge Elizabethan funeral monument, like a six-poster bed, dating from 1592. Two life-sized figures lie upon it, Francis Gilbert of Mumford Hall and his lady wife. Around the lower borders kneel their six children; four of the little statues, the boys, were decapitated by an act of vandalism inflicted by Cromwell's men in their Puritan purges while they were stationed at Kings Tarrant. A portrait of one of their descendants, Sir John Gilbert, in the opposite aisle, dated 1607, bears this inscription: 'Love drawes more neer the life then Paynters art, This lyves but in your eyes; you in my hart.'

Two other memorials attract attention: the effigy of a fifteenth-century priest, Benedict Crossley, who lived from 1435–56; and the fine brass of a knight, Matthew Lance, dated 1439. When the church underwent major restoration in 1855 two skeletons were found under the altar tomb of Squire Lance: a man and a woman. The man's legs were crossed, but neither body was in a coffin. They were laid east-west, not parallel with the church wall, but diagonally across the chancel. But the altar tomb was so decayed that it could not be preserved.

There is a family vault under the sanctuary, and thereby hangs a tale. Mumford Hall was in the hands of the Gardiner-Clarke family for several generations during the nineteenth century, and their remains lie in this vault. Tablets on the chancel wall record their names and dates. The last tablet, however, placed there by her nephew several years after her death, discloses that Elspeth Gardiner-Clarke, the last of her line, was buried 'not far from here'; her remains are not in the vault. Her gravestone, a tall, polished granite cross, stands outside the west window under a yew tree, inscribed 'in affectionate memory'.

The story is that Mrs Gardiner-Clarke, who appears to have been not entirely of sound mind, fell out with the vicar over where she and her entourage should sit during church services. When she died, the vicar said he could not find the key to the vault (it was whispered that he had thrown it, irretrievably, through the grating). Thus her memorial stands apart, a gaunt reminder of an angry feud. Her unquiet spirit still walks, they say, through the gardens at Mumford Hall.

There is a stained-glass window in the south aisle of the church depicting the Sower and the Reaper, 'in loving memory of Robert Stockbridge of Mumford Hall in this parish who died on June 29th 1925 aged 90'. He bought the manor in 1898, on his retirement from a barge business on the Thames, and lived there for twenty-seven years. He was to be the last of the feudal lords of the manor; when he died medieval society came to an end in Swanbrooke Down. His estate – the village – was sold up in lots, and the cottages fell into private ownership for the first time in their history.

The oldest residents of Swanbrooke Down still remember Robert Stockbridge, and many mention him riding though the village in his coach and pair. His horse-keeper's daughter, Ada Brown, showed me a photograph of him which she kept proudly in a special folder, along with others of her father beside his great working horses. Robert Stockbridge's face wears a calm but determined expression; he has a penetrating gaze and a firm mouth, hair receding at the temples, long 'sideboards' along his jawbone in the late Victorian fashion. There is a gentleness and dignity about his demeanour, and Ada's memories are of a kindly, considerate man whom she respected greatly. His benevolence is still mentioned – he built several houses in the village, and constructed road-bridges to replace the fords which flooded regularly. He gave the men a harvest supper every year, and his wife held a Christmas party for the children. She, according to her husband, 'took to the life and the people about. She took charge of the welfare of the village, and although delicate, was not happy unless we had a house full of people'.

When Robert Stockbridge bought Mumford Hall it stood in 1000 acres of farmland, and he became quite a renowned agriculturalist locally rearing stock, winning prizes for cattle and pigs. The house itself, standing just outside the village on a rise, is substantial, but not overwhelmingly stately, surrounded by parkland and outbuildings. In its very early days it was a favourite dowry in the royal gift of the House of Lancaster; in the thirteenth and fourteenth centuries it was in the chamberlainship of the King's Exchequer. At the other end of its history, its grounds were used for training and drilling men for the First World War, and during the Second World War it was occupied by a nursery school evacuated from London.

The house and its 'lord' were central to the lives of the villagers for nine centuries, both in economic terms – the men's employment depended upon it – and in social terms. From Domesday to 1925 Swanbrooke Down was a feudal village. After the First World War, society finally shook off this hierarchical, albeit benevolent, structure. Social mobility is now the order of the day, and the villagers in Swanbrooke Down are more affluent than they have ever been.

Feudalism evokes images of a rural, agricultural way of life, some idyllic, some not so pleasant. Concepts of village life are frequently steeped in mythology; images of the rustic existence are usually coloured by wistful nostalgia. Picture an old gaffer, the 'village character', standing by the lych-gate; thatch and roses, honeysuckle and green lanes; picket fences and a homely inn. A place to 'get away from it all', where time is embalmed, where 'merrie England' exists as chronicled, where the religion of the countryside holds sway under a benevolent godhead in the manor house.

Such a vision was partly invented by the architects and landscape gardeners of the eighteenth century, and encouraged by the novelists of the nineteenth, in response to a particular social climate. Those eighteenth-century architects took it upon themselves to rearrange nature. They designed views from the manor house by moving the farmyard – in some cases the entire village –

out of sight, allowing a few 'merrie rusticks' to wander across the park at a safe distance to impart bucolic flavour. Trollope, George Eliot and Jane Austen imprinted this image on their readers' imaginations, in reaction, no doubt, to the awful truth. Their picture was quite a different one from William Cobbett's whose *Rural Rides* brought him into uncompromising contact with this idyll in all its misery and poverty.

After all, life on the land – for the village's *raison d'être* is agriculture – was far from idyllic. Farm labourers were for centuries not much more than slaves. Freedom and self-respect were the reward only of the few craftsmen (if they were fortunate in their squire), the blacksmiths and wheelwrights and the like, whose skills were essential. They all worked on subsistence wages, in cottages tied to their means of living which could be demolished if the lord so pleased. Beggars could be deported to the next parish, poachers transported to the other side of the world. Once their useful working life was over, the workhouse lay in store for their retirement, hideous places which housed the mad as well as the senile.

The women were also slaves to incessant hard labour; washing by hand; carrying pails of milk from the farm; keeping the fires going all year round; cooking on a meagre budget for their hungry families; sewing and mending; caring for innumerable children and coping with regular pregnancies and early child-deaths, as poignantly chronicled in the parish registers. They were tied to their cottages, in a monotony relieved only by gossip and itinerant traders who called with the necessities of domestic life. This rural idyll was: going to the toilet in a privy in the garden; going to bed early to save lamp-oil and fire fuel; washing in cold well-water; being bitterly cold and damp for many months of the year; and, in return for this, touching their caps, or bobbing to the schoolteacher, the parson (who in most cases didn't help much to boost their self-esteem since the church was in league with the manor house), and the squire.

The horizon of this lifetime was the brow of the hill or the hedge along the farthest field. Within living memory, an occasional trip to the local town or outlying villages in the carrier's cart was the only extension to this universe. Perhaps a Sunday school outing to the seaside once a year, by cart to the railway station. One Laurie Lagden of Swanbrooke Down, who died only a decade ago aged ninety, was born on a farm at Foulmire End, and lived there for the rest of his life. He went to school in Swanbrooke Down, worked in the neighbourhood, and seldom put foot over the county border some five miles distant. He had no hobbies, although he read a newspaper. He kept four cats for company. According to the denizens of Swanbrooke, he was a difficult, bad-tempered man with not a good word for anything or anyone. Is he that gaffer by the lychgate? The invading townies (for such were they perceived to be by the likes of Laurie) saw such a character as a clod, a butt for sharper wits. But as often as not, having taken him for a cross-grained simpleton with an indecipherable accent, they were upset to find that they had been sized up by him as succinctly and with as little charity.

'Merrie England' is always one stage further back in history. The centuries have witnessed the manorial system, villeinage, virgates, enclosures, the burden of the everlasting poor and the inexorable drift to the towns during the Industrial Revolution. Goldsmith's 'The Deserted Village' has immortalised this nadir of the agricultural community.

The fortunes of the village were to change with the introduction of the internal combustion engine. They were, as always, moulded by economic forces. The motor car, new industry, urban culture, a new population, better standards of education, and the widening of social horizons, have all contributed to the immense, and relatively rapid, changes in Swanbrooke Down during the twentieth century. From scythe to combine-harvester; from appalling poverty to social security; from an inward-looking agricultural community to an urbanised commuter-culture. In that span, electricity, mains water, drainage, local services, roads, public transport, radio and television, telephones, computers and fax machines have replaced the do-it-yourself, self-sufficient life the cottagers led at the turn of the century.

For all that, a kind of 'community spirit' still exists in Swanbrooke Down. Village life is still quieter, cleaner and more pleasant than its urban counterpart; it is still in great demand. The price of progress is that the countryside has been tamed, it is no longer a free and natural habitat. The land is heavily cultivated around the village, yet as it nestles in its hollow under a wide East Anglian sky, surrounded by sweeping wheatfields in all their seasonal moods, Swanbrooke Down still has its special beauty.

The life of the village rumbles on, for the most part oblivious of its past, yet inextricably linked with what has gone before. Traces linger in the memory ... Shadows of the past flit across the stream of village life as it continues into the twenty-first century.

THE VILLAGE STREET

Walking through Swanbrooke Down on a late winter evening the sky is clear and bright. It has been a day of exquisite clarity, rare in our winter months, with pale sunshine all day, the air crisp and cold. The sinking sun turns to amber behind a line of trees, silhouetting them in perfect detail against low wisps of cloud; they are etched down to the last twig, as black as black on the skyline. It grows colder. We need to walk briskly, hands firmly in pockets.

The light is fading fast. Everyone is indoors, and we meet nobody. Windows light up, curtains are drawn. The first wood fires of the evening are lit; thin curls of smoke drift from cottage chimneys. The only sound is the swishing murmur of Winter Water underneath the bridge. An owl hoots from the wood on the hill.

As we walk into the village we pass Wilf and Dora's place, a long thatched cottage that housed three families in days they remember, days of working the land with horse and plough, of maypole dancing, fairs and harvest festivals. Days of grim cold and damp, outside lavatories and oil lamps. Wilf still has his first crystal radio set on the sideboard, an object of reverence to the younger generation. They will be sitting by their fireside now, reading, until Dora rises to prepare supper.

Across the road the Colbrookes are listening to the six o'clock news, curtains not yet drawn. Their semi-detached cottage was built by Robert Stockbridge in the 1920s, a plain but pleasing enough design – above all, from their point of view, easy to run; they have retired here from the busy village shop in Haverley. The gas fire is lit and Margery has just come in from an Over Sixties meeting for which she had prepared much of the food. She needs to put her feet up in front of the television before getting their meal; Percy will soon amble down to the pub to meet his friends for a leisurely drink before supper.

The pub is quiet tonight; the only lights are upstairs. Derek the publican and Linda his wife are resting before opening time. The car-park is empty, but by the end of the evening his clients will be parking halfway up the street. Across the road we can see Pauline upstairs in the post office, cleaning out her bed-and-breakfast quarters: she must be expecting a guest.

Walking past the big house on the left where the Gawthrops live, and Clarice's gingerbread cottage on the right, we hear a piano playing. Chopin, and rather well played. Grandpa Walsh is practising for the concert on Saturday; we can see him through the high modern picture-window of Apple Tree House. Next door the strident screams of children interrupt the evening peace.

This is the young end of the village – it is just the way it has turned out. Some of the young families live in original farm cottages newly converted, extended and centrally heated, others in the new houses on what was the farmyard of Pebblegate Farm. In the old days there were just barns and two tiny thatched cottages – and rats. Today there are several quite large, expensive houses with tidy gardens and double garages.

Over the second bridge we go, on to the green and up to the church. St Michael's is by far the largest building in the village, and perhaps the least populous apart from its dead. Its sprawling churchyard houses silent families – the Cakebreads, the Gapeses, the Bushes, the Middleditches. It is a peaceful place. In summer old roses hang over the porch with their heavy scent. Tonight the graveyard is leafless and dark.

There is no street lighting in Swanbrooke Down. Unless the night is moonlit you need a torch to walk down the street – the darkness can be like a curtain, thick as velvet. This evening, however, there is still a vestige of twilight as we walk up

Hawthorn Hill and out of the village by the Kings Tarrant road, to complete our round. Passing the council houses at the top of the hill we spy Sidney in his back yard, humping coal into a scuttle. Edith Spooner draws her curtains stiffly and returns to her armchair in front of the television. We take the road back past Grimstone Hall Farm, where Lilian Drayton saw her ghosts, past the rambling farmhouse at Grinchells Manor with its secret garden, where Timothy, last of a long line of Goodwins, was born, and back down into the village street. In half an hour we have passed all the cottages and houses in the village. Back to Holly Cottage, briskly now, to a welcoming log fire and a mug of tea.

THE VOICE OF A VILLAGE

THE WAY WE LIVED THEN

WILF AND DORA MIDDLEDITCH

Jobbing builder and wife

Wilf and Dora live in Lagden's, a rambling thatched cottage by the ivy-clad bridge. The Lagden family used to populate Swanbrooke Down by the score – in 1858 there were twenty-eight of them in the village; Dora is the last remaining member of her family.

The garden is planted with unusual old roses, Wilf's passion. Now, in early November, one late rose hangs forlorn in the chill sunlit afternoon. Low light filters through the leaves, illuminating their rusty and earthenware colours. Slight dampness rises from the sleepy ground, Michaelmas daisies and white anemones droop their wet leaves among bare brown stems, waiting to be cleared for winter. An ancient wheelbarrow full of fallen leaves rests against the pear tree; there is a lingering smell of bonfire smoke. Three beehives stand by the vegetable plot, for Wilf is an expert beekeeper, but they are dormant now. The only sounds to be heard are muffled drips, and the murmur of Winter Water alongside the garden.

Wilf and Dora have lived in Swanbrooke Down most of their lives – over seventy years. Wilf was a jobbing builder and an engineer until he retired two years ago; Dora has devoted her time to being wife, mother, housekeeper and companion. They are gentle folk, always ready to stop and pass the time of day. They live very much as they always have, with no central heating and few mod cons – Dora still does her washing by hand, on a Monday morning. They are content with the basic requirements, and contentment is a word they use a lot. Their property, at today's prices, would be worth a quarter of a million pounds. That would not particularly impress Wilf and Dora.

We sat around their living-room table, a coal and log fire flickering in the tiny black grate. The room was square, quite small, low-ceilinged; a flowering geranium – Dora's speciality – stood on the window-sill. Evening light slanted through the leaded panes and the lamp in the corner threw soft light into the darkening room. Everything in the room was simple – Wilf made the furniture decades ago: a gate-legged table with straight-backed chairs, a solid sideboard, a china cabinet covered with a runner embroidered by Dora. Fading patchwork cushions in the armchairs, photographs around the walls, ornaments on the mantelpiece. A small television stood in the corner, an old radio on the sideboard. Everything was clean and neat and plain.

From time to time during the evening Wilf limped into the next room searching out treasures to show me – photographs dating back to the turn of the century, a pair of black leather ankle boots his cousin used to wear, primly laced and with steel tips on the soles and heels, made by the village shoemaker Mr Nightingale. And his first crystal radio set which he made in 1925. I was not allowed to go away without a jar of Wilf's honey, either. They talked nostalgically, and not without humour, about seventy-odd years in Swanbrooke Down.

Darvel was all meadow

Wilf Things changed so much in the thirties, what with the radio and the motor car. In our early days it was much the same as it had been for hundreds of years. After the First World War, Jack was as good as his master – he had gone to war and seen new horizons. He wasn't content to be tied to the land any more. There weren't the men about, either, so many had been killed. For a time jobs were easier to get, and women were beginning to work as well.

The war memorial, by the churchyard gate, was given to the village by Robert Stockbridge. It is simply a massive stone which, until 1920, had lain in a spinney near the dairy at Mumford Hall. Inset is a piece of slate on which are inscribed, by a local stonemason, the name of the eight villagers who fell in the First World War. It was carried to the churchyard on a timber-whim – a vehicle for transporting fallen trees. A small group of elderly villagers gather in front of it every Remembrance Sunday.

Forty-three men of Swanbrooke Down, out of a population of around three hundred, went to France. Eight were killed in action. One Leslie Baker, born in 1892, had been recently converted to the Methodist faith by an evangelist called Gypsy Smith, and taught Samuel Gapes in Sunday school. Sam is one of Swanbrooke Down's late lamented 'characters'. His brother Horace joined the Eighth Cycling Battalion of the Essex Territorial Regiment and was severely wounded in the head at the Somme. He returned to Swanbrooke Down a changed young man from the fit farmhand who had been captain of the cricket team. He was unable to work again, and apart from helping out in the Dog and Duck from time to time, the rest of his days were spent at home, tended by a loving wife. Leonard Nightingale, son of the shoemaker, was killed in action after winning a medal at the Battle of Mons.

Wilf I was born in 1911 in a cottage just a mile from here, in the grounds of Little Bendysh Hall. We had quite a happy childhood – my father must have been a little better off than most people who worked on the farms, because he was head poultryman. It was a seven-day-a-week job, so he was bound to get more money. We were the only working-class people I know of that went for a week's holiday at the seaside. We went to Clacton twice, and Brighton once. But my father became ill just before the First World War, and things got harder. So my mother went to work in the Hall – she was cook; she didn't have to live in – our cottage was only about a hundred yards from the house.

We didn't notice the war really, the hardships. Afterwards, when you get older, you think about it, but as children we were quite happy. We didn't have much in the way of toys, but we didn't need them. We had the run of the farm, the run of all Little Bendysh which was three farms, and nobody chased you off.

We didn't vandalise things, but we got into mischief as children do. At playtime, our playground was the lane that runs up behind the Hall, and we used to go up to the top of the lane – it was like open roadway then. When the bell went, we wouldn't go back, and Miss Larkin would come up the lane after us. We used to go back through the rectory garden so she didn't see us, go into school, ring the bell, sit down and wait till she came back!

That's about all the mischief we got up to. She was a funny old girl. She used to make porridge on the school stove. And you know the pointer you used to point at the blackboard? We used to push it up the chimney. And if one of the Jacksons – they were a pretty riotous family – was being grumbled at, they'd throw the inkwells at her! I was only eight when the school closed; we never learned much – Miss Larkin was just the one teacher. After that nine of us came up to Swanbrooke Down school from Little Bendysh.

Swanbrooke Down school, a 'national school', was founded in 1844 at the cost of £314 15s 7d, the idea being to put a stop to the country-wide practice of using child labour in the fields. In 1871 it became a Church of England school, and by 1919 it boasted ninety pupils. Robert Stockbridge was one of the school managers, and Mrs Stockbridge used to call and leave instructions that the children could collect a 'penny poke' of sweets from Miss Giles's shop after school. The shop was one of two in Swanbrooke Down at that time, a tiny thatched cottage overlooking the church green.

The school building, on the other side of the green, had flint walls and a slate roof. Originally it was one room only, but in 1908 a soundproof partition was put up to divide infants from seniors. Many pupils went on to local grammar schools, so evidently the standard of education was reasonably high.

In 1949 the building was declared unsafe, and much to the sadness of the villagers the school was closed. It was sold for £125 in 1954, and eventually demolished. Its site became part of the garden of Pebblegate farm.

Wilf We had to walk about a mile and a half to school, and in most weathers. If it was very rough the foreman at Little Bendysh Hall would get his horse out – it was between a pony and a cart horse; he'd put it into a big trap and take us to school. We didn't often walk along the road, we came along the river, sailing tins or getting in the water! We'd follow Winter Water upstream from Bendysh, through Poor Street Field as it was called then, and into

Swanbrooke Down. We called the stream Winter Water because it dried up in summer and was swollen in winter. We'd arrive soaking wet and have to hang our socks on the fender in front of the big boiler. That was all the heating there was. Sometimes our sandwiches got wet too – there were no school dinners so we took our own.

Swanbrooke Down school was nearly as bad as Bendysh. We did as we liked, more or less. Playtime we'd be up the Elmshaw Lane when the bell went, and we'd saunter back. But when Miss Pumfrey came, we altered our hand, I'll tell you. She wasn't unkind, but she was very strict. You had to stop on the church green at playtime then, you didn't wander off. She came out, blew the whistle once, and you had to line up. Then she blew it again and you had to march in, boys in the boys' porch on the right, girls in the girl's porch. We had reading and 'riting and 'rithmetic. We got to the highest standard you could get up to there, most of us anyway.

You had to touch your hat to the schoolmistress, the vicar and the lord of the manor, or else you were severely reprimanded – 'caught a cold in school' so to say. We had the cane – not real birching, but you really felt in disgrace if you got the cane. Your name would go in the punishment book for the inspectors to see.

Dora The girls didn't get the cane.
Wilf I got it though: I had to go and apologise to Miss Giles for throwing somebody's cap in her garden. I didn't do so bad out of it in the end, because she gave me four toffees! She was lovely like that. It was something to have four toffees then.
Dora She was a very kind-hearted person – she would often say, 'I'll give you an extra one for luck'. Ever so generous, she was.
Wilf But we watched our ps and qs with that Miss Pumfrey!
Dora We girls used to walk three miles to Lillingford to learn cookery.
Wilf The boys didn't learn carpentry or metal work or anything like that, it was reading, writing, arithmetic, and geography and history. We had to find out how to do the practical things at home.

Miss Pumfrey used to do things with us for Christmas. Once we had a metal plate, with the corners and edges scrolled over; we had to paint a picture on there, and put a calendar on the bottom, to take home to our mothers. The girls made things too, like handkerchief cases. Once we made peppermint creams. You never had sweets much, you didn't get money for sweets, or very rarely. If you got a penny you thought you were a millionaire, nearly.

One Christmas my brother and I had a pop-gun each; and one Christmas I had a little train set that went in a circle. We both had these wooden horses – a proper little horse with legs, on a platform with wheels which you pushed along. Those were the only *bought* toys I ever had. All of us had a 'shut-knife'; we got them for a birthday or Christmas present. We'd use them for making bows and arrows and so on. We weren't violent with them!

We also had a Christmas stocking. There'd be a little toy, like a whistle, and a comic, and some sweets, and an orange and an apple. That's the only time you had an orange, at Christmas time – not that they were all that scarce, but it was a treat. And right in the toe was a lump of coal, for luck! We always had a chicken for Christmas dinner – that was the only time we had chicken. My father reared turkeys at Little Bendysh Hall, being head poultryman, but they were for the big houses. We never had turkey at home.
Dora We always had beef for Christmas, because my father insisted on that; and in later years we had a goose. You always had new clothes for Easter Sunday; they used to say that if you

didn't have something new for Easter the birds would do their droppings on you! You had a nice new summer dress, the weather was so nice, and you'd wear it just on Sundays after that. We always had an Easter bonnet, but we didn't have Easter eggs.

Wilf We had a roast dinner every Sunday, with Yorkshire pudding – our family did anyway. And if I can say so you don't eat Yorkshire pudding like that now! You cooked your meat in the tin, and when it was time, the meat was put up on a trivet, and the batter pudding was poured into the fat and juice from the meat. There weren't anything poured off, it was poured in and baked like that. Really smashing.

We didn't go meatless the rest of the week, we had stew or a rabbit or a pigeon. For breakfast, in winter time, we had Quaker oats. We brought sandwiches to school – probably be bread and jam, you didn't get a meat sandwich very often. Sometimes we had meat paste. Can't remember having cheese sandwiches although we *had* cheese. We were never hungry – we didn't starve – we were just hungry like children are! For dinner you had a plum duff or fruit in season, a pudding in a basin with apple or rhubarb or whatever was going, in it. We grew all our own vegetables, or my father did. You didn't think of *buying* vegetables, or fruit. Most people had an allotment, and they'd keep chickens and perhaps a pig, and they'd grow enough potatoes to last until potatoes came again. That was the mainstay. We brought home these sacks full and put them in the cellar. That kept us going.

So the gardens weren't the pretty flower gardens of today, although we had some flowers. There was a pink rambler rose over the front door, I think it was Dorothy Perkins. In the bit of garden out the front, before the vegetable garden, there was a row of pinks, white ones. They weren't Mrs Simpkins – you don't see them like that any more. There were bright red ones, too, cloves they called those. We had one or two rose bushes, but not a flower-garden as such. Didn't have any need – we were busy enough growing vegetables. Some of us had a nut-tree, and we all had fruit trees – Mr Stockbridge gave every cottager a Bramley apple tree to plant.

We made our own games. We made this game with hollow door-keys; we put a string on the handle and stuck a nail in the end. We cut a match-head off to put inside this hollow key, put the nail in and banged it up against the wall and it exploded, bang! Also – this is dangerous but we didn't think so – we used to put carbide in a bottle, screw it down, and chuck it under the bridge, and it exploded. There's all that echo under the bridge and it didn't half make a noise. That was naughty wasn't it! We did it with golden syrup tins too – that wasn't dangerous but it banged. We made a little hole in the bottom of the tin with a nail, put a little carbide in and a drop of water, and put the lid on. You set your foot on it so it didn't blow away and it blew the lid off and – bang! Most bicycle lamps were acetylene lamps then, so everybody had carbide. We've still got one somewhere, an old acetylene lamp.

We made bows and arrows in season. For the bows we'd get a hazel stick out of the wood, nice and straight and springy. There was usually a bit of binder-twine around, and you just bent the hazel over a bit and tied it and it would shoot an arrow quite a long way. You used dead nettles or docks for the arrows – the dried stems because they were light, so you could only do it in the autumn. You put a tip on it, made from elder, so the end was weighted, like an arrowhead. Those were dangerous, if anyone had been hit in the face; but there were no accidents as far as I know.

One boy made stilts and walked about on them. We made whistles; you got a nice smooth straight bit of ash and if you tapped it all round with the back of your knife the skin would slide off. Then you cut a notch in the wood and slid the skin back on again, and it worked just like a whistle.

I used to rear jackdaws. We took them from the nest when they were quite young, and you had to feed them. After a day or two, as soon as you went in they'd open their mouths, they knew you were going to feed them. They got really tame, and they used to fly around – we didn't clip their wings yet they'd always come back. They were tame right through to maturity. I had two magpies I kept a long while, but I had to get rid of them because my father kept young chickens and the magpies went after them.

We used to catch wood pigeons too, we'd soak peas in water and feed them. When they were young you had to open their beaks, to start with. Everybody had a cat in those days, to keep down the mice. My grandfather had a dog, and Dora's dad had a dog called Nigger.

We had hoops in the summertime. The boys had metal hoops,

the girls usually had wooden ones. We had a slider as we called it; a piece of stiff wire that didn't bend, with a hook on the end and a wooden handle. You held the slider in the hoop and pushed it along and it went, you see, you just slid it. We used to trundle them to school – that used to get us along.

We collected cigarette cards too. Players and Gold Flake. Used to have games with them. Your good sets you kept, but you'd always have half-a-dozen odds and ends. You'd hold them in your hand and flick them, and the person whose card went the furthest picked the lot up. You'd go on until someone had run out or somebody'd won them all. You really felt that somebody'd given you something if they gave you a new card out of their packet. Now and again you'd pick up an empty packet hoping there might be a card in it, and if you found one you really were in luck. There were all sorts of sets – Wonders of the World, Gardening Hints, Army Badges, Railway Engines, Sportsmen.

Dora There was a lovely series on roses, and a Do You Know series: 'Do you know the cause of thunder and lightning?' was one of the questions. It was a good way to learn things.

Wilf When we lived at Little Bendysh I didn't know of any people who poached. But there was always a rabbit – there were thousands about till this myxomatosis came in the sixties. Rabbits everywhere. People set snares, and during harvest everybody had rabbit to eat. When the field was ready to harvest the corn would be full of them. There'd probably be two or three guns out at strategic points, because they wanted to get rid of them – they caused a lot of damage to the crops. As the binder went round the rabbits would run out. Nobody went up the harvest field without a good hard stick. They'd wave these long sticks, and shout, and kill them. They'd come home with them hanging over their shoulder on the end of the stick. It was nature raw in tooth and claw, but it was a good meal, a rabbit. There was no sentiment attached, not in those days – anything that was edible was fair game, even blackbirds. And Dora went gleaning, didn't you? I never did.

> Harvest time, and the reaper-binder is at work, drawn by heavy working horses. The rhythmical clap-clapping of the machinery startles rabbits out of hiding; neat stooks of corn are set up like little tents to dry in the sun. Threshing; the dust of chaff and straw; sacks of ripened corn, horse-drawn harvest-carts. The tireless men making massive stacks of straw on the stubble. Casual labour in the village – itinerant 'diddycoys' in to help with the harvest, and the annual ritual of gleaning. Gleanings were the bits of corn that the reaper-binder had failed to pick up, and they were there for the taking. It was usually the children who were sent into the reaped fields to pick up what they could, and they would carry home a supply of corn and straw for the chickens.

Dora We had to wait until the field was cleared, then Millie and I used to go gleaning up the Gap there, a long way. We'd be up there all day, but we'd be quite safe from harm. You wouldn't dare do that now in case you got attacked by a strange man. You brought the corn home, and it would have all those long straws on it, so you'd chop the straws up for the chickens, and that kept them going for a long time.

Wilf In my grandmother's time, when they went gleaning they had the corn milled. They were so poor they baked their own bread from the gleaning-flour. They used to bake once a fortnight.

Dora All day long at harvest time you would hear them calling in the fields, 'Hold tight'; 'Gee-up'. When I was young I used to wonder what on earth they were saying.

Wilf That was to tell the chap loading to hold tight because the horses were going to move; and then gee-up to get the horses going again.

Dora After harvest Mr Stockbridge gave them a 'horkey' – he'd have all the men up to the manor house and give them a harvest supper to celebrate their hard work. They'd be working till after dark sometimes, and the harvest went on for weeks and weeks. They had a good meal and some drinks, which was a great thing for poor people. They'd probably have salt beef and potatoes and peas.

Wilf But the horkey was dying out even in my young days. There weren't any after Mr Stockbridge died; the house was sold and there weren't the men working on the farm.

We had the run of the countryside then, and it *was* countryside. Every field had a hedge round it, and there were lots of meadows; they've all gone, virtually. The fields are all ploughed for wheat and there aren't the trees that there were. Either they've died of Dutch elm disease, or they've been chopped down by the farmers.

Dora It was meadows right the way down to Bendysh, and all the way through to Haverley. It was lovely for our children to play in. Darvel was all meadow.

Wilf There were lots more varieties of birds than there are now, too. You don't see them now.

Perhaps Wilf hadn't been looking as closely as his friend, contemporary and neighbour Grace Braybrooke. She is an ardent bird-watcher and spends much of her time walking the lanes, binoculars in hand. Someone once challenged her with the remark, 'Have you noticed how few birds there are in Swanbrooke Down?' She got to work on what became her retirement project. She sighted ninety-three species. The residents were farmland and woodland birds, the most common being blackbirds, wood-pigeons and sparrows; there were summer and winter migrants and birds of passage. One winter an albino blackbird was spotted by several people.

Wilf We didn't think so then, but the country people were very cruel in a way. They'd no compunction about killing anything. But we didn't normally destroy birds' nests; we'd take just one egg out of the nest, because we collected them. But sparrows and blackbirds were game for the pot! We had sparrow pie, and it was all right – we had only the breast mind you, you didn't pluck a sparrow! And rooks – but the meat is horrible. When the young rooks came out of their nests, before they could really fly, they would sit in the treetops, and the men shot as many as they could – they were very destructive to the crops.

We used to go nutting, and often we'd get a bagful of crabs so that Mother could make crabapple jelly. She made jams too.

Dora My mother made wine from most things – hips and haws and crabapples. The meadows were full of peggles, cowslips they call them now, and she made cowslip wine.

Wilf They were full of wild flowers. You can't imagine what it was like then, the countryside. There were trees everywhere, and lovely meadows. Up the Gap, now it's all fields of wheat, but in those days it was a green lane through the trees, with meadows behind.

The first 'vandal' to arrive was the man who bought Mumford Hall after Stockbridge – he cut down every tree on the estate that was suitable for timber. There was nothing said about it then, but it was just to make money: times don't change much! But the trees grew up again.

We walked five miles to Kings Tarrant if we needed clothes – there were no tailors around – and we only went into Kings Tarrant for clothes. We always had what was called a Norfolk suit for best. It was a jacket with a band over your shoulder, and a belt. Weekdays you usually wore a jersey; we called them 'ganseys'. They were usually knitted at home – my father knitted a couple of ganseys for us when he wasn't well. And short trousers – you never wore long trousers until you left school at fourteen, winter or summer. We didn't find it cold, although your knees got a bit chapped. We wore boots, about ankle height, with metal tips on, because the roads were so hard.

We had to cut each other's hair – you didn't go anywhere to have it done. There was no public transport until the first bus service started in 1929. So Mr Trigg the blacksmith, Mr Nightingale the bootmaker, and uncle Benjamin Lagden, they all had a pony and trap and they'd take folk to the railway station, for a modest charge.

Dora My father kept chickens so we always had eggs. Most people kept a few chickens. In the very early days the fishmonger came round in a pony and trap. The fish was always fresh – it was put on ice and came by train from the sea. There were much better train services then. We had herring, cod, mackerel, kippers – nothing fancy. The butcher came in a trap too, and his meat was always fresh. They had refrigerators in their shops, big ones you could almost walk into. Mind you, we had a lot of salt beef, salted to keep. Boiled salt beef. The butcher came twice a week, so we went meatless some days. Later on we had a different butcher every day, and the same with bread; not the same man, all different tradesmen coming round in their vans. There was a grocery van too.

We had to fetch milk from Pebblegate Farm. Just a pint a day, for myself, my father, my mother and brother. We made our own bread occasionally, for a treat. There were two shops then, of course, which sold most things, typical village shops. She used to have sweets, Miss Giles did, big jars of sweets. I can see her now juggling to get the last ones out of the bottom. She had coloured boiled sweets, and peppermint humbugs, and toffee bars – penny ones and halfpenny ones. And caramels wrapped in shiny paper. I'll always remember her poking her hand down these long jars of sweets.

Wilf Some people kept a pig. I can remember Benjamin Lagden, Dora's uncle, killing pigs along here, at Sparrows Farm. No fuss about it then; he had it out in the yard with a cord over its snout and just cut its throat. No humane business, no stunning it. It used to scream something terrible. Then it was scalded and scraped, and we used every last bit. Lots of lard, there was.

Dora You could hear it as far away as Haverley; you'd hear this pig screeching and we'd say, 'Uncle Benjamin's killing a pig tonight.' There's still a hook in the end room here, where it used to hang head down, and drip. It wasn't lean like they are today – they wanted them as fat as they could get them. The meat wasn't kept long because pork soon goes off; so it was smoked, up the chimney, over the open fire, with a bag over it to keep it from scorching.

Wilf Old Nightingale, who lived in the cottage next to the forge, he made all the shoes for the village, and did the repairs. He used to have the pigs' bladders; they were blown up and dried, and he put that in between the boot-soles – it made a waterproof layer. The pig was food for a long time – you'd even eat the bellies – pork chitterlings. My dad liked those.

When we lived at Little Bendysh Hall there was a wash-house for the two cottages, so you couldn't both do your washing on the same day. You had to light the fire under the copper and boil the water, which took about an hour. Then you put it into the washtub, washed the clothes and hung them out to dry. All the water had to be fetched. You used rain water from the tanks and water-butts for everything except drinking. Here in Swanbrooke Down you had to collect it from the well, but at Little Bendysh Hall they had a water cart that went down to the pump opposite the Rose and Crown. They'd set it in the back yard so we didn't have far to fetch it.

Dora It was so beautifully soft, the water. You didn't like the hard water to do anything other than cook with, and make a cup of tea. My father-in-law collected two pails from the well every night, and that had to last until the next night. Lovely water, mind you. Soft water was used for washing clothes, washing yourself, washing your hair. It made a lovely lather – we couldn't get used to hard water at first because you couldn't get a lather on it.

Wilf We couldn't bath every night – Saturday night was bath-night. When we were children we bathed in front of the fire, in the tin bath. The water was boiled in a big kettle over the fire – you always had a fire going because that was the only means of heating anything. It took at least an hour to heat up. At Little Bendysh Hall we cooked on an open black stove like Miss Braybrooke's, with an oven. The kettle was always on the go.

The toilet was up the garden, a hole in the ground with a wooden seat. It was emptied once a year, twice a year perhaps.

Dora The bucket was emptied every week, perhaps twice a week, but not the hole in the ground – that was done once a year.

Wilf Everybody knew when that was going on too!

There were no separate ones for girls and boys. You had a one-holer or a two-holer – or if you were very posh you'd have a three-holer, one each for the gentlemen and the ladies, and a low one for the children. But they were all in the same compartment. Ours was a one-holer.

Dora When Wilf's aunt came down she said, 'Don't you have a lock on the door?' and his dad says, 'Well I never lost a bucket yet!' In any case you would hear if anybody was coming, so you weren't worried.

Wilf The toilets at Little Bendysh Hall were just like the ones

here: buckets, with a door at the back to get them out to empty them. When the girls went in there we boys opened the door quietly and wiggled a bunch of nettles around!
Dora It was awful at night when it was cold. I got really nervous. When we were first married my grandfather still had nut trees down there, a cob and a filbert. You'd sit down there quietly at night and hear a mouse or a rat gnawing away at the nuts. It was quite nerve-racking. I wouldn't want to go back to that!
Wilf You had to find your way up the garden in the dark because we didn't have torches. The normal thing was to use a chamber pot at night, and the slops were emptied in the morning. Up the garden you had what we called a dungle or a dunniken, and all the kitchen waste went in that hole, with the slops, and that was put on the garden, like compost. If you were ill and had to go to the toilet in the bedroom we had lavender; my mother used to burn a few sprigs. We had no sprays or anything like that.
Dora If you were seriously ill the doctor would come out, or if you were capable you went to his surgery. The doctor had a bicycle to begin with, and then what was called an autowheel, a wheel with a little engine that you clipped to the side of your bicycle, that drove it along. But you only called him out if you were desperate, because you had to pay half-a-crown a visit; a lot of money then. Unless you were very seriously ill you didn't go to hospital; the doctor treated you for everything, not like today, they take one look at you and say you'd better see the specialist! The doctor so rarely came out at night that you would know it was him gone by, and my granny would try her hardest to find out why, and who was ill, because you felt it was pretty serious.
Wilf There was always something to do. Boredom didn't exist as far as we were concerned. We were never indoors – if it rained we'd be in the farm buildings. Wintertime we used to slide, and toboggan – we had a lovely slope at Bendysh. There was the moat and the horse-pond at the Hall, lovely places to slide. Up here in Swanbrooke Down we used to slide on the pond down near the school. We used to paddle in the pond, too.
Dora In the winter we played games round the table. We had to mend things, which kept us busy in the evenings. We always had needlework to do. On Saturdays I had to help my mother clean the brass or the windows, little jobs like that. Never had any pocket money though – never. Didn't expect it. If we *were* bored

it was just the natural thing, you accepted it. People now are not so contented. We had each other for company and we found masses to do. The whole village was our playground. And after all we left school at fourteen so we had to be grown up then.

Wilf We had oil lamps and paraffin lamps for the winter evenings so we read books. I can remember a great occasion at Little Bendysh Hall when my father bought a wind-up gramophone from Gamages, and several records. He'd been up to Smithfield for a poultry show. There was 'I'm forever blowing bubbles', and 'Margie', and a comedian called Billy Williams. They were comic records: 'O for another day at Margate'. It was a great treat to hear a gramophone. Father played the accordion, and we used to do a lot of singing – 'Farmer's Boy', and 'Bird in a Golden Cage'.

Dora Your dad had the first crystal radio set, didn't he? The first time we listened to a radio was at school; the teacher had a two-valve set, and two of us listened one wet afternoon. There were only two sets of earphones and I went in with Effie Lagden. It was something about blackbirds, and we had to write a composition afterwards. We used to sit with your dad's crystal set with one earphone each, didn't we! You couldn't rattle about or you'd shake the 'cat's whisker' off the crystal.

Wilf I suppose I must have been fourteen or fifteen before we had the crystal set. Then I made my first valve radio out of twenties parts. It was the early days of the BBC: 'Hello, Daventry Calling' they used to say. If you went too close to this one it would squeak and whistle and oscillate! You had different coils which plugged in for different wavelengths.

I think this electric light spoilt people's eyes, because you could see perfectly with oil lamps. Your dad even used to sharpen a saw by candlelight, didn't he? We went to bed with a candle, and the street was lit with oil lamps. There was one in the tree just outside Ivy Cottage. The lamps were lit as soon as it got dark – Abel Cakebread came down from the Hall to light them.

In the villages in the twenties and early thirties everybody was the same social level, apart from the vicar, the school teachers and the lord of the manor. All the men earned near enough the same wage. It's very different now! When anybody comes into the village now I always say, 'I wonder what grade they're in?' There *are* different sets, there's nothing wrong about it, there just are.

But there weren't then.

Dora The men did all the gardening, although the children would pick the potatoes up. They never did the washing up, or the wiping up. There was plenty of housework, all the sewing and mending. That was quite a job; we mended everything, we didn't buy new like they do today. As long as you could mend it it was all right.

Wilf Even till after the war, when I was working with my father-in-law, most people wanted things repaired, they didn't want new. Dora's dad was a carpenter and he mended carts.

Dora We were self-sufficient, so when the Depression came it didn't affect us, although the thirties were pretty tough. But that was the same all through the village. You only had the bare essentials, no luxuries. Jelly, or a sponge cake, that was a great treat.

Wilf Life didn't change much when rationing came in the Second World War – we didn't have as much red meat but there was plenty of poultry and eggs. We made our own butter, there were cows on the farm. Up at Bendysh, if they wanted anything extra they got it on the black market. People were pretty well-fed during the war. They were probably healthier than now – you didn't have to worry about putting on weight! But after the war the villages were spoiled because every little bit of spare land – meadow and grass and roadside verge – was ploughed up to produce food for the nation.

Dora I'm glad we've known those days because it makes you appreciate things more. The children now – you can't really give them a treat, can you? Some things were better then, and some are better now. I wouldn't want to be without electricity or water or a toilet, but some things aren't better.

Wilf There wasn't all this vandalism and violence. Not round here, anyway. We had the run of the village, but we didn't vandalise things. Somebody once lit some straw too near a haystack and it caught the stack, but not on purpose.

Dora I don't think children today are so contented; you hear parents saying in the holidays, 'My children are bored'. We were never bored. We were never in the house – only for meals, and to sleep. We were all over, and there was always something to do.

Wilf There weren't the homes broken up then; I think they were more content with each other. Most people married within the village, or sometimes from the next village.

Dora In lots of cases I think they lived unhappily together, they didn't stay together because they were happy, they felt they'd got to. They didn't have the money or the social freedom to break away. I wouldn't say they were all happy marriages.

We didn't see much of Robert Stockbridge. We used to have a treat up at the Hall in the summer, a lovely tea in the garden. They had swings, and there was the lake to row on. The next day all of us children had to write a letter to thank him.

Wilf At Little Bendysh they had a Christmas treat at the Hall. They had a tree, or sometimes a big snowball, and one of the family would dress up as Father Christmas. We had a lovely day. We were all given an orange, although one year – it must have been wartime – we only had half an orange each.

Robert Stockbridge had a coach and horses, then later on he had a car; his coachman went on to be his chauffeur. Mr Stockbridge left him two cars and £100 when he died. Didn't make the best use of it, I'm afraid; he drank it away. Easy come, easy go ...

In the old days, the villagers had to pay a shilling to the lord of the manor for the use of the well. But he died before we got married, and the estate was sold, so we never had to pay that.

The pub was only a central part of life for the older people, in the early days. Before I married, all the lads went there on a Sunday night – there was nowhere else to go. But women never went of course, or hardly ever; it was not the proper thing. It was just beer served then, and there wasn't much drunkenness. The only chaps who got lively were the Actons from Little Bendysh – Sunday nights you'd hear them go home singing. They were very merry. Roy Acton fell off his bike into Winter Water one night! They always took a gallon bottle of beer home, and you'd see where they had dropped it and broken it before they got home. But there was hardly any violence, just the occasional scandal.

The church has never been that important here, only at harvest time. There weren't enough seats then. Religion hasn't played a great part for most people, not in our time. There's never been a great congregation in all our years here.

On one of the chancel walls in St Michael's is a prominent

tablet commemorating the Gardiner-Clarke family of Mumford Hall. When the church was restored in 1856, at a cost of £2394, some £1000 was contributed by R. Gardiner-Clarke, Esq, who also rebuilt the chancel at the additional cost of £600. This generous act led to one of Swanbrooke Down's most notorious scandals.

Wilf My grandmother worked for Mrs Gardiner-Clarke up at Mumford Hall. Once she found a pistol under her pillow. Apparently she said to my mother, 'I'd shoot the very devil if he came to my window!' She fell out with the vicar after she had paid for the chancel to be restored. He wouldn't give her a special pew up there in the new chancel. She wanted to sit there and him to be down in the nave! He wasn't having that, and she stormed out. Soon afterwards some of the church windows were broken, and, worst of all, an effigy of the vicar was burned on Darvel meadow. It went to court, and the magistrate said that if it happened again it would mean prison for Mrs Gardiner-Clarke. When she died, the vicar said he couldn't find the key to the family vault. They reckoned he threw it through the grating! So Mrs Gardiner-Clarke had to be buried outside the vault. But before she died she founded the Methodist chapel in Elmshaw Lane just to spite the vicar.

After her row with the vicar Mrs Gardiner-Clarke never returned to worship at St Michael's. In 1886 she bought, for £5, a small piece of land in Elmshaw Lane. On it she built the tiny chapel that still stands there, and so began Methodist worship in the village. It was opened in May 1887 at a total cost – including the furnishings, the pulpit bible and book of offices – of £299, 4s, 1d.

Many children who belonged to the Church of England went to the Chapel Sunday school, simply because it ran the annual outing to the seaside. A large waggon was borrowed from Mumford Hall, and about forty children were taken three miles to Lillingford Station, clutching their pennies for sticks of rock. On their return it was waiting, and they came home by the light of the oil lamps on the waggon.

Wilf I can remember First World War rationing. We used to go up to Haverley for our rations, to Mr Cork's shop next to the pub. We had so much margarine and so much butter, and we blended it to make one big pat so you didn't have all marge or all butter. I can remember standing in our front garden and watching the search-lights over London. One young chap who worked with my father, he lived with us, and he went off to the war. He was only eighteen. He'd been gone about a week before he was killed.

Dora My Uncle Harry was about the same age, and he was killed in the trenches. His young lady told me she had wanted to marry him, but Granny had said, 'Oh, wait till he comes back' – and of course he never did. She said, 'I wish I hadn't waited, because I might have had his child.' She never had a second chance, there were so few young men came back. So sad.

Wilf My first car was a Morris Thousand traveller; then a Triumph 1300. Had a motorbike sidecar before that too. And an ordinary pedal-bike – we all had those. When I was in my teens there was no other way of getting anywhere. I would bike the five miles to Kings Tarrant on a Saturday afternoon. Didn't think anything of it. If you had the toothache you had to bike ten miles to have your tooth out. When I was a child we walked to Kings Tarrant from Bendysh to shop. I can remember walking along holding on to my mother and my brother hollering in the pram!

Dora You'd be so tired when you came back all the way up the hill on a hot day – you couldn't get back in quick enough for a drink of water.

Wilf I used to do old English country dancing. Mr Stockbridge built a reading room for the village, and we used to have a little sixpenny dance in there. A woman from Haverley played the piano. We had fêtes, and a cricket team, and we played football on a Saturday afternoon. Kings Tarrant had a March fair, a June fair and a November fair. It was a great treat; there was a roundabout, and swingboats. There wasn't any canned music, it was all played on an organ – quite nice tunes they were. You could hear the music in Haverley.

Dora Grandfather and the old people always said, 'We must have new potatoes by Haverley fair' – which was June 18th; we were much more seasonal then. We always had gooseberries for Whitsun; there was a Whitmonday fair outside the Green Man, and us children saved our pennies for months to buy sweets and have a go at the coconut-shy.

Wilf You didn't think about going abroad, and that's not something I regret. I've seen all of abroad that I want to see, during the Second War. It weren't anything startling, not where I went anyway. North Africa especially, and Italy wasn't much better. Very primitive it was, during the war, in the country.

Wilf was abroad for three years, leaving Dora with a four-month-old daughter. He joined the Sixth Armoured Division in North Africa and Italy. He still serves on the services committee of the British Legion.

Dora The furthest I've ever been away from Swanbrooke Down is Yorkshire. I *did* enjoy it. And I went on holiday to London sometimes because I had an aunt in North Finchley. There were a few motor cars around, but not so many as now. It was still all lovely meadows round there. Now it's all built up.

Wilf Everything was horse-drawn, so the blacksmith had a busy time. You saw this great fire at the forge as you came home from school; the door was always open. It was a meeting place for the village, because the well was in the yard. There'd be perhaps half a dozen up there of an evening to fetch water, having a chat sitting on the wall. Alf King, he used to smoke a pipe and that smelt horrible. Once something in his pocket got into his tobacco somehow – they did smoke some pretty awful stuff.

Dora Money didn't come into it like it does today. Children didn't have pocket money, not regular – you'd get a penny sometimes, or a halfpenny. Sometimes I did little errands for the woman who lived at the forge, and occasionally she'd give me a halfpenny. I really thought I was doing well. Miss Giles sold Sharps Creamy Toffees, a penny a bar; one of those was a great treat. She had halfpenny bars as well. Sharps Creamy Toffees . . .

Wilf We were watching a cricket match at Little Bendysh one Saturday afternoon, and a large balloon came over. When it came down over the fields four of us boys ran after it, and we dragged this balloon back. There was a label on it, saying there was £1 for it if you returned it to a certain address. To this day I don't know what it was in aid of, but we had this £1 between us, and we thought we were millionaires!

ADA BROWN

Horse-keeper's daughter

Ada is one of the few surviving links with Robert Stockbridge. Essentially a feudal lord, he lived at Mumford Hall in traditional style, and effectively owned the village. All the thatched cottages, now prettily modernised, were labourers' dwellings – and humble ones – which belonged to the estate. The 1851 census return shows three blacksmiths, two shepherds, a carrier, thatcher, dressmaker, tailor, carpenter, dairymaid, schoolmistress, wool-comber, cattle-dealer and cordwainer living in Swanbrooke Down. Resorting to the dictionary for 'cordwainer', I discovered that he was a man who worked with Cordovan leather, a type of Spanish goatskin. There were seven paupers listed, and one-sixth of the population were labourers – one of whom had nine children. It appears that Stockbridge had the interests of the place at heart; a kindly man respected by the villagers. He is still remembered by the oldest residents, Ada among them, driving in his coach and pair through the village. When he died in 1925 the estate was sold up in lots, and feudal England came to its end in Swanbrooke Down. The village cottages and fields moved into the era of private ownership.

Originally Ada's father was horse-keeper to Mr Stockbridge, and she proudly showed me a photograph of him with two pairs of the estate cart-horses. The family lived in Holly Cottage, so-named from an enormous holly bush, long-since perished, that grew by the front porch. So when I invited Ada to visit me there and talk about those days, she was almost beside herself with excitement. As we sat beside the inglenook, warmed by a log fire, her eyes darted around the sitting room, taking in all the details of change. A light rain descended like mist outside the window; the November afternoon darkened into evening. It was obvious that she was reliving cherished childhood experiences, and our conversation sparked off a chain of memories – prompted by Dora Middleditch, who came too. They had been friends since school-days, and it was Dora who introduced us.

When her father was promoted to foreman at the Hall, the family moved into one of the cottages in the grounds of the big house. Not for long though, for Robert Stockbridge was soon to die. However, these times made a profound impression on Ada. Years later she married a policeman, and they now live in retirement in Lillingford. She is a thin, nervy lady with a ready smile and a shrill voice, talkative and brimming with enthusiasm about the way things were then.

The gay simplicity of childhood

Ada I remember the nice things about Mumford Hall. It was beautiful – it has changed so much you wouldn't recognise it. There was a huge cedar tree on the main lawn that blew down a few years ago. There was a big lake too, and we used to go for boat rides.

A four-hundred-year-old cedar was blown down in a storm in the late 1970s, a sad loss to the landscape. One of its branches looked like a monk's head in profile, and local legend has it that this is because a monk tried to hang himself from it.

Mumford Hall has seen many changes. Domesday listed, it passed through the ownership of the royal house of Lancaster and during the thirteenth and fourteenth centuries was in the chamberlainship of the Kings' Exchequer.

For two centuries it belonged to the Gilbert family, and in the nineteenth century it passed to the Gardiner-Clarkes. The infamous Mrs Gardiner-Clarke died without issue; this was how Robert Stockbridge came to be the last lord of Mumford Hall, as he recounts in his privately printed autobiography, *Reminiscences of a Victorian Gentleman*:

> I was now about 65 years of age and I decided to adopt a new mode of life . . . I had always had a fondness for country life and farming, and being no longer the chief of the business in which I had been engaged all my life, I thought I would finish up away from my old surroundings, and much to the surprise of my friends I bought a place in Essex on the borders of Cambridge and Hertfordshire. I found an old place with a house on high ground and about 1000 acres which I could cultivate. The place was very much out of order and I had to restore, or rather rebuild, the house, farms, and village, and weed out some of the folk living in the houses . . .
>
> After 15 years of it, I found myself with many very nice neighbours, many friends, and a large family of children and grandchildren around me.

Ada Mr Stockbridge, he was a gentleman. He used to go by in his coach and pair, through the village or around the edge of the wood to Lillingford Station. Some people were half afraid of him, but we knew him and he was always very nice to us when we lived up there – although we weren't there very long before he died.

Some people didn't know whether to curtsey or what, they were in awe of him. But he was a gentleman. He had a lot of maids, very nice, quite elderly maids who fussed over you and gave you little odds and ends. When Mr Stockbridge died my father was his foreman and we lived in the cottage up the hill here – it's the only little bit of 'real' Mumford Hall still there.

Dora and I remember walking up there from school with a wreath after he died. We sent a wreath from school – and I remember it ever so well because the laburnum was out. But after he died the link between the Hall and the village was broken.

We used to go for walks around the fields and sometimes we'd bump into his son; with him it was always 'yes sir, no sir'. He was a different kettle of fish; we would run and hide if we saw him coming.

Robert Stockbridge junior committed suicide a year after his father's death. A hush surrounds his fate; only his great-nephew, now living on the east coast, has an account of this suicide and, more macabre still, the suicide note. Mumford Hall was up for sale again.

Ada We saw all the awfulness of the place being broken up – I remember seeing the lots put out in the field.

The 1926 catalogue reads:

Mumford Hall Sale:
7 reception and billiard rooms
18 bed and dressing rooms
5 bathrooms
electric light, central heating
3 farms
cottage property
woodlands
3 fine arbitrary manors and advowson
Hunting; good shooting. 1058 acres
Garage 4 cars
Stabling 7 horses
Pleasure and kitchen gardens
7 glass houses
Park and woodlands
Bailiff's house and 7 cottages
Home farm premises, estate and wheelwright's yard
Fine cedar on lawn a feature
Tennis lawn, ornamental water, rustic summer house
Keeper's cottage

Ada My dad used to ride when he was a foreman, a cob horse, heavier than a pony but not as big as a shire. We used to ride it too. People were busy lotting everything up for the sale, so we went fishing in the lake with the solicitor's son – they had come to stay at the Hall while the sale was going on. We took the fish home because the grown-ups thought we'd like to eat them. But at night when they had gone to bed we crept out and put them back in the lake because we just *couldn't* – we didn't fancy eating them. You couldn't, could you, after you'd fished for them!

When the house was emptied and the people had gone, we kept some of the animals on. The big herds had all gone – they kept a lot of stock, but there were only two cows left after the sale. These 'house-cows' were dreadful animals! We used to tease them, my brother and sister and I. There was a dozen or so cows in Darvel meadow, and they'd all got their names. Ada, they called this cow, same name as me, and we teased her something horrid. She was horrid to us, too! She knew us when she saw us coming home, and she'd chase us up there but she couldn't get at us because of the wire. When she was sold in a lot, we were playing on the school green. They drove these cows past us and this Ada she knew us and we saw her coming; we all darted for the school because we reckoned she was going to get us before the end!

On May Day we crowned a May king and queen. Us children voted for them and twice we chose Wilf Middleditch to be king. We picked the flowers the day before: primroses, bluebells, king-cups, apple blossom and may blossom. We tied them into bunches and tied these posies onto hoops for the girls and wooden staffs for the boys.

After the school register had been called we would walk all the way to Little Bendysh Church for a short service. Then the king and queen were crowned with wreaths of white flowers – although I remember Wilf had a yellow Crown Imperial on the front of his crown one year, that smelt horrible! Then we would walk around all the houses in Bendysh and sing our May songs: 'Early one morning', 'Come lasses and lads', 'Smiling May'. Our teacher played the fiddle, and two of us took a collecting box. We shared out the money. The king and queen got half-a-crown, and a prayer book signed by the vicar. One of Wilf's is signed by the blind vicar.

We walked back to Swanbrooke Down for lunch. By then our flowers were a bit tired, so we'd splash them with water from the stream to revive them, and go off singing around Swanbrooke Down in the afternoon. It was always sunny and we girls wore white dresses and garlands. We'd go as far as Grimstone Hall

Farm then back across to Mumford Hall where they gave us lemonade and a bun. Our last stop was the vicarage where we were given a lovely tea. You can guess that we were very tired children by then!

Those were beautiful days up there at Mumford Hall. I remember all the thick cream we had! My mum had this little bowl with a handle and we would take the cream off the top and turn it into butter. It was beautiful. Until the estate was settled up we would go into the dairy, next to our house; it was all marble slabs, and you had these big pans, and the cream settled on the top. Right at the end we had to feed the milk to the pigs, so that it wasn't wasted.

Mr Stockbridge probably did most for the village. The married men with families usually had a job at Mumford Hall – although often five or six of the single lads might be idle all winter. Their wages were only about ten shillings a week – but the rents were very low, and they could rely on growing a row of potatoes on the farm. They had milk and firewood free, and they could easily get rabbits and hares. The girls went into service at the big house, and the womenfolk worked in the fields when they could – potato-picking, gleaning, that sort of thing.

You'd see the men walking to work early, up the little hill towards the Hall. At 6.30 precisely a loud bell was rung on the farm for starting time, and then again for knocking-off time. If a man was late, he was sent home and told to come again after breakfast. Mr Stockbridge gave his staff their wages and a joint of meat every Friday. But they didn't get much holiday – if Christmas day fell on a Sunday they were really fed up because they were done out of one day off.

Still, Mr Stockbridge treated the people well. He built several houses, a reading room which everyone could use – that's where the post office is now. And the field next to it he gave as a recreation field. Sadly there was nothing about it in his will, so that fell into the hands of builders and you've got two modern houses on it now. He built a little house for the policeman, and both the bridges over Winter Water – before that you had to go through a ford, and the road was often flooded.

Robert Stockbridge was also patron of the church, having the interests of his villagers' souls at heart as well as their material needs. In his memoirs, however, he remarks: 'The Church of England is not in a good way and does not fit the people.' He also comments on the effects of the Great War: 'The years of war have altered the character and outlook of the men. They are more difficult to manage, more discontented ... there is more general discontent as to the condition of things, and, I should think, there is a lower moral tone and less religious feelings and observances.'

Mrs Stockbridge was also active in village life. She had the schoolchildren to a tea party every Christmas, and she allowed the older girls to borrow dresses and bonnets from Mumford Hall so that they could appear respectably dressed in church. The garments had to be returned by Monday morning.

Ada In the springtime Blind Man's Walk was full of aconites and daffodils. That's where people say the ghost of Mrs Gardiner-Clarke walks! We had gorgeous times. Our childhood was good, and I tell my grand-daughter, 'You'll never know', I say, 'the life that we knew.' My son thinks that life now is better, and in lots of ways it is – material ways. But not in the gay simplicity, and simple things. We had a countryside you don't have any more, not in the same free way. It was absolutely lovely. We lived in each season as it came.

When my brother left school he collected eggs at Mumford Hall. They had lots of chickens, all free-range – even the chickens were happy! Anyway, you know what boys are, they only collected half of them. So when I got back from school I went round collecting the rest, up by the lovely fir trees. I used to go and collect the eggs, sit there and watch the clouds.

I feel I still belong in Swanbrooke Down, because the graveyard is full of my family – in each row you'll find at least one member of the family. We all lived here in your cottage. Me and my sister slept in the little bedroom at the top of the stairs, and my dad and my brother slept in the other one, with the old leaded window. There were six of us, including my grandfather. He had white hair and this fine long white beard. He was a lovely old man – he used to sit in the porch underneath the holly on Saturdays and Sundays. Wilf has a photo of him sitting there.

He used to give us a carrot from his allotment when we walked past – it was just over the road opposite the cottage. He would get out his old shut-knife and scrape off the dirt, rub it on his trousers and peel it for us. It was such a treat. We didn't have chocolate and snacks in those days.

When the estate was sold up, my dad could have bought this cottage for £100. But he'd brought up three children and £100 was a lot of money, and he didn't have it.

Holly Cottage was part of lot 17 in the Mumford Hall sale catalogue: it reads as follows:

> A detached 4-roomed cottage and a row of 3 cottages two with 4 rooms, one with 2 rooms. At present let to Misses C. Smith, Jeffrey, Whyman and Mrs Wraights, on quarterly tenancies, at annual rents amounting to £15.
> Area, with garden, 1 rood
> Tithe rent charge Free
> Water from estate well at forge and village pump
> Land tax As assessed

Ada It was quite different then, the cottage. Where you've got your inglenook, we had the old black range with an oven to the side and a hob on top. That's where all the cooking was done, and it was the snuggest room in the house. Your kitchen was what we called the scullery. That was just for the men to take off their boots and wash down after a day's work in the fields. And for scrubbing the vegetables. There was a door at the back to next door's to let the steam escape, and I remember my mother leaning over that door on wash-day and gossiping with our neighbours. We called it the chatting hatch.

Then this room at the end – ooh! it's your study now! It's lovely! It had a mud floor and we kept the chickens in here at night. It was filthy. We stacked hay here in the summer and called it the barn.

The cottage was ever so cold and damp. I remember when we all had the whooping cough, and my grandfather told me how they used to cure it in the old days. I was frightened to death. He said they fried mice with the skins on and mixed them with vegetables and gravy and gave it to the children. And that worked, he said.

You've got it lovely and warm now. We used to have a door at the bottom of the stairs there to keep the draughts out and to keep the heat in the downstairs room.

When Bill Lagden came to repair the thatch once he told us he often used to find dried-out bodies of cats in the middle of the roofing straw. Sometimes he round a rat near it, too. He told me an old wives' tale that the devil demanded his due when a house was finished, and wanted a human sacrifice, but he got fobbed off with an animal. But my father said that the cats were put there to scare the vermin – like scarecrows.

The ancient Egyptians mummified their sacred cats and preserved them in special tombs. Throughout the Middle Ages the cat was regarded as a magical animal – a familiar of witches and an associate of the devil. The ritual death of a cat was believed to enrich the harvest, to protect crops and herds from evil magic, and to bring prosperity. 'Foundation sacrifices' to appease the powers of darkness blended with the utilitarian concept of the cat as a vermin-scarer, and a vague idea that the immuring of a cat in a new building was 'lucky'. The possibility of accidental enclosure of cats in a thatch seems highly improbable.

Ada I used to have to bring my grandfather's beer from the Dog and Duck on my way back from school, in a large square bottle. One day, our neighbours were laying a path outside their cottage and I was playing on the slabs. I slipped and fell and the bottle broke. To this day I have the scar on my finger – it made a really deep hole. My mother asked what had happened and I told her I had just fallen. She bandaged me up and consoled me, but our nosy neighbour – I really hated her – she came round and said she'd seen me playing on the slabs. So when my father got in he gave me a hiding. There wasn't a lot of sympathy around; people certainly weren't soft.

In fact there was a lady in Haverley who put poison in her children's porridge and murdered them! The dog ate the remains of the porridge and it died too. They say the ghost of this dog still wanders around the church.

There's a ghost in one of the big houses at Little Bendysh; she has been seen twice recently. She is a lady dressed in dark colours with a scarf over her head, standing at the foot of one of the beds. Dora's father used to say there was a ghost in the basement at the big house in the village street, and I used to be quite frightened to walk past. I've always hoped I wouldn't see a ghost.

LILIAN DRAYTON

Farmer's wife

Lilian Drayton is contemporary with Wilf and Dora Middleditch, although she cuts quite a different figure. Tall and smartly-dressed, her air is grander and more imposing. There is something of the genteel gossip about her which seemed in accordance with the immaculate hair-do and slightly blue rinse. She was full of stories about Swanbrooke Down, many scurrilous, and a fund of information about local ghosts. She is married to Percy, who retired from farming five years ago.

Lilian was born in 1912, daughter of the local wheelwright,

Reuben Gifford, and lived at Grimstone Hall Farm with her grandparents during the First World War. She returned there for holidays throughout her childhood, and remembers pheasants warning of approaching zeppelins long before they could be heard by human ears. After her parents' death she returned to live at Grimstone Hall Farm with George, whom she married in St Michael's in 1936. Millie Lagden played the organ, and she recalls, 'As the bride was an accomplished pianist I was afraid that I would not do well. I don't really know why I bothered to be nervous; I am quite sure she never knew whether I played "The voice that breathed on Eden" or "God save the King", she was so happy.'

Lilian and George have retired to a small house in Suffolk, near their daughter and her family. The house is full of beautiful furniture and *objets d'art*; it is warm and tidy, with a stunningly equipped kitchen looking out over fields. We had driven across East Anglia through heavy snow which was drifting across the narrow lanes and sweeping high against the banks. A bitter December wind whipped over the fields, shivering bare branches. From Lilian's kitchen we could see the blizzard driving over acres of ploughed land, ridging the brown furrows with white. A low sky was leaden-grey behind the dancing snowflakes, and darkening fast.

Lilian gave us an old-fashioned tea, formally set out on the dining-room table. As she poured from a silver service, she offered us cucumber sandwiches, scones with cream, gingerbread and chocolate cake, to go with our Earl Grey tea. She talked and we listened; she was almost unstoppable. George said his occasional piece, interrupting her with practised firmness. He was a friendly, sturdy person, whose ruddy complexion told of a life in the open air, and he had many memories of farming before it became mechanised. They both reminisced gladly.

Scandal at the vicarage

Lilian There was always enmity between Haverley and Swanbrooke Down. My father used to tell me about it – he died about ten years ago, when he was ninety-three, so he was talking about the late nineteenth century. The young men of Haverley, presumably after they had been to the pub on a Saturday night, used to march to Swanbrooke Down, singing: 'You men of the Down, Come out of your den, Roll up your sleeves and fight like men!' Swanbrooke Down had three pubs in those days.

The oldest house in the village, still known as the Green Man, was the principal rival establishment to the Dog and Duck up until the 1950s. A lovely L-shaped house, it stands across the road from the Dog and Duck, behind the stream and now reached by a narrow bridge. Legend has it that it once boasted a priest's hole. A tunnel is said to have linked the cellars of the Green Man with the wood on top of the hill, and was used by smugglers. Hundreds of sealed stone bottles were found in a disused cellar at the tunnel entrance: when they were opened the wine exploded. The tunnel was, they say, also used for romantic assignations. The third pub, the Ancient Shepherd in Elmshaw Lane, was a tiny cottage licensed to sell alcohol until 1900, since when it has been a private house.

Once a year a Whitmonday Fair was held in the road between the Dog and Duck and the Green Man. The girls and boys raised pennies for the big day by selling cabbage and lettuce plants around the village. Sweets, rock and china ornaments were the main attraction, and a coconut shy was set up in front of the Dog and Duck. A stall selling cockles, winkles and mussels stood in the yard of the Green Man. Music was provided by a concertina, and a broomstick dance was held in the bar of the Dog and Duck on Whitmonday evening. Echoes of this carry through to today, when twice a year Morris dancers perform in the same stretch of the street.

Lilian One day there was a funeral, and all the people from Mumford Hall went along to the church. After the funeral the horse-keeper came back to the Hall to give his labradors a run. He let them out, and the dogs were rushing about enjoying themselves, when suddenly they stopped in their tracks. They stood stock still. The horse-keeper wondered whatever they were looking at; their hair was standing on end. He looked up, and there was this Victorian lady in the garden. It was Mrs Gardiner-Clarke.

Millie Lagden, whose mother worked up at the Hall, says that Mrs Gardiner-Clarke kept a gun under her pillow. She must have been rather peculiar, what with her famous feud with the vicar. She killed herself while they were having a horkey up at the big house. She chose the night of the harvest supper to do her worst. They put her coffin on a canopied hearse drawn by four black horses, and she was buried just outside the family vault. They say her soul does not rest in peace, and that her spirit walks around the lake, through the farmyard and down the Blind Walk towards Darvel meadow. The place is definitely haunted; the family who bought it in the sixties had the house exorcised before they moved in. But I gather that Mrs Gardiner-Clarke is still around – the present owner's wife is dead scared of her, so I hear.

George The horkey was when the farmer and his men would assemble in his house after harvest and have a jolly good feed and keep on drinking until they ended up singing 'For he's a jolly good fellow'. It was a general celebration that the harvest was gathered – and the harvest was an *achievement* in those days. It is so easy now it's all mechanised. But men had to work very hard, and for a very long time, and it was a terrific achievement.

I can remember my grandfather saying that one year the harvest was so good some of the barley at the top of the hill was thrown into the ditch by Madge's Oak, and never carted. My great-uncle was a mill-wright, and I heard him say that there was corn out at Christmas time one year! He used to tell me how he and my grandfather cut the corn with scythes in the very early days – later on they had reapers and binders which they bought piecemeal and assembled themselves.

Farmers don't have harvest suppers any more. Farm workers get paid much better, there's plenty of food about and they don't need it in the same way. It was done when they really enjoyed a good meal; it meant something to them.

In those days about fifty men were employed at Mumford Hall, on about ten shillings a week, and they had to keep strict hours. The bell was rung at 6 am to start the working day – it is still hanging over the granary door. If they were late they were sent home and lost the day's pay. The bell was also rung for breakfast, lunchtime and leaving-off time. They worked a six-day week, and every Saturday morning, weather permitting, the whole farmyard was swept and tidied.

But Mr Stockbridge looked after his men. At Christmas a bullock was slaughtered by the butcher in Lillingford, and each worker was given beef for Christmas dinner. Sometimes the girls were given lengths of serge to make clothes. And if any of the workers fell sick, meals would be sent down from the Hall, and when they were convalescing they would be given milk puddings or egg custards. One chap fell off a ladder and was very badly injured, and he was sent a tonic made from lily-of-the valley-leaves and brandy to help him recover!

Lilian Mumford Hall became derelict between the wars. During the Depression, after Robert Stockbridge died, we had a man there who was very prominent in the Labour Party, and my father was *livid.* This was in Ramsey Macdonald's time, and they used to have labour rallies on Saturday afternoons. It was absolute sacrilege to my father to have such a type of person in the grounds of Mumford Hall! Then a Mr Bickley owned it during the last war, and he disgraced himself by going off with his cowman's wife. We didn't hear any more of him after that.

Then we had someone whose little boy went into hospital for a minor operation. He was a very spoiled little boy and he would not stay in his bed; he caught a chill and died in hospital, of pneumonia. He was buried in Swanbrooke Down churchyard. After that his wife felt she couldn't stay there and they very soon moved way. You'll see his gravestone in the far corner of the graveyard; it says something like, 'To the cherished memory of our glorious little son, who passed to the life beyond in his 7th year.'

When my grandfather was courting my grandmother, she lived at Foulmire End, a very nice little farm. It was a beautiful moonlit night – you could see right across to Bullbrook and along the Elmshaw Lane. They saw a crowd of men carrying a coffin; they were intrigued but also a little upset because it isn't a very nice thing to see. When my grandfather went to see her on the next night they saw the same thing again! Both nights the coffin was taken into the field we call Bullbrook, and across to the church by way of the fields. My grandmother wouldn't go down Elmshaw Lane on her own after that, it frightened her so much.

There was all sorts of awful diseases at that time – perhaps it was the smallpox. A family from Didbrooke, possibly. The parish registers are full of these tragic young deaths.

There were meadows alongside all the lanes in those days; I especially remember when the buttercups came out, and the cuckoo which sang incessantly. All my children were born in May, when the cuckoo was singing! The road through the village was still a track with grass down the middle, and it was so *silent*! Only the clip-clop of horses, and very occasionally a car. And the birdsong, of course. There was a grove of oak trees in Bullbrook field, and it was absolutely lovely. The meadows and the ponds were beautiful, and then a farmer, a relative of mine I'm afraid to say, filled the lot in and ploughed it up. He had all the magnificent trees razed to the ground. We had three beautiful ponds at Grimstone Hall Farm, and my son was very naughty and filled them in. We used to have such fun on those ponds when I was a child; when we had a frost we used to enjoy the sliding so much. They were a terrific help when you had a fire, too, for the fire engines to use, before mains water came.

There used to be thirty-five ponds in Swanbrooke Down. A survey in 1974 reported that fourteen had been filled in, including the village pond. Only four contained unpolluted water, and supported healthy plant and animal life. Duckweed, yellow iris, water figwort, hard rush and water mint were among the plants noted. Mallard, occasional snipe, and moorhens frequented all the ponds, and several species of fish flourished there.

Lilian There's a ghost at Grimstone Hall, but I always felt it was terribly friendly. I liked it. It was very nice to me. I saw it, and so did the people who lodged in the flat at the end of the house; they hadn't known anything about it, so it wasn't their imagination. I first heard this person in 1920, it walked in my bedroom. The date was December 24th, and I thought it was Father Christmas! Then I heard people talking, and I was frightened. So I told my mother, 'There's people talking in the flat,' and she said, 'Of course there isn't, don't be silly, you're making it up, you're dreaming.' But I wasn't dreaming. And when this thing walked into my bedroom I closed my eyes because I thought Father Christmas wouldn't bring me anything if he saw me peeping! But it definitely happened.

I saw things after that too. But before we went back in later years we had the house exorcised. My daughter said that lots of bad things had happened in the house, and she wouldn't let us move in without exorcising it. So they got Canon Williams in, and another local vicar and his wife, and they exorcised it. There were still ghosts there after that – very nice ones, there wasn't anything horrid about them.

Old John Dyer, who lived at the end cottage at Grinchells, he was a sweet old man; his wife was lovely too. He was horse-keeper to my grandfather, who thought the world of him. His wife originally lived in a small town twelve miles from Swanbrooke Down, and he used to walk all that way to court her! Her aunt owned the Dog and Duck, and when she died they moved in to the pub. He became a little too fond of the beer, with it being on the spot all the time. He went from bad to worse, so he gave up his job and that was the end of a first-class horse-keeper. Eventually they moved to Grinchells.

Marrying somebody from beyond a three-mile radius of the village was unusual at the turn of the century. The 1851 census records that 68 of the 84 marriages in Swanbrooke Down had been between individuals living within five miles of each other. Such was the fabric of village life until after the First World War.

Lilian In those days some old age pensioners wore little peaked caps; old John Dyer never took his cap off, even in bed. His daughter told me that the night he died he kept saying to her, 'What is this wonderful light in the room?' She said, 'There isn't a light, father,' and he said, 'There *is*! There's this wonderful light, what is it?' That was just a few hours before his death.
George My father's men used to thresh peas in the barn, with flails – sticks about six feet long, with a hinge at the end and another stick attached – and they would wallop the peas to de-pod them. A whole gang of men used them. I think they sang so that they had a rhythm, an ordered sequence of bringing the flail down; they did it all through the winter.

I remember what they used to call 'hossing' peas in the barns. A horse went in on the loose peas, still on their stalks, in the barn. The horse kept walking round until it was up at the top of the barn with the mountain of peas beneath it. It was amazing how they got the horse down: the creature would sit on its bottom, put its front feet forward and slide down at a most incredible angle, in control all the time. I've seen the horse descend at the most acute angle! I never missed it when the horse was due to come down – it was fantastic. The peas were used for seed.

They were hard days, but people had marvellous tables. Food was very cheap, and milk was free for a lot of us. Rabbits and hares were easily obtained, and most cottages kept a pig or a chicken. There was plenty of wood so they had lovely fires, and coal. I have bought coal for twenty-seven shillings a hundred-weight, delivered, when I was running my mother's farm. And we used to brew on the farm, hundreds of gallons of beer. We had all the tackle.
Lilian It was the beer that kept them going, scything the corn; definitely the beer. They used to have little barrels on their backs.
George In those days there were so many horses. They reckoned that the pre-requisite for running a farm was four horses to every hundred acres. We had seven men working at Grimstone Hall and the farmyard was a lovely place. We had a horse-keeper just after the 1914–18 war who was very keen – he kept beautiful horses. Then suddenly, within a week, we had four horses die. They couldn't make out what was wrong – they just dropped down dead. They found he'd been giving them arsenic to make their coats shine – it's an old trick. I suppose he gave them a bit too

much ... Needless to say he was not in his job for very much longer after that!

Lilian I remember one day when I went down to the cottage at Grinchells, in the days when they had fly-papers. I'd just had a perm, and I was going out that evening, to a dance – with my husband, of course; young blood ... I was so pleased with this hair-do I went to show the Dyers. They always had these fly papers up around the house. I said, 'Goodbye, Mrs Dyer, goodbye, Mr Dyer,' and made my way out, but instead of turning my back on them, I was backing out to the door. Suddenly the worst happened and I got caught up in these awful fly-papers. I got home to my mother and she said, 'What *have* you done to your hair' It was all covered in flies! We rectified it as best we could!

Alfie Dyer's father had two marriages, two births and two deaths in a year. I don't know of anybody who can equal this. Now you'll say, 'However did he do that?' Well, his girlfriend became pregnant, so they married, then she died and the baby died. At the same time Mary Lagden became pregnant by him and so he had to marry her! And him a churchwarden ...

But the most famous scandal of all was the Moat Farm murder at Haverley. It happened at the end of the last century but people still talk about it. This very charming and romantic man called Dougal met a spinster lady – she was about fifty-six at the time – who had been left a lot of money by her aunt. Something in the region of £7000. She succumbed to his charms, and they bought Moat Farm with her money. While it was being renovated they lodged with a dressmaker in Kings Tarrant.

Well, it turned out that Dougal was a forger with a prison sentence. Whether Miss Holland discovered this, or whether the romance just went sour, we shall never know, but after about three years the lady disappeared. Dougal kept on signing cheques in her name but he was so smarmy and self-assured that tongues didn't start wagging for quite a while. Anyway, the police finally caught up with him three years later, busy courting another lady and using forged £10 notes.

Since there was still no sign of Miss Holland, the police dug up the entire garden around Moat Farm, to grave-level, but they found nothing. It was only when they started making house-to-house enquiries that a farmworker remembered being told to fill in the open drainage ditch which crossed the farmyard. He remembered it distinctly, even the date, because that ditch had been there since time immemorial.

So they started to dig. They'd gone almost the whole length when a piece of cloth came up on the fork. Then they unearthed her boots. She had very small feet and her friend the dressmaker recognised them. Then they found the body with a bullet hole through her skull.

The dressmaker identified Miss Holland's underwear too, because she had stitched it herself. The corpse was wearing an old-fashioned bustle, which the dressmaker also recognised. Her damning evidence was sufficient to convict Dougal of murder.

Samuel Dougal was hanged at Chelmsford Gaol at 8 am on July 14th 1903, to be remembered by the locals as the Haverley Murderer. Miss Holland's remains lie in Kings Tarrant cemetery, her grave tended with care on the instructions of distant relatives. Moat Farm is now a private home.

MILLICENT LAGDEN

Thatcher's daughter

The cottage where Millie Lagden was born eighty-odd years ago stands empty now. Halfway down the village street, next door to the pub and opposite the post office, her tiny semi-detached house stands back from the road, up a gravel drive. Recently modernised, a bland exterior reveals no trace of its rustic origins; no timber beams, inglenook or thatch. All has been covered with plaster and paint, neatened and improved.

Millie no longer makes her slow arthritic way across to the post office to collect her pension. She finally opted to move into old people's flats in Kings Tarrant. A skip stands in the drive piled high with rubbish; already somebody has plans for Millie's cottage. Memories of her lifetime there will soon be obliterated.

It was a windy afternoon in late December when I knocked at her front door. The first snow had fallen that night; the village had awoken to a white and silent world, and seemed to have decided to hibernate. Nobody was around as I walked down the street through the still lightly falling snow. Underfoot it lay thick, reflecting brilliant light up to the laden trees as the sun struggled through peach-grey cloud. It was bitterly cold, a north-easterly wind whipping over the land forming a crust on the snow.

As I waited – for Millie's arthritis doesn't permit speed – I watched sheets of newspaper used to insulate the porch windows rustling in the draught. Millie welcomed me in, and we sat beside her electric fire. Hair wavy, snowy-white, complexion clear and creamy, her elegant woollen dress enhanced her bight blue-grey eyes. She clearly relished her subject, talking easily and with an engaging smile. Her childhood memories were happy; an only child, she had plainly been devoted to her parents. The cottage was much changed from her description of the past; no trace of the kitchen range, the indoor washing lines, the copper, or the door at the bottom of the stairs to keep the draught out. Now it had fitted carpets and central heating, electricity and simple but functional fifties furniture.

She sat in her armchair, gnarled hands moving to underline her words, crossing and uncrossing her legs. Exuberantly she evoked the past with a realism not untinged with sentiment.

The threat of the workhouse

Millie We used to to gleaning right up the Gap along the footpaths, nearly as far as Little Bendysh. Us children would go off in the morning because the mums couldn't come till the afternoon – they had a midday meal to get ready for the dads. We took a bottle of lemonade and some sandwiches which were supposed to be for midday; but by 11 o'clock we usually decided we were hungry and thirsty so we demolished them. We stayed in the fields for the rest of the day, and we were perfectly safe. If a child was out these days and you hadn't seen them for three or four hours you'd start to worry.

Wages were small, but most people had their own hens and some of the more adventurous had a pig. You had to have a long garden to keep them away from people because they do whiff a bit! Grandpa Lagden always had one at Sparrows Farm when I was little. When it was killed they didn't waste anything except the hide. There'd be the sides of bacon hanging upside-down near the chimney, and we all had a joint, and chitterlings. I never saw the pig being killed – I couldn't have borne that. They had a proper man to do it and I believe it was all over in a second. I remember seeing Grandpa wheel somebody's dead pig in his wheelbarrow along the street, to his barn at the back of Sparrows. That's where he used to put the pigs into a copper of boiling water so that he could skin them more easily. Then he hung the carcass in what was then called the brewhouse – it's the dining room now!

We loved going into the forge with its bellows and furnace, and Mr Trigg the smith didn't mind us going in there. He didn't look a bit like a blacksmith, he was smallish, quite unassuming, but very strong. The first time I saw a hot shoe clamped on the horse, with all the terrible smell, I hid my eyes. Somebody said, 'You silly donkey, just you look at the horse!' The horse was standing there perfectly still; so I thought, well it can't be hurting him. The horses were shod in what is now Mr Gawthrop's garage; it was only big enough for two horses at a time.

We were encouraged to pick up horseshoes in the lanes and fields, because Mr Trigg would buy them for a penny. He had a pony and trap for his business and for transporting people to the station, and he used to drive the blind vicar to Bendysh to take services there. He kept his pony in the recreation field.

Mr Trigg came to a sad end. Apparently he became very depressed, although nobody knew why since he appeared to have no problems at home. One day he went out to clean up a shed at the rear of the forge, and the next day he went back in there and hung himself from a beam. His assistant, who had lived at Sparrows Farm, moved to Didbrooke and opened a forge there, and the villagers of Swanbrooke Down took their horses to him to be shod for many years.

Millie I was born in this house. I think I am the only person left who lives in the house where they were born, except for Rex Vickery, but that's a younger generation. The school here was quite strict, although things got out of hand at one point. Then two friends took it over and one was an absolute gorgon! For a while even the boys were afraid of her. But we respected her and we soon realised it was for our own good. I think most children got the same reception as I did; if I went home and said I had been given some punishment, all I got was 'Well, I suppose you asked for it. What do you think we send you to school for!'

But the headmistress was good. Nobody was allowed to leave school until they could enjoy reading a book, and they had to count well enough to know that they were giving the right money, and write a letter to apply for a job. We concentrated on the three Rs, history and geography. We had concerts and plays, but all the rehearsals had to be after school hours.

The school day started with assembly and a hymn, and then until 10 o'clock it was Scripture. We learned lots of the Bible by heart; not parrot-fashion, it would be explained with its inner meaning. So it became part of our thinking. It was definitely a religious influence, not a social thing like it sometimes is today. Every child should be taught these things, and then when they are older they can examine it, and choose whether to take it seriously. I think church schools were a good idea. We had to go to church on Ash Wednesday, Ascension Day, days like that – only for half a day, we got the rest of the day off, so that was a bonus. We went to Sunday school every week.

We were brought up strictly in regard to manners and morals, at school and at home. My father was one of six boys and two girls, so children had to be kept in order! When we were small you didn't ever call elderly people by their Christian names. But since everybody called Len Cakebread 'Len', I did too. Then once, when I was in their house with my mother, I called Mrs Cakebread

Bertha. My mother boxed my ears! She said, 'Mrs Cakebread to you! Don't ever let me hear you say that again!' And do you know for the rest of my life I called her Mrs Cakebread. She used to say, 'You call Len Len but you never call me Bertha.' So I said, 'Don't you remember when I got my ears boxed for it?' And she said, 'You never did!' – she'd forgotten completely.

Len Cakebread has assumed legendary status in the village; he was even known as 'the uncrowned king of Swanbrooke Down'. He died four years ago aged nearly eighty, and everyone who remembers him has a Len story. He was a village 'character' of the old school, and to those who knew him his demise was the end of village life as it had been for generations.

The eldest of four children, Len Cakebread left Swanbrooke Down school at the age of thirteen because 'they couldn't teach me any more anyway'. He went to work at Mumford Hall under Robert Stockbridge, and after the latter's death became farm manager at another farm in the village. He spent his last few working years employed by the county council, and became a familiar figure keeping the roads tidy.

In 1928 Len married Bertha, who had also been born and reared in Swanbrooke Down. She was sixteen years older than he was, and had been widowed during the First World War. She was a laundress, and helped keep the church clean; Len was churchwarden, bellringer and parish councillor; he had strong words to say about the demolition of the school in the 1950s. A footballer in his youth, Len became in his maturer years umpire of the village cricket team, an imposing, generously-proportioned figure whose judgements nobody challenged. During the Second World War he joined the fire service and was called upon to deal with several incendiary bombs dropped near the village. Len and Bertha had no children, but one wartime evacuee ended up spending several happy years with them.

Len's door was always open and not many hours passed without a visitor, especially after Bertha's death. He was well looked after by his neighbours and counted himself blessed to have such good friends. He hardly ever went out of the village; after being taken to Derbyshire by some villagers once he was heard to remark, 'I wondered where on earth I was going up all those steep hills.'

Swanbrooke Down, so they say, will never be the same without Len's comfortable, corpulent frame leaning over the garden gate, ready to share his earthy wisdom and his fund of dubious stories with whomever was passing.

Millie In those days the people we had to respect, and sometimes we liked them a lot, were the doctor, the vicar and the schoolmistresses. Master Stockbridge, too, of course. I suppose the Stockbridges were fair, but they were a little bit Victorian. Their employees, even in their private lives, had to do what they thought the squire would approve of. He greatly disapproved of gardening on Sundays; but they *had* to garden on Sundays – they didn't even have Saturdays off when I can first remember. So gardening was done on a Sunday, I can assure you.

You had to remember that he was the squire, and Mrs Stockbridge the squire's lady. When they drove through the village the boys had to doff their caps and the girls had to curtsey – so whenever we heard horses coming we'd make a dive for the nearest hedge and hide! When I look back and remember the maids and the staff there, it was just like *Upstairs Downstairs*! They always came to church on Sundays, the Stockbridges and family in the first two rows, the staff sitting behind. We had to behave ourselves, because we were all in the choir, sitting up in front of him in the stalls; we knew we'd catch it if we didn't. They had a party about once a year, for any celebration like when there was a new king or queen. Each summer the children were entertained to tea on the front lawn of the Hall. School closed early and we each had to take a mug for lemonade. Mrs Stockbridge gave us bread, butter and jam, and rock-cakes. They had swings put up in the park, and there were boat rides on the lake. But I wasn't very old when Mr Stockbridge died so I don't remember all that much of it.

The land was sold off to different people and one tragedy was that a timber merchant bought some and chopped down *beautiful* trees. At Sparrows Farm there was a huge, lovely walnut, the first to come down. The row of trees alongside the recreation meadow, mostly elm, all came down. That was sad because it was only for money.

We weren't hungry; our back gardens were our allotments and we grew all the vegetables we needed. The foreman at Mumford Hall overestimated the number of Bramley apple trees they needed for the orchard so all the cottages were given one. We had a Victoria plum tree too, so we had plenty of fruit.

Breakfast had to be porridge when you were little. When you were old enough to rebel you had an egg. Dinner at midday had to be the main meal because the dads came home at noon, and there was always meat and ample vegetables; it might be mince, or liver and bacon. While Mum had apples, either off the tree or bottled, we had apple pudding, or apple pie and custard. Mum fetched the milk from Grinchells Farm every other day, so there was plenty. Tea was very ordinary – bread and jam or, in the winter, toast; and when a pig had been killed there'd be lovely dripping-toast.

We kept warm because there was always a fire on the go. After dad died it was such a nuisance cleaning the chimney that we had the old-fashioned range taken out and an electric cooker put in, but it was never like the old open fire which made the room so lovely and warm: warmth which went on right after the fire had died down and you'd gone to bed – we always left the stairs-door open. If my dad said, 'Let's have a baked potato for supper', there was no problem, you just popped it in the oven; you couldn't put just one potato into an electric cooker, could you, not unless you had a lot of money! We put hot bricks into the grate to take to bed instead of a hot water bottle; we wrapped them in newspaper, then in a piece of flannel, and they kept hot for hours. Mind you I used to kick them out of bed and they made an awful clatter.

Although I was securely tucked in so that it wouldn't happen, I usually managed to find a hole somewhere.

Mum did all the plain sewing – turning sheets to middle, and mending dad's shirts, and cutting towels off and making collars of them. But she was no good at making dresses for me, so they had to be bought. I had one cousin older and bigger than me and I got her clothes handed down, which was most useful. My shoes were like the ones Wilf showed you – black leather ankle-boots with laces, made by Mr Nightingale. We needed them because the roads weren't made up.

Daniel Nightingale, born in 1870, was first apprenticed to an undertaker, where he survived a practical joke played on him by his colleagues: they threw him into a coffin and fastened the lid down. Subsequently apprenticed to a shoemaker, he set up business in one of the cottages next to the forge, and used to walk to the outlying villages to pick up shoes to mend. When he needed leather he would take the train to London from Lillingford and buy his goods in Petticoat Lane.

Children were always welcomed in his workshop and he would sit them on high stools and give them little tasks while they watched him work. The boys were given knives to sharpen, while the girls were allowed to clean his lamp-glasses. He worked long hours, often by the light of an oil lamp or by candlelight.

The more mischievous boys used to tie Daniel Nightingale's apron strings to his cobbler's stool, so that when he got up he took the stool with him. Nonetheless he kept apples and pears in drawers for the children. By all accounts he was an excellent shoemaker; the shoes hardly ever wore out, they were just outgrown. The ankle-boots Wilf Middleditch showed me looked, in spite of their great age, almost new.

As his business flourished Daniel Nightingale acquired a pony and trap. He was a regular down at the Dog and Duck, and although a diminutive size – only 5′ 3″ – he wore enormously long shirts, the longest in the village, he was proud to claim. A fellow-villager who was well over six feet challenged him, and on measuring, Daniels's indeed proved the longer. He and his wife Lydia brought up six children in their four-roomed cottage. One of his sons, Leonard, affectionately nicknamed Ding-Dong, was killed in action in World War I.

Daniel's parents lived next door to them in Stocks Cottage. His mother was the local midwife and also administered country remedies when villagers fell sick, since calling out the doctor was only resorted to *in extremis*. After their death, the Nightingales' new neighbours, a couple called Smith, moved in with a lodger named Harry Brooks. Mrs Smith did not permit her husband to sleep in the house so he was sent to the garden shed every night. One evening he fell into the stream outside the Green Man, and was found there dead the following morning.

Millie When I was old enough to knit I did all the knitting for Mum and for me, and I quite liked it – I even knitted all our vests. At school we had needlework lessons and how I hated them! We used to make *dreadful* chemises which were a sort of slip, sometimes with sleeves, that went on under your vest. They were made of calico, and as scratchy as heck, even after they'd been washed. We were always made to buy them after we'd made them which was adding insult to injury. And summer knickers of the same material. So by and large I was scratched from my neck down to my knees! It didn't encourage me to like needlework.

Washing clothes was a palaver. I can still see my mother's poor hands at the end of a wash-day. She had a big wooden washing tub, and Dad would fill the copper for her on Sunday, ready for wash-day Monday. We had large tanks then for soft water, and it was lovely for washing in. In the summer when it was hot – and believe you me the summers really *were* hot – Mum would get up early and light the fire under the copper, boil the water and bail it out pailful by pailful as she needed it. She used soda, and her hands used to be red and raw, but she never grumbled. She was a jolly good washer. The sheets were beautifully white, and that was using just soda, none of these detergents. We had a line up the end of the garden, and sometimes she'd have two line-fulls; there were two beds each week, and in the warm weather it had to be a fresh shirt for my father every day, a working shirt and another when he went for his drink at night.

He was a thatcher, Bill Lagden his name was, a real character. He always went around on a bike, he never had anything else. People thought he was very grumpy, but he wasn't, he just wouldn't take any nonsense. He was kind to me, and there wasn't a better father anywhere. He was a regular at the Green Man until that closed, then he went to the Dog and Duck for his drink, every evening at five past seven. You never quite knew what he was going to say next. They called him the tap-room philosopher! There was a story that once he was sitting at the bar making a case for the earth being flat, and the person he was arguing with pointed at the full moon: 'Look at that, Bill,' he roared, 'You'll agree that the moon is round?'

'O yes,' says my dad, 'I'll grant ye that. But so's a penny!'

A thatcher's work was even more seasonal then than it is today. Bill Lagden would collect his long wheatstraw from the fields at harvest time, for before combine harvesting the corn was cut in one piece, with the straw intact. He treated it in the traditional way, still used today. He piled up the straw and turned and tossed it with a hayfork until it gleamed. Then he would throw water over it and stamp it down hard. The next day he would pull neat handfuls out of the pile ready for thatching. His tools were simple: he had a short-handled metal rake for combing the straw once it was in place on the roof; a wooden mallet for driving in the spindles; a cutting tool which looked like the end of a scythe, and a pair of small hand-shears to trim the thatch at the end of the job.

Harvest was Bill Lagden's busiest time, because the farmers wanted their cornstacks made weatherproof until the threshing machine came around to deal with them. He would work from early morning until late evening in the fields, his balding head turning mahogany in the sun. The water he needed had to be brought on the horse-drawn water-cart which plied between the well and the fields all day long.

Once cold weather came and the wheatstraw had been frozen it was no use for thatching, so Bill Lagden turned to his winter occupation of making spindles – the pegs which keep the thatch in place. These are made from poles of hazel which had to be cut into 20-inch lengths. He would sit astride a long wooden bench, using the other end as a chopping block, and split the poles into four with a special 'bill' or chopper to give them sharply pointed ends. These were then soaked in a tank of water until they were pliable enough to bend in half without snapping. He would make enough to see him through the busy times in the year ahead.

Millie We always went to Mrs Nightingale, the shoemaker's mother, if we were unwell. My granny's remedies were pretty good too – they had to be, she had eight children to bring up, and they were all healthy. But then the food in those days was so much purer. I only remember going to the doctor once but I don't remember what for. Mum chickened out, she wouldn't take me, so Dad got Grandad's pony and trap and took me. But mostly the old wives' remedies seemed to work. Granny mixed up 'Granny's Lotion' – she got the recipe from the gypsies, she'd listen to them for hours. It certainly was good, and it definitely worked.

One of our treats was going to Kings Tarrant in the holidays; we walked there and back. Going was all right, we ran down the hill. Coming home was different, we were tired and irritable and we whined and moaned because it was all uphill. Nevertheless we were quite ready to go again when there was another holiday. I used to think it was great fun looking around the market. We had to buy most of our clothes there.

I began to go further afield when I went to work and had the money. The first Woolworth's I ever saw was in Cambridge and it was great – I thought I was dreaming! You could see a lot in Cambridge – I went to my first theatre there. But you had to earn your own money to do these things. I worked at the electrician's shop in Kings Tarrant as a ledger-clerk until my mother fell ill, and then I had to stay home with her. While I was home I had an opportunity to do a few hours for a chartered accountant. After that I was able to find someone who would look in and see that my mother was all right, so I worked part-time for two years. I had to stay at home for the third year of her illness. When she died the chartered accountants gave me a full-time job and I was there until I retired.

I've never been out of this country – I didn't even get to Cornwall and Devon until I'd been retired about three years, and I love Devon! It's beautiful. I've been nearly into Wales; I stayed quite near the border. Scotland I don't want to go to, and Ireland – no. There's only two places I'd like to go to, I always have, but I'll never get there now. I'd love to go to Austria in the spring and see the wild flowers, and I'd love to go to Vienna to the New Year's Day concert. I look at it every year on the TV and do I wish I could be there! I've never really wanted very much to go abroad – my friend and her husband used to invite me to go with them but when I kept on making excuses they stopped asking me. Looking at countries abroad on the TV I don't think I especially want to.

I read an awful lot of books and I'm glad I did. It's a wonderful hobby when you start reading the right sort of books. As I was an only child there were lots of hours in the winter when Mum would be sitting sewing, and Dad with his 'head stuck in a book' as Mum would say. So I read too. I started off with Billy Bunter, and then the mistress at school started a little library for us; we paid about a halfpenny a week towards new books, and she introduced me to authors I hadn't even thought about. I was reading Dad's blood-and-thunders which weren't good for me, so she introduced me to Charles Dickens and I've never tired of those. Whenever there's one of his plays on the TV I wouldn't miss it for anything. Dad loved Dickens too – I introduced him to *The Old Curiosity Shop.* I sat him down to it and he just wouldn't stop until he'd read it.

When he went on holiday once to his sister in Finchley he brought me *Oliver Twist* back: talk about *me* giving *him* sweets for his birthday . . .

I was allowed to read until eight o'clock in bed, because we were reading by candlelight and it was bad for the eyes. I was reading *Oliver Twist*, and I wouldn't go to sleep until Mum and Dad had been in to say goodnight. Well, I got to the part where Bill Sykes was about to murder Nancy, and I thought, 'I can't go to sleep until I know what happens!' So I waited until they'd settled down, put my slip-mat against the door, lit my candle and got back into bed with the book. Poor Nancy got murdered and I was too scared to put the book down. I was too scared to blow the candle out, so I had to call Mum to do it. And of course she couldn't open the door because I'd put the mat against it. Was I in trouble! I thought I'd be banned from reading in bed forever.

I had a vivid imagination as a child. We were always hearing about ghosts because several places in the village are supposed to be haunted. I didn't believe in them then, but I think I've got an open mind now. I'd have to see something to believe in it, but I don't actually want to be convinced! I don't know anybody who is convinced that they've seen a ghost. Perhaps you've got to have an open mind about spirits of the departed. Granny Lagden used to tell a tale of how one woman, driven to suicide because her husband was such an old devil, cut her throat in the outside toilet at Sparrows Farm. She assured me you could still see the bloodstains on the floor. But she never persuaded me to go and look – so I didn't believe her! Another lady who lived there suffered bouts of depression, and one day, when her husband had gone to Mumford Hall to collect the milk, she jumped down the well in the garden and ended her life.

Church was a very important part of village life in those days. The vicar was connected with the school because it was a church school, and he was an influential person and tried to give people the right ideas. He was respected, and if you respect a person you're inclined to follow their example. When I was at school there wouldn't have been much going on without the church and the school. The first time I saw the sea, when I was eleven, was on a choir outing. The schoolmistresses were responsible for getting us mixed up in all sorts of things – they took us to our first pantomime. We used to take a penny a week for about two months beforehand and that was meant to pay for it. That was ridiculous, it didn't. But it gave us an independent feeling. When a child left school they were interested to help them get something they wanted to do.

There was always carol-singing before Christmas, which originally consisted of one or two children tapping on the door, singing two lines of 'Away in a manger' and starting to giggle. Then the school organised it, and we did it to raise money for something worthwhile.

I always had a Christmas stocking, and a present by the side. Since the time I can remember I always wanted an annual for Christmas. They were on show early in the shops – not so early as these days though! I'd start looking at them in Kings Tarrant to see which one I was going to have. I would spend a lot of Christmas Day looking through it quickly, then spend the rest of the year reading it again until I got another the next Christmas.

The stocking had the usual things: a bar of chocolate, a sugar mouse, an orange in the bottom, and little things Mum had picked up. We always had a Christmas tree – usually a bough of spruce which Dad would pick out of the hedgerows. I decorated the house with paperchains everywhere.

Chicken for dinner was a luxury. You had to wait until one of your hens got too old, and you could boil it. But chicken with sage and onion stuffing, that was *the* Christmas dinner, and always home-made Christmas pudding afterwards. And some mince pies if you'd any more room. That was at midday. Being in the choir, there was a service in the morning and a crib service in the afternoon. It was a major part of Christmas day and we sang all the old carols, to let rip. But you didn't expect to spend so much of the day in church as you did Easter.

Easter was a religious holiday. Easter Sunday was even more important than Christmas, even if it wasn't as popular. You spent Good Friday in church; Saturday you decorated the church, and it was quite a performance. The school children all had their parts to play and we used to do the tall candlesticks at the ends of the pews. At Eastertime we could sometimes find palm – that's pussy-willow – and hazel catkins, and usually there were a few daffodils about because I'm sure the weather was kinder then. We always found plenty of trails of ivy which we'd twist round so it would look lovely.

Our favourite time for decorating was harvest time. The old man's beard had gone fluffy by then and you could wind streamers of it round with sprays of rose hips and little bunches of corn which you'd pinch from the field when nobody was looking; we enjoyed that.

People kept talking about Munich, but I never really thought war would happen. That Sunday morning the vicar terminated the service and told everybody what had happened. I just couldn't believe it. We had evacuees of course, and we did our best to make ends meet with the rations. In the winter that was pretty dreadful. But it was amazing how different people were during the war. Everyone put themselves out to help everyone else, as if we had all been brought down to one level.

It had its humorous side; I was clerk to the parish council which meant we had to see about dishing out gas-masks. Jimmy Woodcock, who lived in Holly Cottage, had a tremendous bushy beard. He had been a labourer at Mumford Hall, but he was retired and spent much of his time keeping the churchyard tidy. Anyway, do you think we could get one of these gas-masks on him? So Mr Ashton said, 'It's no good Jim, you're not going to get into this.'

'Well I've got to have one. I'm going to take it home.'

So off he goes with this silly little mask. Mr Ashton said, 'It's no good, we've got to get him something', and they got him one of the outsize industrial ones. Mr Ashton took it to him in this great box to make sure he knew how to get it on. He said, 'You're OK now, Jim, so give me the other one, will you please?'

'Well', says Jim, 'I don't know where I put that!' And we never did find it. It did have its lighter moments.

After the Second World War many more people came to live in the country. Some of them had come here during the war with their children, and they liked country life so they stayed. Lots bought cottages to get out at weekends, and it grew and grew until you had an entirely different population.

So the war was responsible for a lot of change. So were the car and the radio. I can remember the first car in the village – it belonged to the vicar. I used to ride in it when we went to sing in Bendysh church choir and I thought it was great! For ages after that if you heard one coming – they were pretty noisy – you rushed to the window to see it – it was a special occasion!

The radio made the world smaller. It was maddening during the war, though, because as soon as enemy aircraft approached the coast the sound faded practically to nothing, and it was always in the middle of Tommy Handley or some other programme I wanted to hear!

As far as contentment and happiness were concerned, yes, they were 'good old days'. Living in the country, we had enough to eat, even if that was because of our own efforts. We had every reason to be content. Employers in the country weren't the dreadful people they have been made out to be.

It's a two-way thing. I can see my mother's red-raw hands, and then I think of the washing machine in the kitchen. I couldn't do without my spin-dryer now, but in rainy weather in the old days the washing would have to keep going out and being brought in until it was dry. At night there were lines across the sitting room, to finish the drying when the fire was made up at bedtime. So there's good and bad. Running water and electricity have made life simpler and more pleasant.

On the other side, some good things have gone; contentment is one of them. So many people are never satisfied. Perhaps some of them have so many advantages when they are very young that they grow up taking them for granted. They have many more choices to make. Our life was wonderfully simple. When girls left school, they only had one choice of employment – domestic service. I suppose the war altered that, because factories sprang up and employed them. Once the war was over they weren't going to do people's housework again. If they like it as much as I do who can blame them!

There was no old age pension; the first pension Mum and Dad got was five shillings each! Before that, an overseer used to decide which old people were in need of parish relief, and they had to go along to the yard of the Green Man to meet the Relieving Officer, who would give them 2/6 and a loaf of bread a week. Curiously enough, this village overseer also decided which stray animals in the village pound belonged to whom. If you hadn't got grown-up children to help financially, or take you in, it was the workhouse.

That was a terrible place. the local workhouse was at Kings Tarrant, and there was another at a small town twelve miles away. People used to walk from one to the other past New Farm where my mother lived, which was one of the first houses they came to. They were always at the door begging for something to eat or hot water to make tea. My granny was like my mother, terribly softhearted, and they got more out of her than she could well afford; they soon find out who they can con! They then walked through to the workhouse in Kings Tarrant and had a meal. They had to do a little job, something in the garden for the men, the women had to scrub, to pay for their bed and board. Then they made the journey back to their own workhouse. The system had to be changed eventually – they'd never have got away with it for ever. Just because you're old it doesn't mean you should be swept under the mat.

I had to go inside the workhouse in Kings Tarrant, because the lady my mother worked for all the time she was in service, she died there. I hated going. But my mother religiously went to see her every week, and in the holidays. I had to go with her. There was this horrible smell of carbolic. The walls were dark green and the rest of the paint was dark brown and there would always be poor old dears on their knees scrubbing all these stone passages. It was a horrible place. But they were fed, and looked after, and after all they had nobody else. But what a way to die. I'm quite sure people weren't unkind to them like the old days, but it was no picnic. The part that frightened me, because I was only a school girl, was that people who were really round the bend were mixed in with all the others. There was this old lady who'd make a dive for me and pat my head. I was scared *stiff.* Mum said, 'Don't be silly, dear, she just likes your hair' – but I was terrified.

Nowadays it's a hospital, all nice and bright. They've had buildings added, and it's lovely and warm. The long passages are glassed in, so you get any sun there is. When I think of those days, bitterly cold in winter, it is one of the good things that that has gone.

It has to be part of a natural change that village life isn't a community any more. I don't see why we can't all get on together, but then we are all different. People have a different way of life now because they are affluent. I'd have a car if I could afford one! People buy a house and it's theirs to do what they like with. If you don't like it, just let it be. You can't be romantic about the past. Lots of things make me sad, but there's nothing you can do about it, you just have to accept it. The surface may change, but human nature doesn't change. Doesn't improve, either.

I was reading a book in which the Master of Fox Hounds had seduced the kitchenmaid and she'd been turned out of the house. Wilf said, well that happened in everyday life, and Dora said it couldn't have done. She doesn't like to believe anything bad but of course it did! In those days all that sort of thing was suppressed, but it happened. I don't think morals have changed a lot. Everybody had their own standards or non-standards but the difference is that things that weren't meant to come into the daylight never did come into the daylight.

Today you've got the added misery of drugs. In the old days a pint of beer was a pint of beer and men could drink a lot more of it before it affected them – a lot of it was water. I can't ever remember seeing drunken men in Swanbrooke Down. Let's be honest, they couldn't afford to get drunk! There was a lot of home-made wine, and some of that was pretty potent! Dad made wheat wine once that burst in the night, went all over the larder it went off with such a bang. It would have been jolly good stuff if it had kept another week!

Dora was always the good girl and I was the tomboy. I could climb trees as well as her brother. We had stilts, and I wasn't content until I could walk on them. We used to cross the stream in front of Holly Cottage – all the carts went straight through there, and it had a pebble-stone bed. So Dora's brother said, 'I bet you can't go through there on stilts.' So of course I did and went flat on my face! Served me right. One thing he was so pleased about was that he had a penny-farthing bicycle, which he rode as easily as you would ride an ordinary bike. And I *could* not do it! I could *not*. I used to stand it up against the side of the house while I got on, and the first turn of the pedals and I was on the ground again!

I was rather afraid of horses so I never rode them; all the farmers' horses were put out to grass in the meadows, and it was lovely to see these big working horses, heavy horses. They had Suffolk Punches at Little Bendysh Hall and they were magnificent.

GRACE BRAYBROOKE

Schoolteacher

She sits by the old black range, stretching her hands towards the glowing coals. It is a dreary January morning, and her tiny cottage is shaking off the chill of the night. Grace Braybrooke, offering me a chair opposite her, proudly shows me a new electric radiator which, she says, makes all the difference to coming downstairs in the mornings.

Her cottage was the old post house where, until about 1950, the post office ran its business. It is an ancient two-up, two-down semi-detached cottage adjoining Len Cakebread's, lath and plaster with a reed thatch. A long, narrow back garden runs up to a hedge of tall trees which shield it from the fields. A beehive stands at the top of the garden; like Wilf Middleditch, Grace is a dedicated bee-keeper. In summer the garden is full of cottage flowers and herbs; today there are only a few aconites and a clump of hellebores. Winter jasmine knocks against the window panes.

Grace is eighty-five, although it is hard to believe. She is tall and gaunt with a dignified, upright bearing and hair pulled back into a bun. Her lined, aquiline face has the indefinable air of a 'lady'. She is often to be seen striding through the village, binoculars in hand, in pursuit of her favourite pastime – bird-watching.

A retired schoolteacher, a spinster, she is a self-confessed loner and has lived on her own since her sister died many years ago. She lives simply, shopping at Haverley every Friday, attending church on Sundays, tending her garden and her bees. The waterproof jacket on the back of the kitchen door, the wellington boots by the step, are the give away – for above all Grace loves to be out of doors. She is interested in everything to do with nature and the countryside; this constitutes her companionship and communion.

On the windowstill overlooking the street there always stands a plant or a vase of flowers. As we talk a single amaryllis is bursting into bloom, luminous pinkish-scarlet. On the desk is a posy of jasmine and snowdrops. In the autumn a stunning display of nerines is shown to advantage in the leaded window-frame, in late summer it offers a vision of old roses to passers-by. Today the view from the window is sunless. That special English brand of January greyness has descended. It is damply, bitterly, cold; we sit as near the fire as we can.

Grace's story nearly spans the century. She 'only' came to Swanbrooke Down in 1950, for which she apologised and called herself a 'newcomer'. Her experience as an Edwardian vicar's daughter was spellbinding, and forty years was time enough to tell a tale or two about life in Swanbrooke Down.

Lasting values in natural beauty

Grace I was born in Wardingham vicarage in 1903, about five miles from here. I was the fifth in a family of seven. My father was vicar of Wardingham, which in those days was a small village with Sir Bernard Rolfe as squire at the Hall. Practically all the men in the village worked on his estate. He had paddocks, so there were grooms as well. He started a lavender factory, and the well-known Wardingham jam factory, all for the village. The men who didn't work in these special places worked on his outlying farms.

My father was on good terms with Sir Bernard, who was a very kind man – we got presents from the Hall, and from the jam factory. My father would take us up to the Hall to meet the butler; he showed us the gold plate in the safe once. I was meant to be very impressed by that; it was very interesting – but gold has never had the same effect on me as silver. Sir Bernard had an aviary, too, which my father used to take me to see, and we played in the gardens. So we were quite closely connected with the Hall.

Sir Bernard Rolfe was very particular; he liked things to look well. The vicarage was a big house on the side of a hill; there was a front gate, and all alongside the gardens, down to the bottom gate which my father went through to the church, there was a white painted fence, behind which was a beech hedge. Sir Bernard liked it to look nice as he passed by, so, although we had a full-time gardener, and two maids in the house, he sent his gardeners and painters up to paint the fence and clip the hedge! Then he would drive past in his carriage and pair with a coachman and a footman. That was a lovely sight; he had beautiful grey horses. I remember him as an old gentleman in a top hat and yellow waistcoat. His coachman and footman both had the same yellow waistcoats and top hats; even the gamekeepers had these yellow waistcoats! He had between six and ten grey horses up in his stables.

As time went on, he had a car – a Rolls Royce; so the first car I ever drove in was a Rolls! But that meant he got rid of his carriage, and I was sad, because I loved horses. I was taught to ride by a groom at the Hall, who showed me how to ride side-saddle; it was not considered ladylike to ride astride. So instead of

this lovely sight of the carriage and pair, the car would go past at its stately pace, sending clouds of dust over the garden because the roads weren't tarred. In spring when the trees came out the new leaves would be covered in dust until the rain washed it off.

Sir Bernard died in 1924, and the estate was sold up. That was the beginning of change in the village; there wasn't the same feeling at all. Previously we had gone up to the Hall for village parties, and functions like the Mothers' Union, but then the main gatherings started to take place in the village hall. His daughter – who was my godmother – ran them.

I was brought up in a regular Church of England tradition, my father being a vicar, but it wasn't overdone. We didn't go to church until we were old enough to understand what was going on, and my elder sister saw that we behaved properly. We went to matins, and occasionally to a children's service – he was very keen on getting the children to church. On Good Friday and Holy Innocents' there used to be a number of children in the congregation, which only happened in Wardingham. Somebody from the next village came to the service and was quite surprised to see all the children. As they went out of church on Good Friday they all had a hot cross bun, and on Holy Innocents' Day a bag of sweets. Some people would say that was bribery, but my father used to say it was a reward for going to church, and anyway it got them into church and that was what he wanted.

In those days the girls sat on one side of the aisle, the boys on the other, and parents with babies and younger children at the back. The vicarage family sat facing the altar under the pulpit, with the Hall pews facing the other way. That's all been altered now. Sir Bernard himself didn't go to church, but his daughter and her family, and any people staying there, used to attend.

It was a very structured society. The factories had been created for the local people, which was a bit unusual. They grew lavender in the fields and made lavender water, but that factory ceased a long time ago. The jam factory is still going. But the people were content – Sir Bernard was a good master. It was a kind of feudal arrangement and most people lived in his cottages. There weren't many houses in those days; the farmhouses were very nice, but nearly all the houses were either smallish houses or cottages, with quite a few living in each one.

I didn't go to the village school because we had a governess, the postmaster's sister. When my brother and I were old enough we went to the high school which had only recently opened when I started at the age of nine. By then I could read and write and do some arithmetic and I found my level soon enough. It wasn't a very big school to start with, just a few hundred pupils, and it was nice and modern. We wore uniform, and there was never any trouble, perhaps because the classes weren't very big. We were naughty of course and I wasn't a saint. I was athletic and thoroughly enjoyed games and that's what I remember most, playing in the hockey and tennis teams. I was very happy at school, yet I was always very pleased when the holidays came because I loved being at home.

We had a live-in nanny, and the governess came daily. The governess came from Haverley. For us, Haverley was the back of beyond! I don't know how she got to Wardingham and home again because there was no transport. My father had a pony and trap and when we were older we all had bicycles and travelled everywhere on them. My father had a bicycle and later on an autowheel, and he did quite a lot of walking as well.

It was a lovely part of the country, round about Wardingham. I remember how *quiet* it was. Just the clip-clop of horses, or very occasionally a car. Now you hear traffic all the time, and the hum of the motorway in the distance. As long as I can remember I've been interested in anything to do with the country – as children we spent a lot of time roaming the lanes and looking at flowers and birds. There were more pasture fields, because paddocks were needed for the farms. There were cornfields too, and paths across the fields, and woods on the Hall estate. It was all well kept, the hedging and ditching were immaculate. The horses were still working, so it was a different countryside. After the First World War things changed – because of the car, and because Sir Bernard had died and the estate was broken up.

Our upbringing was fairly strict, but in no way irksome. I adored my father and I couldn't bear to do anything that made him reprimand me. We did as we were told. It was strict, but not alarming; in those days children did behave better. I remember my father saying there were three men in the village whose children had better behave themselves: himself, the policeman and the schoolmaster! We didn't have vandalism, and I don't remember teenagers being tiresome. When children left school they immediately went to work, so they had something to do and they behaved themselves. Boredom never reared its head – we used to wander along the stream and in the woods and fields – we weren't trespassing, we were allowed to. There was never any question of not going out because something might happen to us. We went for miles on our bicycles, and walked perfectly free. We used to birds'-nest, pick flowers, play in the stream, and I really had a happy childhood because I was so fond of the country. I had siblings, a big garden and quite a lot of animals. There weren't many other children our age but we didn't miss them. We came over to Kings Tarrant for parties because my grandfather lived there. We had very few parties at home.

My upbringing was in the context of village life, and my father impressed on us that we were to be polite and helpful to the village people. In the 1920s all the old people respected him. The women curtsied to him, and the men touched their hats. When we were out with our father elderly women would bob, and he would speak to them – as we did too. They used to come to the vicarage to see him in his study. It was a big house, and from the front door the hall led straight through to the garden, with his study on the right. There was a seat in the hall for anybody who wanted to see him. We were told not to run to the nursery past anybody sitting there without stopping and speaking. One day my brother and I were going down the hall and an old lady called Hilda

Cooper was sitting in the chair. She had come from three miles away. The older women all wore black in those days, and a shawl. Hilda had on a hair-net of thick crocheted cotton or wool – they said she put it on in the autumn and took it off in the spring! There she was, and we knew that my father was buying turkeys from Hilda so we stopped, as we had been told to, and said, 'Good afternoon,' and then, 'and how are the turkeys, Mrs Cooper?'

'Aarrh, they do greuse and they sots everywhere!' by which she meant, 'They are growing fast and sitting down all over the place.'

Not long after that my brother and I were coming up the road from playing in the stream when we met Hilda Cooper again. And she gave us a curtsey! We were absolutely thrilled, and told my father, 'Hilda Cooper curtsied to us!'

'Well, that's very kind of Mrs Cooper, and I hope you were polite back.'

'Oh, yes!' I don't suppose we were, but we were so thrilled! I shall always remember her bobbing to us.

Until five or six years ago there were two or three old men in Swanbrooke Down who always touched their hats – one of them was Wilf Middleditch, the others have died. Nobody in the village would do that now.

In our village, war didn't seem very close, except for the men who had joined the forces. I had just gone to school when the First World War broke out, and we went to school by train: one mile to the station, five miles by train, and about thee-quarters of a mile to walk to the school. The thing I remember most vividly was the trains being crowded with soldiers – we could only just get on. I remember rationing, but we never went short of anything. Meat was difficult to get, but we had a village shop and we could get most other things there. The butcher came once or twice a week, the baker came, and we normally had butter from the farm. We had a sizeable kitchen garden so we had all the vegetables we needed, and an orchard for fruit, so there wasn't any difficulty with food.

My three elder brothers joined the forces and the eldest was in the Flying Corps – it wasn't called the Air Force then. One day my brother and I were going across the fields and we saw an aeroplane doing stunts over the vicarage. We realised that it was my brother and suddenly he looped the loop. I remember the fear then, that he had gone out of control. We started to run home, but instantly he righted himself and went off and everything was alright. I don't remember being frightened by anything else. It was the Second World War when the fear of invasion really occurred.

My sister bought this cottage in 1950. There are a lot more houses now – I counted twenty-seven houses and bungalows built here since, not counting the four new agricultural cottages up Elmshaw Lane, or the council houses which were built just before we came. People with children were moving out of the cottages next door to go into the new council houses; they were bigger, they had bathrooms and were more convenient. That meant that older people like my sister were coming to live in the old cottages. It's rather amusing because the people in the council houses called these the slums!

There were no houses next to the post office, that was the recreation field. A lot of the old cottages have had additions recently – most not spoiled but improved. This is one of the few that hasn't been altered. It is about 300 years old, and it is the same as it was in 1950. Just before my sister bought it, electric light and drainage and a septic tank had been put in. Apart from that this part hasn't been altered. There's still a copper in the kitchen (so-called!) and this mid-Victorian stove. When we came there were several still in use in the cottages, but as soon as they changed hands the stove was taken out. I have rather sentimentally kept this one, because when I'm gone it will come out. It's rather attractive, and has been used for nearly a century – you can still use the oven; it will cook a quiche, and mince pies or sausage rolls, and the hob will heat a kettle. You will notice it hasn't got a well with a tap for hot water, as the later Victorian ones did.

Even though my sister and I were 'foreigners', there was still a sense of close community in Swanbrooke Down when we came. My sister was the eldest daughter of the vicarage; she had the way of getting to know people and very quickly got into village life. Everybody knew everybody else then, there was no question of having to live here for twenty years before we were accepted! I was speaking to Mrs Gapes in the street one day, and I didn't know whether she knew who I was; she was rather a formidable lady in black, with a large hat, and I said, 'I'm Miss Braybrooke's sister.' 'I know who you are!' she said.

The Cakebreads were the most entertaining neighbours. I found them increasingly so after my sister died, and we got to know each other better. Len used to tell me yarns. Bertha liked to know everything. She used to say, 'Naturally I never gossip', but of course she did! Len was working on the farm so I only saw him at weekends and holidays, but when we both retired I used to hear these stories. There's one I particularly remember.

There were allotments up Elmshaw Lane, and a villager who I'll call Jack was planting potatoes there when he had a friend from London to stay. This friend went and watched him planting.

'Why are you so careful to plant the potatoes the right way up?' he asked.

'Ah,' said Jack, 'if I planted them the wrong way up, they'd come up as artichokes.'

The London man simply did not believe him. So Jack said, 'You plant this potato upside down, at the end of the row, and when you come next time you'll see it has come up as an artichoke.'

The man did as he suggested, and after he had gone Jack took out the potato and planted an artichoke. When the man came down again he said, 'What about that potato I planted?'

'Well, you come and see, it's come up as an artichoke.' The man from London looked at it.

'Well,' said he, 'if I hadn't seen it with my own eyes I would never have believed it!'

They were real Essex people. Mrs Cakebread had some nice expressions. I once asked her if she had been gardening.

'Not really,' she said, 'I've just been a-dibbin and a-dobbin round.'

Essex had its own vocabulary in those days; Wilf Middleditch made a list for me of all the old words he could remember. It contained expressions like 'shonks' (feet), 'scrotch' (a forked stick), 'jinney-bob' (a wren), and 'dummy-dors' (bumble bees). Potatoes were generally known as 'taters', and when you were frozen cold you were 'froor'. An 'orkard hoss' was a wilful horse, and the 'owd diddycoys' were the old gypsies. A 'yellum' was a bundle of straw used by a thatcher, a 'sheen' was a threshing machine, and 'sheening' meant threshing the corn. Phrases were shortened into single words, like 'giss', give us, 'dint', did not, and 'thissul', this will. One villager would frequently be heard telling another to 'git orf of it'.

Grace In our time there haven't been scandals or misfortunes here at all, so I imagine the gossip was fairly trivial. I've never seen a ghost, but I wouldn't be a bit surprised if I did. I would never be surprised if someone said people came back to these cottages. I've had a feeling sometimes, but that's all very intangible.

Bird life hasn't changed much since I've been here, certainly not since I started birdwatching when I retired in 1969. I personally haven't seen as many as I did in the early years, but that's partly because I haven't watched as much. It's not until you really watch that you realise what's around; that's when you come across the migrants and rarities. Last summer I had what I call an acute attack of dotterel fever, and spent most of one weekend watching them in a field near here.

My beekeeping started in rather an extraordinary way. I was a schoolmistress in Herefordshire during the Second War. I had a spaniel for twelve years, and when he died I missed him very much. In the village there lived an elderly beekeeper who came up to the school once a week to take the boys for walks to learn about butterflies and to see his apiary. After the dog died the headmaster said, 'Why don't you keep bees? Mr Rowland will probably let you have some, and would help you.' The idea appealed to me, and Mr Rowland sold me some bees.

Bees are fascinating. Last year was quite different from any year I've ever had. First it was wet and cold, then it was warm, then it turned cold again. A lot of people lost bees; I didn't lose mine but they got weak. I didn't get much honey, but I kept the bees. I read about them – Wilf lends me his books, he's got quite a library. But as he says, 'There are plenty of books about bees, but the bees don't read the books!' They carry on in their own sweet way. If bees make up their mind to do a thing, they'll do it. You just have to put up with it. Beekeeping is one of the most interesting things I have ever done, and it isn't all that easy! I brought them with me when I came to live here. I used to go to beekeepers' meetings, and watch demonstrations. You never stop learning about beekeeping.

Beekeeping has been practised in Swanbrooke Down since Domesday; Cold Spring Farm had three hives at the time of the survey, which would have been 'skeps' or straw hives. These were used until the middle of the eighteenth century, when moveable frames were patented. This meant that honey could be extracted and the frames returned without unduly disturbing the bees. Previously they had had to be killed to get the honey out of the combs. Straw skeps, however, were seen in Swanbrooke Down as late as 1935, hackled and potsherded just as they had been in Saxon times.

Swanbrooke Down's beekeepers bemoan intensive farming which has deprived their bees of the nectar from pasture land, in particular from clover. In the fifties Wilf's average yield per hive was 120 pounds of honey; now he counts himself lucky if he can get one-fifth of that. In a bad year the yield may go as low as twelve pounds per hive.

Traditional beekeepers still use two important old customs: 'tanging the bees' and 'telling the bees'. 'Tanging' is banging a large iron key on a metal tray when a swarm emerges from the hive. This was supposed to make the bees settle, and also served to warn neighbours that a swarm was out, and that the owner knew about it. 'Telling the bees' is explained in an old Essex verse:

Marriage, birth and buryin'
News across the seas,
All you're sad and merry in
You must tell the bees.

Grace I talk to the bees: I like these old superstitions. When the master of the house dies you tell the bees – it's to do with ownership. When my sister died, I told my bees. They say that if you don't tell them they fly off. There have been cases when bees *have* flown away. In the olden days, long before I was beekeeping, if a beekeeper died black crêpe was put over the hive, and they were told. It's like people who talk to plants and care for them; they respond to the care. It seems to work.

Wilf Middleditch is one of the great characters of Swanbrooke Down. He is a real craftsman, a carpenter among other things, and he made all sorts of things for my sister. He had a *feel* for these cottages and made things for them that blend in. He is a true countryman, the only one left in Swanbrooke Down. Wilf *is* Swanbrooke Down for me. I got to know him through bees. He said to me once, 'Why don't you bring your bees here?' I said, 'My sister doesn't like bees', so he said, 'Put them up the top of the garden out of her way.' So I did. He's a staunch churchman, too. He was churchwarden for twenty five years.

The church is far less important in village life than it used to be. Maurice Mansfield is a very nice man, very kind, but he doesn't live in the village, he doesn't get to know people. He comes on a Sunday, takes a service very nicely indeed, and goes away. The congregation has definitely diminished. In my father's time far more people went to church, and there were two or three services on a Sunday. I don't think that he is altogether to blame, because a vicar of three parishes hasn't time to get to know all the people, but I think that is rather sad. The festivals – Christmas, harvest and Patronal Festival, Easter – are all well attended. But not many people go regularly any more. About half a dozen of the regular church goers have left the village, and nobody has taken their place.

I have lost touch with Swanbrooke Down because of increasing old age. Fortunately the people coming in are younger, with families. All the village events used to be organised by the oldies who'd been doing it for years, but now a younger generation has taken over and the various societies are run by younger people, which is excellent. About twenty-five years ago there was only one baby in the village, and a few children up at the council houses. The other night I counted seventy under fifteen! The village needed new life. You can't stand still, or you start to go backwards. I still like

Swanbrooke Down very much; I like the people, and I like getting to know the children.

When there was a school here, children were made to behave; they were taught manners. It is much more lax now. A lot of the trouble in the schools today is due to lack of discipline and manners in the home. I never taught in a state school, and I wouldn't like to nowadays. I taught in boarding prep-schools, and I was fortunate in teaching in two good schools under very capable headmasters. We didn't have trouble – you had individual problems of course, but not the wholesale difficulties they seem to have now. My theory is that it starts in the home.

Public morals are immensely different from the way they were in 1903, although human nature doesn't change much if you look at it historically. People have always done wicked things, but we didn't know about these things. The media do make it much more widespread. You knew of difficulties and things that went wrong in a little community, but you didn't know of the awful things that went on all round the world. I don't know whether it's a good or a bad thing.

It's easy for the likes of me to say, 'Oh, things were much better in my young days.' But the sixties were a good time; we had got over the war, and people were better off. Now there seems to be a constant urge to grab for money. Everything must be money and you *must* have things that money buys. My greatest pleasures have been natural beauties, flowers and birds and the things of the countryside. Not what is bought, but what can be appreciated in nature. But with increasing old age I'm much narrower, because I don't do so much. And I'm a bit more critical of the things that go on. I have travelled, and met people, but you wouldn't say that I've had a wide experience. I'm not very good at getting to know people. I observe them. But certainly the last few years I've met fewer people.

Money seems to be today's religion. Money is the god. That's not in my nature. I've never had a lot of money, far from it, but I've always managed to be very interested and happy on a low income. People spend so much more now, and more time chasing money. They must have things 'to keep up with the Joneses' – even more so than in the past. That's quite obvious in the village; when so-and-so has a new kitchen, or a new car, we must have the same. If you don't keep up, you fall behind. The amount of clothes these younger women have compared with what we had! When I was young money went so much further – my father's stipend was pretty low, in fact my salary at school was higher, but at the vicarage we had a house-parlourmaid, a cook, a nurse, a full-time gardener, a man to dig the garden, a boy to clean the knives on a Saturday and a man to pump the water to the top of the house. All these people to be paid, and all of us children to educate. Yet my father managed – I can't think how. But the cook would get perhaps about £40 a year, her keep and uniform. Things were so different.

I find it very difficult now to cope with what has to be done in the house, building and repairs – the cost seems terrific. I haven't much money, but I can manage. However, the last five or six years the price of everything has gone up, and my income hasn't! Yet that doesn't worry me because I don't crave for things that can be bought. I would like a nice car and a nice kitchen, but I can manage without.

One has to be careful about repeating things about people. I know it happens everywhere and to some extent it is the spice of life; every village has its stories. A lot of it used to be covered up. I think the general feeling is to be discreet – you've got to be in a village. I think Millie Lagden could tell us all sorts of things, but she won't!

I remember Lilian Drayton telling me about the women who lived in cottages like this, with their men who worked in the fields. In the afternoons the women would put on their clean white aprons and stand at the doors gossiping. A woman's day then was unrelenting hard labour. Getting up early because the men went off at the crack of dawn, getting the children to school, getting the food, getting the washing done – they deserved their gossip! Without an hour off in the afternoon life wouldn't have been worth living.

The washing was a real drudge, but they were such good washer-women! Bertha Cakebread was marvellous. All her linen was marvellously white. She did washing for the Hall too. How they managed with the farm labourers I don't know; their filthy trousers and shirts – awfully hard work.

It's a misnomer calling the farm labourers unskilled – those men could drive a binder, control three horses, attend to all the intricate goings-on in the binder and mend it when it was broken. They were far more skilled than these 'skilled mechanics' who sit on their backsides on a tractor. They do it well, and they *are* skilled in their way, but these men that did all the work with the horses were really very skilled. They were proper countrymen – they did the hedging and ditching in the winter and they knew what they were doing.

Until fairly recently there were six farms in the parish, with the farmers living on their own land, in their farmhouses. Now there are only two. All the other farmers have moved on or died, and the land has been sold. When we came here they were starting to use tractors, but when we were children at Wardingham it was all horses. It all happened so quickly – the mechanisation of farming happened in twenty to twenty-five years. But it was a very hard life these ploughmen and people on the farm had – by no means a rural idyll.

1903 to the 1980s; we are talking about the end of feudal England to getting to the moon – in seventy five years. Television would have seemed like magic to them, and I often wonder what they did in a cottage like this; there'd be several children and what did they do in the evenings? The men got up at dawn: a horseman, for example, would get up as soon as it was light, and feed and groom his horses before he set out to plough all day. After that he couldn't have had energy to do anything but eat and go to bed. The children could read but there wasn't much else to do. In the daylight they had their skipping and tops, hopscotch and conkers, but very few other games. They made their own occupations, so they were never bored. Now children are taken everywhere in a car. Sometimes the boys next door are driven to the end of the road to catch the school bus. They have got used to having amusements provided, they haven't made them for themselves, or they soon lose interest in them if they do. We had to make our own amusements; there wasn't a choice. They have a choice, and they choose the human option. On the other hand, they have far more opportunities than we had, both at school and in the village.

CLARICE PENINGTON

Novelist

Clarice Penington is known to most of Swanbrooke Down as a 'character'. Even at her great age, of which she is uncertain but which must be well into the ninth decade, she strides around the village with a tiny dog in tow. She is an unusual not to say eccentric figure, tall and thin with a neatly cut fringe and smooth gray hair falling on to her shoulders, usually dressed in a tweed suit and brogues. Her memory is failing and you have to catch her on a good day to get coherent sense; her behaviour is mildly dotty from time to time as a result of this decline in her faculties. Soon after our talk (which was on a relatively good day), I met her by the bridge clutching an enormous rat to her bosom. 'My sister said she was going to kill the poor darling,' she said, eyes burning with indignation. 'It's such a sweet little thing but she says I have to turn it out of the house. So I'm taking it up into the fields – do you know of a place where it might be safe?'

Decades ago Clarice was married to a senior BBC producer, and was herself for many years a successful novelist. She doesn't write any more, saying she has achieved all she wanted to in that field. Her eccentric vagueness tallies with a story told about her: how, when first married, she roasted a turkey with all the innards still inside it. Local legend has it that she had an equally dotty sister, who lived along Elmshaw Lane. Nobody ever saw her out of jodpurs, riding boots and hunting jacket. She wore her hair very short in a bob. This androgynous figure, it is said, kept a horse in her sitting room. Or rather, she had the living room divided by a stable door; she lived in one half, the horse in the other.

Clarice, now widowed and her son living in London, lives alone in a classic 'gingerbread' cottage, an old thatched place by the church, full of beams and nooks and crannies. The outside walls are deep pink, with blue window-frames, and china cats sit on the windowsills. In the large garden, overlooked by the church, stands a brightly-painted gypsy caravan, eye-catching to sight-seers as they walk beside Winter Water, alongside her hedge.

I visited her on a bitter January morning. The street was deserted. A curtain of greyness had descended over the village, and the drizzle fell faster and colder as I walked. The muffled squelch of my footsteps was the only sound to be heard in the early morning stillness. Cottagers were huddled indoors against the freezing weather, not tempted to stir from their cosy rooms into that bleak rainscape.

Clarice greeted me warmly and the cottage felt friendly. It was furnished with traditional cottage-style ornaments, books and rugs and lamps. The little dog, after greeting me noisily, settled her feet.

Looking back to old-fashioned ways

Clarice We bought this place when it was falling to pieces. We'd been looking all day for somewhere to live here, because we liked the look of the village, and we needed a place where we could get away from London, where my husband was working. He pointed to this cottage and said, 'We must have it.' I said, 'Darling, where's the money coming from?' 'I don't care, we must have it!' – too ridiculous, just like he used to be! We hadn't a penny in the bank. Anyway he got round his father to lend us enough to buy it, although he was very much against it. 'It's all falling to pieces, it's ridiculous, the whole thing.' He was a very old-fashioned old man. However we didn't mind because if you love a thing enough there's always a way, and we weren't going to allow it to fall to pieces. We wanted to build it up like it used to be and I've always maintained that if you want to do a thing enough you can do it – if you're prepared to work. You've also got to have faith in yourself; that comes first. You have to get outside of yourself and have a good look, as if you were a stranger. People who really want to achieve something go to a lot of trouble to get there. But the majority want to talk about themselves so much that they never get round to it!

My father-in-law and his old-fashioned family were very 'in' with the church – they had this one son and he was extremely spoiled. We lived opposite them in Blackheath when I was a child, in a wide road with trees, and I loved looking through the window at Christmas time to see all the presents being delivered over the road. My mother used to say 'Good gracious, that boy is spoiled. Look at all that stuff going in this morning!' She was as fascinated as I was.

My father died when I was tiny and although my mother could have married again – she was a young woman – she thought it was wrong to marry somebody else and have the children brought up by him. So she brought us all up herself. She took us to places she thought we ought to see – there were five of us. It must have been in the late 1880s – it's such a long time ago now, I can't remember exactly. Looking back it seems very, very old-fashioned.

London was completely different then, and it was a tremendous treat to be taken there. We used to take the train up from Blackheath; we had no car. I remember London as the place where there was lots of noise and lots of toys and all the things young children like. It was very exciting to go shopping with my mother, and things were so cheap compared with now.

We were definitely disciplined at home, but it was right; it did work. I was threatened with boarding school because I was being really naughty. My mother became quite frightening in her anger with me for behaving badly with people who took me out, so she put her foot down. I remember being taken down to the playroom by my father when I was only about four or five, to be whipped, because I had behaved badly at table. Looking back it's fascinating, but horrifying in a way. How did we ever get through that?

But we were taught good manners – not to start eating before the grown-ups, for example. We were particularly told to be polite to anyone working for us – none of that business, 'Bring us this and bring us that!' They were all treated as important people – as indeed they were. They had a lot on their plate; the tables were beautifully kept, and the houses looked after perfectly. Often it was people with very little money who kept things so lovely. So our manners were pretty good, although I remember being shut up somewhere because I'd said something awful.

Some people are right for village life, and for the ambiance of a thatched cottage; others think they are but they're not. When we came here the village was still very much a community. There used to be a lovely little shop where you could get anything. It even had trousers and shirts, which my husband was sometimes seen in! It had practically anything you could think of, all in that tiny place. Two women friends ran it beautifully – better than any man could have.

We came here during the Second World War. I used to be very

worried about leaving my mother in her flat in London, what with the air-raids; she was frightened, so we brought her out here. But she was never happy, because she didn't like the country. She said she liked to see her fellow creatures, and she liked things nice and up-to-date. She was longing to get back to London.

It was a country village altogether, then; you only had to walk a very short way to get into the fields, and the meadows were lovely. They had sheep at one time, and I used to watch the men rounding up the cattle in the evenings and bringing them back to the stables. Tom Goodwin was still using horses on his farm, and my sister and I were allowed to drive them in the harvest fields. I suppose it must have rained sometimes, but I remember only sunshine at harvest-time, especially during the rest-times – blessed intervals when we relaxed our aching limbs and quenched our thirst. Tom's sister brought us out jugs of tea, and thick, really satisfying sandwiches. It was *real* country. I loved it. Now, when harvest comes, I try to shut out the racket of the combine, and to hear instead the gentle clap-clapping of the old reapers.

We did a lot to the house, and considering we didn't have a lot of money at first, it turned out to be a brilliant investment. Then we looked about for a real gypsy caravan and found the one in the garden. We used it to keep my collection of china animals in, and we put visitors up in it.

The cottage has a good feeling, a quiet atmosphere. We were very lucky; it has been a retreat. I had to be in London quite a lot, looking after my mother, so I was backwards and forwards, but it was very nice to know that after being in London for a while there was this, even if I had to come to it alone as I very often did. The only trouble is that I feel there are ghosts all around, and I don't like being here alone, especially at night.

It was our cosy place to come to at weekends. My husband drove us down in his motor – a Lanchester with pre-selective gears. During the air-raids it became a place where we could get away from the bombing. This was a farm cottage in the old days, with almost exactly an acre of land, including a fruit and vegetable plot. We loved working there. I decided to make a cottage garden and started by planting a periwinkle hedge along one fence. I put lots of different sedums underneath it, which climb through the rockery, and a special viola that a friend gave me. Halfway down the garden there used to be a beautiful Victoria plum tree, but it was blown down, so I covered the stump with clematis. There are violets all around the stump, white and purple ones, and I planted a circle of crocuses too. Some people say sparrows eat only the yellow ones, but I have found that they eat my purple ones and leave the yellow ones alone!

There's a low wall at the back of the garden, and I planted cyclamen underneath that, and aubretias along the top. The wallflowers do well there, too. Then I planted beds of lilies – some cardiniums, and lots of nerines which do very well there. I love my Crown Imperials in the spring, yellow and rust-coloured. I moved a rambling rose from the front to the back of the house, *Felicité et Perpetué*, and it is scrambling everywhere now. I've planted roses everywhere – old-fashioned ones that smell wonderful and have spectacular hips in the autumn.

I never liked the pub, I'm not really sociable; but my husband was very popular down there, he was good at talking. I hated it, I never liked drinking, so I was the wrong person in the wrong place, until I got down to my writing. Life isn't like magazine stories with happy endings, so I thought I'd write, if possible, about life as it was, and let them return my stuff if they didn't like it. In fact it paid off. 'Happy endings' is a lot of rubbish – at least a lot of fictional happy endings are!

We were the first commuters in the village, and the village

reacted badly. Didn't like us at all – 'Those people up from London' – and they showed it. It was an agricultural village, with very few people working outside the village, and I suppose we were perceived as being in a different class. They were thoroughly suspicious at first. Sam Gapes, who lived next door to Wilf Middleditch, he didn't speak to us for years, even though he was often in the pub at the same time as my husband. He was on the local fire service with Len Cakebread during the war, and there's a story about how he got back from a wedding reception, still in his best outfit and probably one over the eight, and was called out to deal with an incendiary bomb. 'Leave 'un to me,' he said, 'I'll put the b.... out.' Whereupon he picked up a great clod of mud and dropped it on the German squib! On another occasion he was tracking down a parachutist when he was on sentry duty in the pig-sties at Mumford Hall – this was when we were expecting to be invaded at any moment. He stalked it with the utmost stealth, and became paralytic with laughter when he discovered that his parachutist was one of Mr Bickley's cows! But he wouldn't have anything to do with the likes of us.

Sam Gapes, who died two years after Len Cakebread, appeared in the Dog and Duck shortly after one o'clock every day to enjoy his pint (or two). He was born in Swanbrooke Down in 1902, went to the village school, and worked at Mumford Hall until the late 1920s. He was also delivery boy around the village, and delivered meals to Miss Giles the schoolmistress when she became unwell. Between the wars he was a keen member of the cricket team, and belonged to the men's club. He became the village barber, and on a fine evening you would often see him cutting a customer's hair in his back garden. He was a regular at the pub for over sixty-five years, a keen card-player and also a gambler – he went to the races at Newmarket as often as he could get there. He lived in his simple cottage, now being renovated by a local builder, with his disabled brother Horace who had been wounded in the First World War.

Clarice Some were very nice, and welcomed us, but very few.

Arthur Bush, who lived next door to Sam Gapes, was quite friendly, but then he was a Londoner too. He had been born in Finchley, and came here because his grandparents lived here. Arthur's mother was a Middleditch, and very proud of the fact that Middleditches had been in Swanbrooke Down since the beginning of the eighteenth century – they used to farm on Mouse Hill. Arthur was a prisoner of war in the First World War when he was only seventeen. He was unwounded though, and when he came back he started his own dance band – he was a brilliant pianist. He spent a lot of time out of the village, which was unusual in those days. He was a regular down at the Dog and Duck just like Sam.

But mostly the reaction was: 'They from London!' – with a sniff. It didn't last long though. Wherever people came from, whatever their language, my husband could get on with them. He was pleased to meet anybody, always interested. Naturally it's also the way you take it yourself. It's probably best to try and believe that people are 'real' people if you can only get to the core – instead of all this snobbish nonsense, which seems to be a very English thing. It's extraordinary to me, that people who think that somebody is out of 'their class', won't speak to them! I suppose it's upbringing. I still remember being pulled here and pulled there by my nanny and being told not to speak to people. None of this nice friendliness which is there if you want it. Snobbishness like that must be based on fear; it's also to do with people being too conscious of themselves.

But then other people started coming into the village, not 'real' people – people with plenty of money but not much sense. Then there are some who come for a little while, sell up and move on. The village used to be a place where everybody knew everybody, and all the children went to school together – it was one happy family. However, change was inevitable. It seems that fewer and fewer 'real' people come into the village. What do I mean by 'real' people? I think you sense it more than know it, you feel it in the blood.

Children today don't get the discipline in the early years and then they go off the rails later. I often watch the children and wonder what they're being taught and what they're allowed to do and what they're not. It seems that they can go ahead with practically anything. Although it's true that there *are* some very good mothers about these days, and fathers take their part more than perhaps they did.

Most people were brought up in a Christian tradition – they were very keen on the children going to church, so we were made to go; in a way I think it was good to have that discipline my mother was so keen about. There are basic moral rules in Christianity, like treating others as you would like to be treated yourself. They caught us early.

The media have had so many effects – it may be excellent for some, not so good for others. Children watching TV all the time is not a good idea. Surely they should be looking outwards to the world rather than inward. The way people behave has changed so much. There was nothing wrong in how strict people were; it was in our own interests. We weren't allowed to go out alone, since there were nasty people about who would have taken children off if they could. Once, walking home in Blackheath, I had to go through an avenue and a man came up very close on his bicycle, and said, 'You ain't got much clothes on, you'd better come out in the country.' I was frightened to death. But that was in London of course.

I'm not a very friendly person, so if I don't see many people and they don't come to see me it's my fault. I've been awfully selfish in wanting to be left alone. It's difficult to find a kindred spirit. I'm naughty about village activities and functions – when I went to the last bazaar I was only thinking about finding something nice and getting away quickly. And I won't go out at night. I'm still driving my car although my son isn't very keen on it!

PERCY AND MARGERY COLBROOKE

Grocers

Percy and Margery Colbrooke retired to Swanbrooke Down after a busy life running the village store in Haverley. Not that their pace has slackened much. They immediately became involved in village activities, and Percy is a regular at the Dog and Duck. He follows the lunchtime tradition of Arthur Bush and Sam Gapes who used to tread a daily path towards the inn for a pre-prandial pint. Percy now follows, punctuating his well-ordered day with a get-together in the public bar. His stooping figure passes my study window at twelve-thirty sharp two or three times a week. His lined face is as near as a human face can get to a likeness of Jeremy Fisher; his speech is precise, wry, with a Northerner's directness – for Percy comes from Manchester.

Margery is a committed member of the WI, and helps to run the Over-Sixties club. She is spry, neatly dressed, with a kindly manner and, one suspects, a heart of gold. A regular church goer, she is the first to be enlisted for bazaars and functions. Often the house seems full of very young children – Margery has become surrogate granny for numerous toddlers.

The Colbrookes are my neighbours, and early one bitterly cold morning in February, as I returned from walking the dog, I spotted Margery coming out of her back door. A light drizzle was turning to sleet, and there was ice on the path up to her house. She was making for her shed to collect kindling. I asked whether she and Percy would like to give me an interview. She accepted with enthusiasm, and within half an hour we were sitting in their front room by the gas fire, with coffee and biscuits. Outside, sleet pattered on the road, the wind whistled round the house, and it grew as grey as twilight. Margery lit the standard lamps and turned up the fire.

Their semi-detached house stands opposite Wilf and Dora's. It was built for the village policeman by Robert Stockbridge in the early 1920s; a small, box-shaped comfortable house – ideal for their retirement, they told me, because it was so labour-saving. The back windows look out over the fields. Their tiny garden which they tend immaculately is a cascade of colour in summer. Today only a bank of green hellebores shiver in the freezing wind, and clumps of snowdrops catch the eye amongst leafless shrubs.

Percy 'opens the batting' with his customary twinkle (he is a man of metaphors), telling me of his army days in Sierra Leone, where he was posted from 1932 to 1948, and of his involvement with the Freemasons, which began between the wars.

A Contented Retirement

Percy I started working in the cotton trade in Manchester after the First World War but I had no fancy for it; it was collapsing rapidly and I could see little or no hope there. I had no wish to enjoy unemployment in the north of England, and I thought the south would be better climatically – not quite so damned cold. I also thought – and I was right on this one – that agriculture would have a longer innings in the general prosperity after the war-scare than the manufacturing industry. So I finished up in Haverley.

The shop had been in existence for donkey's years – the deeds went back to the 1700s, and it had been a shop most of that time. When I bought it, the place hadn't had a lick of paint for over thirty years. There were two electric lights in the back shop, one in the kitchen and one in the living room; you went up to bed with a candle! There was one cold-water tap in the kitchen, and a red sandstone sink. The old-fashioned copper boiler was filled by hand on a Monday morning. You lit the fire underneath and then you turned out because you needed another bucketful of coal, the heat was so terrific.

I had it stripped out and started from scratch, put in electricity and central heating. I never made a huge living and it took quite a long time to pay off the bank loan, but it was a comfortable living, a going concern. It was one of four shops in the village.

Margery Percy's mother was widowed and he was her only son, so she came to live here. She wasn't very enamoured of the place having come from the hills of Derbyshire – she thought this was very flat and uninteresting. When I first met her, she said, 'Do you know, this is the most *immoral* place I've ever come across!'

All the scandals that used to go on! Somebody from the local wheelhouse did time for embezzlement. While he was in jail they had to sell the house, and his wife had to live temporarily with a neighbour. Granny was shocked – she thought that anything slightly amiss was *immoral*!

Being behind the counter we picked up the titbits. A lot of time is wasted in a village shop, with all the gossip. On the other hand there are some people, especially in those days, who, if they didn't speak to the grocer, the baker or the postman, wouldn't speak to anybody all week. A lot of them were very isolated. One young wife I shared the toddlers' school run with, who lived in a hamlet two miles away, said to me, 'If I didn't see you in the morning, I wouldn't see a soul all day.' It's different now because everybody's got cars.

Percy The population has changed too. Then, most people worked locally, on farms. The main landowners in Haverley had four farms, and about fifty-six employees between them. When mechanisation came the workforce shrank. So offspring drifted away from the village, and they continue to do so. Of the few original Swanbrooke Down people left, their offspring have almost all drifted off. Villages used to be made up of generations of families. You try to sort out the pedigrees of the Lagdens in Swanbrooke!

Margery There are still some Swanbrooke people in Haverley, so there's a close interrelationship between the two villages – or has been.

Percy A few fights now and again! They used to get bored, and have what they called a sod-fight. Great muddy turves off the grass banks – sloshy!

Margery There was great rivalry between the young men, between the villages. That doesn't really happen now.

Certainly life in the village has changed tremendously in the thirty years I've been associated with it. I'm a townie, from Richmond in Surrey. The movement of the population has altered the whole atmosphere. People weren't moved about so much by their jobs. We did have people who went to London every day, but not many. There were a lot of retired people in Haverley – more retired than commuters. The younger element were closely connected with farming. A few people cycled into Kings Tarrant; some people walked to work outside the village. There was none of this shifting around, families moving in and going again within three-four-five years. This had an effect on the schools, and the village way of life generally.

Percy One of the changes was the EEC policy, when they started building food mountains. In the old days the farms in this area grew mainly peas and potatoes. The ground was suitable, and pea-picking time – about the middle of July – there was a tremendous influx of diddycoys and gypsies, and there was a lot of casual labour employed. Village womenfolk used to turn out for pea- and spud-picking. There's many a child in those days was kitted out for the winter from his mother's 'picking fund'. You see hardly any of that nowadays, it's all mechanised.

Margery It's years since they've grown peas by any great acreage here – they might have the odd field, but that's usually for stock feed. Since then the rotation of crops has altered a lot because they grow much more rape. They always had a good harvest of barley and wheat here. They didn't have many sheep, and not a great many cattle.

You don't get the casual workers now. They had a hard life, too. I always remember one woman, she'd been out on the fields all day long, and was absolutely gummed up with mud. She'd come into the shop and say, 'Oh excuse my dirty boots and my muddy hands.' And I would think, gosh you're braver than I am, I wouldn't go out and pick those spuds.

Percy Peas were used as an alternative crop to keep the land in condition. They were originally picked by hand, then that was mechanised, and then they concentrated on areas near the freezing plants, near Lowestoft. Birds Eye had a big plant up there. This place was a bit too far to get the crop to the freezers.

Peas were a dicey market; if there was a glut the price went down and they weren't worth picking, and if you kept them you could only throw them away. The EEC altered things in that they are paid guaranteed prices if they sell the barley or wheat into intervention. So farmers said, 'Right, to hell with peas!'

Margery The shop was still a viable concern when we sold up; we were ticking over, we made a living, but we were very conscious of competition from the supermarkets and bigger chainstores.

Percy There was a tendency for the small country shops to die out. As I said, there were four of us in Haverley, and when one of them gave up he gave me first option on the newspaper round, so I did newspapers, in Haverley and in Swanbrooke Down, for seventeen years.

Margery Of course we're imported into Swanbrooke Down, Percy coming from the north and me being a Londoner, but we settled, and I'm very glad we didn't move away to Suffolk as we thought we might. But to come to such a small place, after our large house in Haverley, takes a lot of getting used to. I kept bumping into doors and furniture because we'd had so much space there! But it's much easier for older people to look after a smaller property, so we stayed put.

Percy It'll see my last few years out!!

Margery We feel at home here; having done the newspaper business in Swanbrooke Down for years, we felt this was an extension of Haverley.

Percy There was a tremendous amount of speculation about who would move in here, and I know that the Middleditches were terrified they were going to have a lot of teenage bee-bops with radios and record players at full blast. When they saw it was a couple of decrepit bits of old fungus they came over with flowers!

Margery We had a right old welcome. Perhaps people felt we weren't going to live it up and have all-night parties! But we were extraordinarily lucky, we've always had lovely neighbours.

Percy This is the nicest end of the village!

Margery It couldn't be a nicer corner, and there's a lot to be said for having nice folk around you who get on with what they want to do, yet you know that if you were in the slightest trouble somebody would come to your aid immediately. Percy's sister and brother-in-law live on the outskirts of Wolverhampton, in quite a pleasant part. They've been there for twenty five years and they hardly know their neighbours. They're both getting old and they're not in the best of health. If we were in a similar circumstance we'd have people popping in to see if we were OK, and we'd never feel alone. But they are really out on a limb. Here in Swanbrooke it is friendly without being intrusive – you feel you could turn to anybody, or even without turning to them they'd turn up with something.

Percy It wouldn't be quite the same in Haverley: Swanbrooke Down is a compact village – Haverley is really a number of little hamlets dotted over a pretty large area, and there's not quite the same co-operation.

Margery On the other hand, we've looked at life in Haverley from a different angle because we were always busy behind the counter and our contact was with folk coming in to us, or people we delivered to. Some of these folk I saw twice a week, and they might not see anyone other than the coalman or the baker in between, so we got to know them very well. But our life was almost 99% working. You had very little spare time for the casual 'come on in and have a cup of tea'. So we didn't see that side of village life.

When Percy went into hospital for an emergency operation, so many people came to my aid. Some young lads who used to borrow our loft to practise for their band came round and said, 'Can we help with the newspaper round?' All through the winter those boys helped me sort the newspapers. They were absolutely splendid, out of sheer good nature. I don't know what we would have done without them.

Percy We've been here nine-and-a-half years, and it's amazing how busy we have found retired life!

Margery I certainly have! I knew quite a lot of people, so I did get involved. When you retire people seem to assume you've got all the time in the world! Of course it's much better to have plenty to do. There's never a truer saying than the less you do the less you want to do. Busy people always have time, they *make* time to do things.

I've always been a very keen WI member, since I joined in 1952 when I came to Haverley. While the children were tiny it was difficult to get to a meeting, although I kept up my membership. As they got a wee bit older I joined Swanbrooke Down WI because it was an evening meeting.

I became secretary while I was at the shop, and I've been president for many years. While we were at the shop Percy was secretary of Haverley village hall and I helped him. Since I retired I help with the Over-Sixties – I'm secretary of the rural association and that combines all the Over-Sixties clubs in the district. We don't *do* a great deal but it keeps everybody in touch, and one year we had a day of talks, like a seminar, of interest to the elderly. We also have a handicraft exhibition for all the local groups. Our local club is very successful; people are allowed to do what they want. A lot of people only see their old friends twice a month at the club. They have a few outings, and play cards and dominoes. Our present chairman is very good – she'll organise a whist drive or a beetle drive, and they try and do something of interest. There's enough to keep them going without being too *organised*!

As you get older you don't always want to have a lot of set things to do. Old people don't want to be hurried all the time. 'We must finish at four o'clock because the transport is coming.' They don't want that, they'd rather take it in slow easy stages.

The young people here regard the WI as the old fuddy-duddies, which is a pity because a few more young members would help lift the whole concept. People in Swanbrooke are quite different from people in Haverley – they would want something more exciting. But the WI still is really very go-ahead; I can't think of one other women's organisation that has its own college, as we have at Denham. It is a remarkable institution and I would hate to see it fade out. I can't see that happening, although we might have to change a few things. But I wouldn't want to change it altogether; the principles behind the WI are very good.

It was a great joy to find we had a few young families around here. Percy used to collect two little ones, take them to playgroup at 9.30 and collect them at 12 o'clock. Those children have not forgotten! 'Big Brooke' they called Percy, and they've still got a very soft spot for him. It must be fading in their memories now because they were only very tiny when he took them, but I think they remember just going hand-in-hand with him down the street. It was a lovely picture.

It was something we had never been able to do before, because we hadn't yet got grandchildren. A lot of families round here, their grandparents lived far away, so we became substitute grannies and grandpas. Soon we had an invitation to go to the grannies and grandpas tea party at their school.

Percy It was one of the funniest things I can remember! These two little kids had invited us. One of their mothers was expecting her third baby, so a seat had to be kept free for her. More people turned up than anticipated, so I was put into that seat. I got some odd stares!

Margery We were greatly touched to be invited. The children met us, and showed us their classrooms and their work. Before long we were surrounded by children! It was great, we had so many extra children, all anxious to show us their work. We were quite overwhelmed, and felt it was a great compliment. This has been the lovely feeling ever since we've been in Swanbrooke, it's been almost a joke with our family, that all our little neighbours pop in to see us. If there's a birthday there's always a little tap at the door to wish us happy birthday, and it's lovely to be remembered. It's very pleasing to have this attention from the younger generation!

Percy I'm doing what I want, if I want, when I want, and I'm not tied to that clock. Except about half-past-twelve when I go out for a pint! It's not a daily habit – twice this week, might be four times next week. There's a story there, Margery, you'd better tell how the 'committee' came to be formed.

Margery Dear old Sam Gapes, you could set your clock by him going down to the pub every lunchtime. When Arthur Bush died, poor old Sam was getting a bit past it too. He used to potter down there but life was getting more and more difficult for him, so the old boys were not the regulars they had been. Soon after we got to Swanbrooke we got to know a widower called Dennis, who lives alone up on Hawthorn Hill and he's got time on his hands. We gave him a lift home from shopping one day when it was pouring with rain. He said he went down to the Dog and Duck every lunchtime and took his newspaper. If there was anybody to talk to that was fine, but if not he'd read his paper. So I said to Percy, 'Dennis seems very lonely, and Sam's gone now, and there aren't many village people going down the pub now.' I said, 'You'd better go down and have a chat with Dennis. I'm sure he'd enjoy a bit of company. And then Dennis and Percy formed the 'committee'.

Percy A friend of ours from Haverley used to have a roving commission around the pubs, but he gradually got roped in with us at the Dog and Duck. He must have enjoyed our company, because he came more and more often. One day we had a real laugh. There was an obsolete notice still up on the board outside the pub; I twigged that it was out of date as I was going in, but this friend went in through the back entrance. I knew he could get a bit ponderous and long-winded, so I said to Toby, behind the bar, 'You want a clip behind the ear for neglect of duty, the place is getting scruffy. Have you seen that ruddy poster on the notice board there, it's three weeks out of date! They're too lazy to take the darned thing down!'

Well, we got pontificating about this; we went on and on. Toby Wagstaff, who's never lost for words, said 'What!' he said, 'I've been hauled up in front of the committee!' And that's how it all started. Subsequently another old chappie joined us for a natter, the chap who used to play the piano for the playgroup, he would come in for a pint to revive his fading tissues so he got 'ex officio' on the committee as well.

Margery It's a nice little set-up down there. Arthur and Sam were almost the props of the public bar, so it's nice that it's carrying on.

Percy Sam was a character, you know. When my son and daughter went down to the Dog one Christmas Eve, very soon after we moved here, Sam was there. At that time my son had been appearing on TV in *The Old Curiosity Shop.* Sam hadn't seen our children for some time – he knew them as little ones, but they had been on their travels. Anyway, Sam was cogitating, he'd been looking in their direction as if to say 'I think I know who they are but I'm not certain'. As he got up to leave, he looked at them and said, 'Are you Mr Colbrooke's son?' and he said, 'Yes that's right, Sam, I used to deliver your newspapers.' 'They tell me you've been on the television,' he said. 'I unt seen it; unt got a television I suppose that's why.' And he stomped out. The kids came back here doubled up, and my son said, 'As long as I've got fans like Sam I'll never get a swollen head!'

Len Cakebread was a character too – we've lost quite a few of the good old characters in the short period we've been here. Len didn't move far but by jove he knew everybody's movements. I popped in now and again for a chat and it was surprising, if you sat down with Len Cakebread for half an hour, how many people popped their heads around the door. He had a regular clientele. The lady across the road from him was very good to Len after Bertha died. The amount of food she took over was nobody's business. One day Len was going to collect some plums from a local orchard, and she said, could you get me five pounds of plums, and he got them. She wanted to pay for them, and he exploded! 'After all you've done for me! Me to take a penny off you for five pounds of plums!' They could hear him over at Little Bendysh!

He was a great storyteller, but secondhand they wouldn't amount to much. It was his timing and his delivery – it was in a class of its own. That's like a lot of these old people, if you talk to Arthur King in Haverley, he could tell you a fund of stories, but they would never be the same if we related them.

Len was very fond of his food – he didn't go short. Many of us thought when he lost his wife he'd be like a ship without a rudder, but Len got down to it and you should have seen his breakfast! Sausage, bacon, egg, the lot, and a mountain of fried bread to help it down. He didn't starve, no doubt about it.

You never heard Len complaining, never, and that's something, because many people that age have a lot of trials and tribulations. That's why people popped in to see him – he always had a cheery word and you knew you wouldn't have sob-stories slung at you; you'd probably have a joke and a jolly good laugh.

Margery There aren't many of the real old Swanbrooke folk left. Mabel Hutchinson was a Cakebread; she's one of the older originals.

Percy The odd building keeps going up where there's a bit of spare ground, and a large number of houses have changed hands since we came; this comes back to the ebb and flow of the population, which must have an effect on every village or town. It certainly hasn't helped community feeling. Some newcomers regard the village as a dormitory. They go out first thing in the morning and they get home God knows when at night, half past seven or thereabouts, and they have virtually no opportunity of seeing anybody in the village.

There is a great divide between one end of the village and the other; a lot of people on Hawthorn Hill really don't know who are living down this end, and people down here wouldn't know who lives on Hawthorn Hill. Folk who weren't born and bred in a village have a different outlook on community life. If you've been used to town life where you can isolate yourself if you want, and you can be extremely lonely, you may want to continue like that. My feeling is that the newcomers come out at weekends and think, how lovely to get out of London and home to that sort of environment, wonderful! They can afford to buy the properties, but are they able to contribute very much to keep that sort of atmosphere? I suppose the answer is, not until they start having children.

Margery Children make your finest contact with friends, this is what brings it all together. Having seventy children in the village now is a help – the mothers get to know each other. Moving to a new area, if you have no children, it's difficult to find a footing. If you've got children, it's open sesame.

There was a playgroup party once when Humpty-Dumpty went on strike. Humpty-Dumpty absolutely refused to jump off the wall! She sat there scowling, with her thumb stuck in her mouth. We've had some laughs. Things like that have kept us busy.

Percy People over the last thirty or forty years are better off, comparatively speaking – thinking of the days when the women-folk used to go pea-picking and the rest of it. That income was essential for the family budget. Nowadays the urgency isn't there – neither are the peas!

Margery The standard of living generally has gone up, no matter how much people grumble about high prices. We are warm, we're comfortable, we've got washing machines.

Percy Everybody's got cars, and there's much more part-time occupation for womenfolk.

Margery Not only that, Percy. If we cast our own minds back, while the children were little I was washing everything by hand. Just think of what was on the shop shelf in those days, too, and the variety of food now!

When I was first married, Percy's mother lived with us. I can remember her absolute joy when she managed to get half a sheep's head, and she made brawn – mind you I couldn't have dealt with it. That was a treat! And half a pig's head – we had the bath chaps – I hadn't a clue what 'bath chaps' were. A lot of people today wouldn't have any idea either.

It's a different world, and what amazes me is that it's all happened in my lifetime. Foreign travel has had a tremendous influence. That is one thing I regret, that my youth was mainly during the war and therefore I was not able to do the travelling young people do nowadays. Not that I'm grumbling but you do feel you have missed out on that side of life. But it's not all that essential.

Percy What has just come to my mind is that in Haverley the dustbins were emptied only once a month! We burnt most of our rubbish in those days, and tins and bottles you had to stash away as best you could; vegetation, tea leaves, outer cabbage leaves, they went on the compost heap.

Margery We didn't have as much, either – we are a throwaway society now.

Percy Those kitchen ranges would burn a brickend! Then came packaging when self-service started, things had to be pre-packed and we had more to throw away.

Margery Up until then there wasn't the packaging round everything.

Percy We had to weigh up the sugar.

Margery And all the dried fruits. We had huge drawers in our back shop, deep ones full of soft brown sugar, currants, sultanas, raisins, rice, demerara. Once when there was a sugar crisis we had loose French sugar delivered and we had to weigh all that up. That was a chore – a session of weighing up fruits and sugars and biscuits. Our half-day closing was spent weighing up!

Percy Biscuits were all loose in those days, in big square tins. We had a special stand, and these tins slotted in at an angle; you raised the glass-fronted lid and weighed out the biscuits. We had to have some lard and butter loose, too. The butter ration fluctuated. If it was 4 oz per person that was alright because you'd just chop a half-pound block in two. But when they reduced it to 3 oz it was a bit of a headache. They carried on importing it in 56 lb blocks. A number of grocers used to alternate it – if it was an odd number they'd make it 2 oz this week and 4 oz the next. Of course if you were a family of four it didn't matter anyway, you'd get a pound of butter.

Cheese always was in blocks – as a matter of fact we made our name in cheeses! Right to the end, we'd take cheese in bulk and sell it freshly cut, and I still maintain that's the best way to have cheese.

Margery After we'd sold the shop, people used to ask, 'Which wholesaler did you get your cheese from? I'm pretty certain one or two of the local shops had the same source of supply, but we kept our cheese in the cellar. It was never refrigerated. This is the great difference. Percy's Tuesday afternoon job was to go down into the cellar, and he'd be down there for ages skinning cheeses. They used to come in round wooden crates, covered in mould, and with muslin covers. We had to scrape all that mould off, and get the muslin off. It was a very messy job. He would halve the

cheese, and a certain amount would be kept in a wooden box upstairs, for current use. It was kept as you would keep it covered in a cheese dish. We never allowed it to be exposed. We kept it in wooden boxes in the cellar, too, and only cut off more or less enough for each day's supply. If need be we'd have to go down and get more.
Percy You'd feel sorry for yourself at the end of a hot summer's day when you'd get the pea-pickers belting in at the last minute and you'd run out of cheese so you had to go down those steps again and cut some more!

EDITH SPOONER AND MABEL HUTCHINSON

Labourer's Wives

Hawthorn Hill seemed deserted in late afternoon, as February merged into March. A savage wind tore over the bare fields around the houses on top of the hill, banging the wooden gate back on its latch behind me, and breaking up heavy cloud which had hung over the hill all day. Watery sun filtered through, momentarily lighting a clump of creamy crocuses in the border that led up to Edith's house. On the other side of the path a cherry tree stood in the middle of a fenced lawn. Shivering with cold, I knocked at the door.

Edith Spooner is a tiny woman in her sixties who suffers from multiple sclerosis, although there was no sign of her pain that day. She led me to her sitting room at the back of the house, which looked down over the fields into the valley. Mabel Hutchinson rose to greet me; one of Edith's closest friends, she is well into her eighties. A large, forthright woman with a ready laugh and a jolly manner, she was eager to join in the discussion, and to contribute her memories of working 'below stairs' at Mumford Hall just after the First World War.

Edith's back garden was entirely given over to vegetables, neatly dug ready for spring sowing, with just a few leeks and cabbages remaining from the winter crop. Beyond, a great sweep of winter wheat ruffled by the wind; the land was punctuated only by an occasional tree. Swanbrooke Down nestled in the valley, its smoking chimneys just in view.

Edith still manages to do housework for a couple of folk in the village. She is married to Walter, who is usually to be found on a Monday night playing cribbage in the Dog and Duck. On a Tuesday night he goes to Elmshaw where a regular darts team spends the evening. Walter has worked for the past forty years on Rex Vickery's farm. Due for retirement next year, he is known to villagers as 'the man who cuts the green'. Their two grown-up daughters have left home now, and Edith felt regretful that the community spirit of old had died out, and that village life had been supplanted by something less substantial. She felt isolated, she said, a statement with which Mabel agreed. Mabel's husband is crippled with emphysema, and it was clear that the two friends were hanging on to memories of when the community had operated in a different – and in their view a better – way.

Isolated in a community

Edith When I first came we had two shops and two pubs. There were five butchers and three grocers delivering, and two bakers doing a round, so we weren't dependent on transport. The motor car was the end of village life; if you haven't got your own transport now, you've had it, living here.

I've lived here for forty years. During the Second World War I joined the services, and met my husband in the ATS. After we were demobbed we came here out of the blue, because we couldn't get a house in Wiltshire. The only way my husband could get a house was to move here as an agricultural worker. I rang a friend who lived in the one of the cottages down by the brook in the Dip – where the big house is now. She said the other cottage was vacant and there was a farmworker's job to go with it. One of my daughters was born in one of the cottages, and the other one next door. The cottages were quite sweet but it was a job getting a pram across the stream because there was only a little narrow wooden bridge.

The Dip and the Gap are often mentioned by the older

generation in Swanbrooke Down. The Gap is a grassy footpath opposite Lagden's, where the Middleditches live, leading uphill across the vastness of arable fields. Once, this was a 'green lane', a grassy track that led through meadows and woods over the hill towards Kings Tarrant. They remember bluebells, wild flowers through the summer, climbing trees, playing in the woods and resting on mossy banks. Today the fields are almost bare of trees; only one meadow and one hedgerow remain. Wind sweeps across the cleared, 'cleaned', cultivated land; a solitary lark still nests in the corn each summer.

Edith I was brought up in the country, and it was nice – I wouldn't want to live in a town. I went to a village school, and then as you become a teenager village life is dull so you want to do something else. We didn't notice how hard times were, as children. My father was a farmworker, and if it rained he got sent home and quite often you had bread and sugar for supper because there wasn't anything else. But I didn't notice that life was hard. It was probably my mother who noticed it. I didn't know any different.

When I came here just after the war it was all green fields and cattle. The cricket field was a meadow, and Splash Wood was across the hill. The fields across the front of the council houses were meadows with cattle in – my husband came here to look after livestock. It was lovely looking out and seeing cows in the meadow; there aren't any left now, nowhere in the village is there any grazing. No meadows or woods where children play Red Indians!

We were probably poorer than we are now, but we didn't really notice it, because if you went down the village with a pram there was always somebody with prams and children and if you were bored you went down the road for conversation. There was quite a strong sense of community then; now if I go down the village I only know a few of the old ones like Mr Middleditch. Everybody's very friendly up here though; they don't interfere, but if anybody's ill everybody's very helpful.

I'm afraid there is a feeling of 'them and us' – we're a little group on our own up on Hawthorn Hill. It was stupid building up here, cut off from the village. So we've made our own little

community, but that's not as strong as it was.

My husband was on the village hall committee for years, and also on the parish council. Although we're not churchgoers, I wouldn't want the church *not* to be there. My husband still cuts the graveyard and the greens, but we thought it better if younger ones did the other jobs now. He still works for Rex Vickery – he retires next year. He just accepted the farming changes as they came along – he was a bit disappointed when there weren't any more cattle, but farming is a business, isn't it, so you just carry on.

We'll stay here after he retires – after forty years you get used to a place! In any case there isn't anywhere to go – they don't build houses that OAPs can afford, and we're still council tenants. A lot of people up here have bought their houses from the council, but they're still the same people.

The cottages in the Dip were lath and plaster, thatched, quite nice. But in the end I was glad to move out because rats from the farm ate their way through the lath and plaster into the house! My baby daughter was crawling on the floor one day, and I saw a rat running along as well! I rushed out to the shed to get something to knock it on the head with and if I'd stayed in the shed I probably would have been able to hit it because it went back that way!

The Dip was the site of the last of Swanbrooke Down's slums until the mid 1950s. It is a piece of land down by the stream in front of Pebblegate Farm farmyard, on which stood two ramshackle labourers' cottages. Thatched, beamed, rustic, they were alive with rats and chill with rising damp. Rats were such a scourge that the council offered a penny a tail, so labourers brought them in from the fields to supplement their meagre earnings. Benjamin Lagden collected the tails on behalf of the council, and kept them in an out-building at Sparrows Farm. A favourite trick amongst the children was to steal some from his store and produce them later for more pennies.

Rex Vickery's father pulled the derelict cottages down in the mid-fifties and built his own house there, one of the first of Swanbrooke's suburban dwellings: large, warm, solid, comfortable and functional.

Edith Complaining about the rats was how I managed to get a council house – it was really difficult to get them then. But up here the wind blows! It was sheltered there; you could sit on the doorstep and see the apple blossom.

You had to go out to the tap for water. We boiled everything up on the kitchen range. We had seven cats that lay under that range – such lazy creatures I had to set mousetraps on top of the range at night!

It was hard work bringing up children in those days. Everything took longer. Washing was something! I bought unbleached sheets because they were thicker and cheaper; once I put them in bleach, and the sink ran out and this sheet looked like somebody'd been sick! I daren't hang it on the line until I'd done it again.

The kitchen range cooked smashing cakes. We started our hens as day-old chicks, and kept them warm on top of the copper, so the range was a busy place! We had fresh eggs, and eventually we ate the chickens.

We had an outside loo, and a beautiful cockerel in the yard. I enjoyed eating him for Christmas! I used to take a stick with me to the loo because he used to chase me! But he was beautifully coloured – greens, blues, reds – lovely. We grew our own vegetables – we still do, enough for the year round – so we ate quite well. But you weren't so extravagant with the meat. Being a cowman my husband had free milk from the farm, so we just had to buy meat and that was expensive even then.

When we first went to work in the big houses, you didn't go past that green baize door! The war ended that, took people out of domestic service and put them into the factories. I think it's a good thing that that's gone; although I go out and do domestic work here, I please myself. In those days that was all the work there was in the villages, so we had to put up with being bossed about. When she was fifteen my sister's job was to fill up all these paraffin lamps, and instead of topping them up she just twiddled around with the can and wondered why people got annoyed! A fifteen-year-old *is* going to get bored with that.

That social snobbery hasn't gone though – it's still pretty class-ridden, although not quite as bad. In those days you could tell the farmers' wives and doctors' wives just by their dress. Today you can make the transition – then, if you were born behind that baize door you had to stay there! We are still quite divided, definitely, but by different things, like what jobs people do and how much they earn. But it's still true that we're all the same inside.

The countryside was nice in those days – there was the maypole and daisy chains every first of May, and all the village turned out to see the schoolchildren doing their thing. The May king and May queen went in the procession and you all wore daisy chains, hoping they wouldn't break on the way! We always had oak-apple day on May 29th; it lasted until twelve o'clock, and if you didn't have an oak leaf on you, you got pinched! I used to hate it – they would take the leaf off me and I'd get home black and blue. If you had an oak-apple you were king for the morning! It wasn't around when my children were small, and a lot of people have never heard of it.

May 29th was traditionally oak-apple day, a loyalist celebration of the anniversary of King Charles II's restoration to the throne. The legend goes that the king, fleeing from the Roundheads after the Battle of Worcester in September

1651, hid in an oak tree at Boscobel near Wolverhampton. An oak-apple became the symbol of royalist sympathies, and was worn by the loyal on Royal Oak Day. Oak-apples, being the grub of the gall-wasp, are plentiful in spring and early summer and those found without either an oak-apple or oak leaf were not merely to be pinched, they were to be beaten with stinging nettles.

Edith At harvest-time Daniel Nottage used to go around behind the threshing machines on his bike. His boss on the farm gave him a caravan to live in, and he asked if he could park it on the cricket field for a few weeks. It was still there when he died thirty years later! He was well-liked, was Daniel. Mrs Gibbs who owned the Dog and Duck bought meat for him, and people gave him winter clothes. Poor chap always seemed to be black, from the threshing machines I suppose; he had no place to bath so all he did was wash in a bowl – and not all that often. It was difficult to tell if he was coming or going, he was black all over! He was a very pleasant man, and everybody was kind to Daniel Nottage. He was a great darts player, too. He had cats for company, and when he died there were all these empty cat-tins; he fed everybody else's cats! Strange life, but it suited him and he was happy that way.

Len Cakebread was our roadman and very good at his job – all the ditches and hedges were in good order. He would lean on his shovel and chat to anybody coming along the road, so he wasn't exactly a commercial proposition. He knew everybody, and everything about everybody!

When I first came to Swanbrooke Down all the houses were workmen's cottages. The shop and the cottage next to it, where the doctor lives now, was four cottages then. Old Mr Stone who ran the shop, he was a curmudgeon; always glowering at you when you went in. The children used to put bangers through his letterbox. Most of the cottages belonged to Mumford Hall, and now they're being sold for *vast* sums. That has cut through the community.

Some changes are to be regretted; not the washing and that side of it, but the landscape that's gone. And children today don't know anything about little chicks, for example. To them a chicken is something in a plastic wrapper on a supermarket shelf.

When my children were small we had rabbits and a goose called Gussie, and tortoises. Children don't have all that now.

They used to have whist drives in the village hall – they don't have them now. We get invitations to the various do's, but I'm not sure we can really afford them. They are a bit expensive. When there was a village function years ago, everybody baked, so it was all home-made stuff. Then people started to go to work and didn't have the time. But over all it's still quite a nice place to be – not the friendly place it was, but still a nice village. If you've got children you mix in with the youngsters coming in; otherwise you don't have so much contact, you lose it.

A silence fell. Mabel Hutchinson, at the other end of the sofa, caught my eye and smiled, recognising that it was her turn to speak.

Mabel My husband was from Hoddesdon and came to work at Mumford Hall, where I was a parlourmaid. He did general maintenance and later on he helped in the gardens. We met one night when he was walking along the hall and I called to ask if he could get the curtains down in the toilet upstairs – it was too high for me to reach. He had to stand on the toilet. He got the curtains down, sat on the windowledge and when he jumped down, the pin of the window-latch went right up the back of his trousers and split them all the way up. He landed with his head almost in the toilet and both buttocks showing. I screamed with laughter and never stopped for days afterwards.

We wore a black-and-white uniform some of the time, then we had purple and white which was rather nice. Mr Holmes who owned Mumford Hall at the time was just an ordinary person really – not very grand. But it was hard work. We had to be up by six in the morning, and when they had parties you went on to near six o'clock the next! In shifts of course – but it was a busy household.

As house-parlourmaid I was responsible for the bedrooms, and for waiting at meals. We had to do household work too. My sister was kitchenmaid. It was a busy time but it was enjoyable. We met a lot of people we would never meet now – they were friendly, and we didn't feel we were 'below-stairs'. It was a beautiful house to work in – Mr Holmes did it up in what was modern then. Of course I had known Mumford Hall long before I started there because my grandfather worked in the gardens, so did my father. It still seems like home – or it would if I went up there. I haven't been since the new gentleman came. I understand it has altered quite a bit.

I am a Cakebread, and my mother's family was local as well. She lived next door to the post office. I was born next door to Millie Lagden, in 1906. It was two houses then – now it's been joined into one. When I was five my mother and father were keeping house at Mumford Hall, and she didn't send me to school because of the long journey down to the village. They had the school inspector up to enquire why I wasn't at school. I would be playing around the gardens with Dad.

It was very rural then, yet the village looked much the same as now, except there weren't so many houses. There weren't those houses next to the post office: that piece of meadow was the village playground. We couldn't get up to much mischief – my mother could see us all the time! But Mr Stockbridge didn't say anything about that meadow in his will, so it didn't get left to the village. He built the post office of course, as well as Mrs Thake's house and the policeman's house. The little room at the end of the post office we used as our community centre – we had Red Cross meetings there in the war, doing needlework and rolling bandages.

Mr Stockbridge was a nice old man, and Mrs Stockbridge was a lovely lady. They had a big family, including a grandson whom they brought up but he has died now. Mr Stockbridge was respected in the village – he was the Squire.

Robert Stockbridge built, in the twenties, two pairs of semi-detached cottages, one opposite Lagden's, the other behind it on the other side of the stream. They are simple, square constructions tacked together to make rectangular houses, of brick rendered with plaster, and tiled roofs. One was built specifically for the village policeman – one of the few amenities enjoyed then and not now. He also built a 'reading room', in the cottage adjoining what is now the post office. This turned out to be a misnomer since not many of the villagers were interested in reading, much, after they left school at fourteen. Some could hardly read at all. This room, with a great open iron stove in the middle, became a meeting place for whist drives and concerts. Sixpenny dances were held on a Monday evening, with Ivy Igglesden from Haverley on the piano. During the First World War it was used for meetings of Queen Mary's Needlework Guild, when lady members sewed for soldiers on the battlefields. Strips of linen were rolled into bandages, and swabs made from terry-towelling. The ladies sewed pyjamas and knitted socks for the troops. When they had worked for over twenty hours they were allowed to buy a special badge to commemorate their war effort.

Stockbridge also built two bridges across Winter Water, one at the bottom of the green, the other at the crossing between Lagden's and Holly Cottage where the road divides into Little Bendysh in one direction, Haverley the other. No longer was the road impassable after heavy rains, no longer did the houses flood as the stream spilled over its banks in winter. The fords at either end of the village were a thing of the past.

Mabel I remember my father being called up for the First World War; he was gone two or three days and we thought he was gone for good. Fortunately he was discharged and came back. The war brought people in to buy up the cottages when the estate was sold. My father had the opportunity to buy his cottage, since Mr Stockbridge owned most of the village. Apart from that, the old thatched cottages were snapped up by people from London, as the older residents died off.

The farming was all done with horses – we often say now, when we see the tractors rolling by, we can see one particular old gentleman, quite a country yokel he was, ploughing his furrows. He had to walk with one foot on the plough, one in the furrow. It was all done by hand. I often think the farmers don't know they are working nowadays. They were out in all weathers – none of this sitting in the cabin of a tractor or combine.

Hawthorn Hill used to be a field and us children came up here gleaning. We called it Little Cricksie then – quickset is another name for hawthorn. My dad used to thresh the gleanings out for the chickens. We were allowed to glean after the farmer had cleared his shocks off.

Mabel still uses old Essex words. When I asked what a 'shock' of corn was, she replied that it is local dialect for a stook or little stack, and went on to let me into other secrets: 'slud' is mud, a 'hoddedod' is a snail, and to 'shamp' is to tread heavily. Then she told me some words which are simply pronounced differently: 'bud' is bird, 'hin' is hen, 'peg' is pig, 'farden' is farthing and 'lebum' eleven. All the older generation pronounced threshing 'thrashing'.

Mabel We live in number 13, and we moved here on Friday 13th July! It was a brand-new three-bedroomed house, and we never thought we'd get it. But the person offered it turned it down because it was number 13. It was a real luxury to have mod-cons after our tiny old cottage. The thing I enjoyed most was having a bath properly. We had had to bath in one of those long sink-baths. The tap was in the yard, so we had to fill the bath from the electric copper. We accepted it – what you didn't have you didn't miss. But when I think of all the buckets of water I have carried round from the tap in Mr Thake's backyard . . .

We had to mind our ps and qs at school – you got your knuckles slapped sharpish if you didn't. It was a Church of England school and we had to go to church during Lent. We used to play rounders on the village green: that was our playground. There was only a little garden and square inside the schoolyard.

I have been connected with the Methodist church all my life. I was organist at the chapel in Elmshaw Lane for many years. Methodism was just getting round the villages in those days, after the fame of John Wesley, and his brother Charles who wrote all those lovely hymns. I suppose it was a novelty and something different – anyway it caught on and was very well-attended. The chapel is 101 years old this year – but there's no congregation now so I'm afraid we are due to close. But as the minister told us last Sunday we shouldn't think so much about buildings.

It was a surprise to hear Mabel mention the Wesleys as if they were so close in time. But her grandfather was alive at the end of John Wesley's life – he died in 1791 – so the connection was obviously real to her.

Wesley's message moved plain folk deeply; his brand of Methodism was about a way of life devoted not only to religious observance but to self-discipline and selfless work for others. John Wesley was not just a great missionary preacher, he also had a genius for religious organisation, so the movement spread fast through village communities everywhere except Scotland. His uncompromising ardour for the salvation of souls was attractive to the poorer elements in England's structured society; it spoke to their condition regardless of birth, it cared for them. It also gave them other interests besides the material, and thus gave them a self-respect they had previously not known. As part of a general movement of non-conformism which was emerging in the eighteenth century, it provided the less well-to-do with a democratic organisation, religious, educational and political, of their own.

The Methodist chapel in Swanbrooke Down closed this year due to lack of attendance.

Mabel Len Cakebread went to chapel too. I went to school with him. He was our roadman, keeping the village tidy. You miss those sort of people. He didn't mind what he said, that was the funny part. I remember one Sunday night when he came to chapel and the minister gave us all a lift down the road. Well, Len was very fond of his food, and because he had been ill he had to go on a diet. He went on and on about it. 'Well, I don't know,' he said, 'I was always told you should never let your backbone touch your belly-button.' Our minister just rolled up with laughing. I thought it was quite embarrassing really, because I didn't know how he was going to take it.

His backbone never did touch his belly-button mind you. It was sad how he died, although it could have been much more serious. He had started to light the oil stove, fell and knocked it over – evidently he was in the process of lighting it when he had his stroke.

What I remember about village life was the well in front of the forge. The men always went down with their buckets after they came home from work. They would talk over the day's doings. I used to love listening to them – they were earthy men, always laughing and making jokes. They talked of the land, village affairs, and the latest cricket match, which was a matter of life and death! I didn't always understand what they were saying, but they were kind to me and pulled my leg.

That well supplied the whole village. My father would fill two buckets for the copper for washday. The copper was up at the top of the back garden – it seemed a long way! These coppers were big, built-in with brick, and they were either copper or zinc. We lit a fire underneath.

The men used to sit along the wall and jaw half the night; all the gossip went on there. Talk about women gossiping; the men were just as bad! I went down with Dad sometimes, mainly to see

that he didn't fall down the well. I hated him opening those lids – they opened back from the middle to let the bucket down. When he leant over to drag it up I was terrified he would take a header down the well. The people here now wouldn't know *how* to fetch water – there's a marvellous spring in the village but they would want someone to collect it for them. There was a roller and heavy chain which had to be wound up – there was a handle on both sides but most of the men did it with one handle, especially if there was no one there to help.

We ate well. My father grew all the vegetables in his allotment; the International Stores used to come round in a van, and an old gentleman who had a shop at Haverley walked to the outlying villages in all weathers to pick up orders. Then he would deliver them in his trap. A baker came round pretty often – now we have no baker, just a milkman and a coalman. A butcher and a fishmonger used to come round – even if it snowed and you couldn't get up the hill they got there somehow! Supermarkets have killed that. Now we have to get to the shops on the bus or in a taxi. It has become a pretty inconvenient place to live.

Our main entertainment was the piano in our own home. As the buses started coming through we sometimes went to the pictures. We played our own games – skipping and hopscotch and anything that was going. The wood up at the back was full of primroses. They say a tunnel started there which went to Moat Farm – there is a mound in the grounds. We would go there for Sunday school outings and they said there was a connection between the two, and that King Charles went from one to the other when he was in hiding. How true it is I don't know.

I can remember going to Kings Tarrant in a donkey cart. The blacksmith took people to Kings Tarrant in a trap. An uncle of mine was coachman up at Mumford Hall and he was allowed to take my family and one or two others to Kings Tarrant in a waggonette. We children sat along the side. He put up at the Rose and Crown to rest the horses. Going to Kings Tarrant once a year was our outing. We went there for clothes, but not very often. There was a shop called Street and Robsons. You didn't pay at a desk; they put the money in a little cup with the bill, pulled a chain, and it ran along a wire to the office. They put the change in and it came back to the counter.The building was burnt down and some other shop has taken its place.

I remember my mother walking to Kings Tarrant many times. Millie Lagden's grandmother lived at New Farm and every Sunday morning Millie's mother went to see her. She walked down Long Lane, spent the day with her mother and walked back. Never knew her miss, winter or summer. The workhouse was a dreaded name for everyone. My mother died in one. It must have been dreadful, feeling that once you became dependent and poor that was your fate.

I remember when we first had mains water; we had a pump and stand-pipe in the front garden just by the fence, and Mr Lagden the thatcher and Dad shared it. It was marvellous to have that pump there, so they didn't have to lug buckets back from the well.

Dad wouldn't have electric light. He didn't believe in it. We had lamps on the table and when we were larking about, Dad used to hold on to the lamp and say 'Be careful! You'll knock the lamp over.' We did get electricity in the end. All the cooking was done on the old black range though – it took longer but it was just as good.

When people were ill they went to Mrs Nightingale, the village nurse. She attended all the births, deaths and funerals. She wasn't trained but she knew her job – the doctors were very glad of her knowledge of natural remedies. She came to our house quite a lot – there were four of us and she attended each birth.

The blacksmith was fun to watch. There were a lot of horses and at night they turned them into the meadow below the keeper's cottage. At five o'clock when they knocked off work the horses were let loose to run down the road and they would dive straight into the field. The horse-keeper came behind but they knew where to go. There would be six or seven great big farm horses, and the dust they used to kick up! You couldn't see for a little while after they had passed by. I remember going into the harness room where my uncle the coachman kept the brasses. It was all green baize and horse brasses. I look at horses now and I can still imagine the smell of that room.

I know that things have to change, and I'm not criticising, but a lot of people here now couldn't care less what goes on in the village. It's just dashing off up to town in the morning, and back at night – the village is just a lodging place. There aren't many left in the village whom I knew in my youth.

There is a feeling of two communities – us up here and the village down there. These houses should never have been put up here really; but there is 'them and us' in every village. Some of us meet people at the do's and they say, 'Ooh, where do you live?' 'Up at the council housing.' The conversation tends to peter out. We have all said that they don't want to know the people at the council houses until they want someone to work in the house or garden. I have heard the remark, 'Surely someone up the council houses wants a job?' With a house and garden this size we don't have a lot of spare time, although I did work at one of the big houses for some number of years. They were good friends to us and I could always ring them up if I wanted a natter. They took me backwards and forwards to the hospital when my husband was ill.

There's a lot of jolly good youngsters about today, but there's a lot of the other sort too. In my opinion – and my son agrees with me – National Service did them a lot of good. The youngsters where he works, he says they haven't a clue of their responsibilities to anybody. There has never been much discipline for that generation; there isn't much at home, there isn't the church and there isn't the army – so where is it? The parents are all out at work. Our taxi-driver told us about the little blighters he takes on the school bus – the under-elevens. Their parents go out to work leaving them to get themselves to school, and they get to mixing drinks from the cocktail cabinet before they set off! By the time they get to school they can't stand up.

Our life was much simpler, we didn't have these choices. I feel quite sorry for children now, they have so much put into their heads so early. I don't think they are ready for it. They just grow up too quick. Going to these bigger schools and taking them away from the village doesn't help – I think it is wrong. You can't tell me that when there are a thousand children in a school they are all individually known by their form-master. They are going to write their own little notes to say they have permission to go down the town, and get away with it. With my teachers, my goodness you had to mind your ps and qs; and I don't suppose we were any more angels than they are. We needed that discipline and so do they.

JOAN TRIGG

Widow

There was an illusion of spring the following day as I walked up Hawthorn Hill again to Joan Trigg's house. A bright cold sun illuminated peeping flowers in cottage gardens as they basked in the rare spring sunshine. If you go right up the hill, past the houses, and take a footpath across the fields, you get a bird's-eye view of Swanbrooke Down, lying snugly in a dip, sheltered by sloping fields. The church tower rises high over the cottages, and several great trees throw their shadows over the quiet street.

Joan lives at the far end of the semi-circle of houses on the hill, and beside her path runs a long, wide border thickly planted with herbaceous plants. Some glorious hellebores, pale-green, cream and pink, luxuriated in the sunshine, and snowdrops, tiny tulips, scyllas and grape-hyacinths were beginning to show. This strip of garden was planted by her late husband, who was gardener at Mumford Hall. He was her second husband, a man of few words, in marked contrast to her lively sociability.

For Joan Trigg is the archetypal English village person: active in the WI, churchwarden and ex-parish councillor, she runs meals on wheels and is involved in Amnesty International. She is a craftswoman, as her sitting room bears witness; although simply furnished, it was full of patchwork cushions, collage pictures, canvas embroidery and even pewter doorplates – all made by the indefatigable Joan. She is seventy-four although you would never guess it. She rushes around in her little red car, immaculately dressed, neat grey hair in place, mustering support for the latest WI event or fund-raising effort. The first time I was ever introduced to her, in the post office as I was buying stamps, she practically press-ganged me into doing for meals and wheels. Everybody knows Joan, for she is ubiquitous. Most villages have at least one of these ladies, who for many people epitomise English village life.

Joan moved to Swanbrooke Down during the Second World War to escape the blitz in London where she was working. A doctor's daughter, she was brought up in Leicestershire, but having moved into the first of the council houses to be built in the 1950s, she has remained there. Like many of the occupants, she has bought her house – rather against her openly-admitted left-wing tendencies.

We sat at a solid square table by her back window and looked out over the garden to the fields. A bank of cloud emerged over the horizon as we talked, threatening the bright day. But still the furrowed fields were deeply lined with shadow, and the bare trees stood traced against the blueness of that cold sky. March was leonine.

What will happen when we're gone?

Joan I've lived in this house since it was built in 1951 – nobody else has lived in it. I count myself one of the older generation now, although I'm not Swanbrooke Down-born. So many people have been and gone in this place – it's terrible.

There were far fewer houses then – down by the bridge there was just the farmhouse and two little cottages in the Dip. The other farm cottages were at Mumford Hall. Although I was married to a farmworker, we never had a farm cottage and I was a little bit envious of the others, because they didn't pay rent. I had to pay a pound a week rent, out of seven pounds a week. My husband worked on the farm and he was an extremely good gardener, so the lady of Mumford Hall leapt on him and made him her gardener. That's why our garden is so lovely.

It was amazing how little money we had, but we managed. We

didn't run a car, and I didn't have a telephone when we first married – nobody did. Mabel Hutchinson's sister had the first telephone, and when I started work in 1961, in the training centre for mentally handicapped children, we were on a shoestring. But I did get a telephone because I had to be in touch with work.

Occasionally we organised outings to Cambridge – shopping, and sometimes the cinema. Kings Tarrant had two cinemas once. But these were rare treats. We had a simple life and didn't expect too much. We were used to living on war-rations; they didn't stop fully until about 1952.

Joan had copied for me a list of her weekly wartime rations, which she had kept. It reads as follows:

1/10d worth of meat (about 9p)
4 oz bacon
2 oz butter
2 oz marge
1 oz cheese
8 oz sugar
2 pints milk
2 oz jam
½ fresh egg
egg powder to the equivalent of ¾ egg
1 tin canned food (included canned meat, fruit, fish and vegetables; *or* 1 packet of breakfast cereal or biscuits)

Bread, potatoes, fresh vegetables, flour, oatmeal, fish and fresh fruit (apart from oranges) were about the only important foods not rationed.

Joan We never had holidays, not like people nowadays. We used to go to my parents, and sometimes they would take us to Cromer. When I started work it was a bit easier, but I must say wages weren't very good – they offered me £3 a week in the Health Service! Once I became a teacher and on the Burnham Scale it was different. Finally a friend gave me a little car, an Austin, and I became mobile at last, in about 1966.

Because these houses are outside the village, it's always been 'them and us'. I cannot get people up here to get involved in the village. They live their own little lives, they earn their money and they spend it, and that's it. There's no community life up here, we never do anything together. I've lived next door to the Hutchinsons for thirty-odd years, but they hardly spoke for years. We've got a bit friendlier lately, however.

But we all know each other and I can call on them for help if I need it – sometimes it's difficult to manage on your own. We are friendly, but we don't organise things together any more. People just chat over the fence.

Edith Spooner used to organise outings, and the WI organised events. Some people up here used to belong to the WI but now only Effie Lagden and I do. People seem to live their own lives now much more. The church has an average congregation of twelve or fourteen. Only a handful go to WI meetings. The village hall committee is there to promote social functions and I have been on it since it was formed. We used to have proper village do's. People were much simpler types. We had a women's cricket team; we played the men once and it was very funny. We had bicycle races, and a pancake race on Shrove Tuesday which still goes on. We used to go to the Essex Show, and once we went to a Garter Ceremony at Windsor Castle. There were Over-Sixties parties, coffee mornings, beetle drives, classes, and a regular fish-and-chip supper. Some of the girls – not girls any more – they met on Thursday afternoons for a cup of tea, but I was out at work. Also I was looked on as a bit of an outsider because I wasn't local – I wasn't quite one of the gang.

In the old days we had the recreation field, a lovely cricket meadow. We had fêtes there, and sports days, and the children could meet there. Today they don't meet up because they all go to different schools. Once this place was full of children; the green in front of the council houses didn't have trees on it, it had swings. And of course they could go roaming around the countryside. I used to go mushrooming in the cricket meadow in the early mornings, and down Long Lane you crossed the field and there were hedges where you could pick blackberries by the ton. Then the farmer chopped the hedge down. All those sort of changes haven't helped, ever-bigger fields and so on. I blame the local farmers partly – they have torn down a lot of hedges in the interests of bigger machines and bigger crops. At least they can't cut down trees any more, not without getting into terrible trouble.

A spinster called Miss Dalliday, who lived in what is now the Colbrookes' cottage, was an amateur naturalist with a keen interest in wild flowers. Before she died in the early 1980s, she recorded 250 species of wild flowers growing in and around Swanbrooke Down. She discovered many chalk-loving species including the now-disappeared musk mallow and henbane. Old man's beard and dogberry grew alongside dewberry, and in the banks flourished mignonette, hairy violet, salad burnet and milkwort. She recorded eyebright, red bartsia, dwarf thistle and rough hawkbit. Cowslips, a few primroses, bluebells in spring; scabious and hoary ragwort in late summer. Wild herbs – thyme, marjoram and even basil – flourished on the edge of the chalk-pit half a mile outside the village. She found an early purple orchid and the common spotted orchid, and once discovered the common rock rose in a field hedgerow. The chalk pit has since been 'cleaned up' and many of these species have vanished. The narrow verges alongside the open fields and underneath the few remaining hedgerows suffer from the spraying of the crops; wild flowers are struggling for survival around Swanbrooke Down.

Joan The presence of more money has made a difference, I'm sure. People who never had two pennies to rub together have far more now. How they spend it is another matter – they may hoard it under the mattress for all I know. But they've got the money; many earn lots. The ones who go up to London do, and they spend a great deal. The pub never used to have so many cars – now you can hardly drive through the village. There were two pubs, the Green Man, as well as the Dog and Duck, and people went for a pint; but now every night there's a roaring crowd in there, very often the same people, and they have their circle of friends, and they give little dinner parties. Never in a hundred years has anyone up here given a dinner party.

We were content with our life then. I was fortunate because occasionally my father helped me out. He wasn't rich, but he was a doctor, and he bought me a washing machine. I would never have been able to afford it. One of my brothers gave me a second-hand spin-dryer. Before that I had a table mangle! Money didn't worry me too much.

We all used to go potatoing. The first year I was here I was on my own most of the time, because everybody was out in the potato field. I got quite worried – there was only one old lady up here, and no telephone. When my daughter was old enough I went too, and made enough to buy clothes for the children, that was the aim. I once went pea-picking and that was terrible – I didn't go again. But I liked the potatoing, and one was always able to bring a few home. So we managed.

I don't think people of that age-group, with young families, now, are as content. There's one girl who, whenever she has something new, tells everybody how much it cost! It would never occur to me to do that – unless I thought I'd got a bargain. People didn't moan, provided they could make enough to live on. We didn't go anywhere much – you were lucky if you went for the day to Clacton. We organised the village trip to the seaside, and the children rushed off with their buckets and spades and had a lovely time. We just hoped the weather would be nice. But I've never been to the seaside on my own with the children. My parents took me to Guernsey once. But once I had two children we didn't go anywhere. The first time I went abroad was in 1971 and that was to Gibralter because my eldest brother was stationed there. There was a long period of not going anywhere, which I regret. Nowadays people go bombing off two or three times a year – a weekend here and a trip there.

I just have a feeling that things have gone up to a high point, and now they're balancing out and coming down again. I may be wrong. I don't know a lot of these young people intimately.

When I was young and carefree I never went to church. I had no religion, I was very socialist, very active politically. I don't know what started me going to church, the process was so gradual. I didn't have a sudden blinding light! The children went to Sunday school. They sang in the church choir, so I got more and more involved and finally I went along to the parish AGM. The vicar at that time was never in the village, and never visited anybody to my knowledge. He and his wife never even shopped locally. Somebody at this meeting proposed me for the PCC. I was just getting to my feet to say, 'I'm very sorry but I'm already on three other committees', I was working at the time and couldn't manage it. The vicar leapt up and said, 'I'm afraid that's out of the question. Mrs Trigg's children go to the Methodist Sunday school and she doesn't come to church every week.' There was an appalled silence, I felt awful. Everybody felt awful. Then old Charlie Cook, who's dead now, sprang up and said, 'The children go to the Methodist Sunday school because there is no church Sunday school.' And I said, 'A number of people here don't go to church every week!' I got letters of apology from members of the church, and I'm a churchwarden now.

There were more people in church in those days, and we had little fêtes in the vicarage grounds. People like to *see* the church there but aren't prepared to do anything about it. I never feel there's quite the same feeling in the village now. People are very nice and I like them, but we're not the close-knit community we were. Most of the village were the same social class – I was not because I had been to university and was a doctor's daughter. But I married a working-class man, which lowered me to a no-man's-land in between. A little bit difficult at times, but I got on with everybody, I always do unless they're really awful. The village was more spread out because we didn't have all these in-fill houses.

We led such a simple life. We had two shops and a decent post office. We had two butchers calling, and I would leave a tin out with a note to say what I wanted and he would put it in! I used to reckon I could get my meat and my fish for a pound during the week. We ate simply but well – we had lots of vegetables in the garden, and strawberries and raspberries; I didn't buy much fruit, fruit was a luxury even though it was cheap. The fish man came, the greengrocer came, the Co-op grocer came – he had a system of two books, and you gave him the order for next week. There was milk every day from Jack Jacobs. Nowadays there's only milk every other day, and it's not from the village.

Bertha Cakebread was affronted if she didn't get a visit from somebody every day. She never went out, although she belonged to the WI at the beginning. I occasionally looked in on her, sitting just inside her front door as she always did. I visited all the old people. There were so many old people in the village when we were living in Bendysh and I wanted a house here in Swanbrooke Down, that I made the rounds making enquiries. I discovered a number of cottages here all inhabited by one very old person, and I had plans about marrying them off to each other to get a cottage. It never came to anything, naturally. I wasn't very serious about it!

Nowadays it's difficult for local people to get places to live – they are driven out of their own villages because they can't afford the done-up cottages. One of the houses up here on Hawthorn Hill was valued a year ago, then again this year, and it had gone up by 100%! It's terrible to think that the cost of things is so great now. My meat and fish cost a pound, my groceries another pound, and of course school was free, milk was free, sixpence for school dinners – half-a-crown a week for the children's dinners. I go out with a lot of money in my purse and come back with nothing. I don't know what I've spent it on – probably things I shouldn't! But I'm not throwing the money around – occasionally I like to buy a little plant for myself, but I have to think twice.

Waldo the Pole worked at Mumford Hall – there were several Poles working there. Waldo got one of the cottages at the bottom of the Hall drive. Before that he lived in the Dip; people moved around the cottages in those days. I remember I gave him an old kitchen table. He was fairly friendly with my husband, but my husband was a bit wary of him because he drank so much. He once came up here, sat himself down, produced a bottle of whisky and proceeded to drink it. He made my husband drink it too, and gave me drinks. When he had to totter off to the loo I'd pour it back in the bottle because I don't like whisky very much. Once he drank so much he slept the night in the chair. After a while he didn't come – I think my husband choked him off. I didn't know a lot about him except that he had once had a wife in White Russia – and a daughter still supposedly somewhere, but nobody as far I know succeeded in tracing her. He used to weave his way home from the pub on a bicycle. Then they told him he couldn't come to the pub any more.

Long ago they had a Christmas Club at the pub, the Thrift Club they called it, and I thought I would join to save a bit, because I never had any money at Christmas. I applied and was told that I couldn't. I went down and made a terrible row. It was because they thought my husband drank! I made a fearful scene, and it turned out to be a misunderstanding over him and Waldo, because they were both Poles. They were so sorry about it. My husband had never been in the pub except for a meal once! He didn't drink much at all – we would only have a drink at the weekend.

Mrs Rush, there was a character for you. She seemed to spend her time making cakes. I don't know *why* she made all these cakes! Fred smoked, so Fred had to sit in the kitchen, and she sat in the living room! She was a scream; but she was very kind-hearted. She didn't go out much, although at one time she belonged to the WI. Fred Rush worked in her garden. He was a lovely old-fashioned man; he wore gaiters, breeches and gaiters. I went to see her once and he said, 'She's gone out in the *motor*!' That took me back to my childhood.

Arthur Stone kept the little shop, The Stores it was called. He came from London and had a strong cockney accent. His wife was rather prudish. She ran the library until Miss Braybrooke took over. It was in the village hall on a Wednesday afternoon. The books were changed every three months and there was this tremendous *do* when the delivery van was coming, and we went to choose new books. Once I chose *Women of Rome* by Alberto Moravia, but she snatched it out of my hands and wouldn't let me have it! She died before he did and he carried on, but then the shop closed and he got chest trouble and went to live in Kings Tarrant. Once we were having a cheese and wine evening and I was secretary, so I was deputed to sell tickets round the village. I went to see him and he said, 'Just a minute, Mrs Trigg,' went into the shop and came back with a large piece of cheese. 'Do you know what this is?' 'Yes, it's cheese.' So he said, 'I have not been asked to provide anything for this cheese and wine, so I'm not going to buy tickets.' Unfortunately he took umbrage very easily. Somebody had decided to get the cheese from cash-and-carry instead of the local shop. We used to get the wine from Kings Tarrant, but now we get it from the Dog and Duck. We thought it was better to get it in the village. In those days some people, outsiders, didn't realise this, and it led to bad feeling.

What we say at the church and even at the WI is 'What will happen when we've gone? Who is going to run village functions?' It is nice when you can get a few younger people to join – because there is something for everybody.

THE WAY WE LIVE NOW

SIDNEY AND GWEN PILGRIM

Gardener and wife

Spring has come early to Swanbrooke Down. The March morning is bright, crisp, blue. The midday sky is cloudless; delicate pale crocuses and golden aconites, now nearly over, bask in unexpected sunshine. Walking up to Hawthorn Hill you see clumps of snowdrops in many of the cottage gardens, and the first tiny irises. Even the birds, singing loudly, are deceived into early display by this apparition of spring.

It is noon, and the village bustles with activity. A couple of cars draw up to the pub, and a young family sits at an outside table. A couple of folk nip into the post office before it closes for lunch; the builders are still at work on Sam Gapes's cottage. The low bright sun casts long shadows across the street. There is a feeling – deceptive no doubt – that winter is over.

Sidney and Gwen Pilgrim live in number 1, Hawthorn Hill, on the edge of the semi-circle of council houses, more than half of which are now owner-occupied. They are country people, with true solidity of character. It is hard to believe they are grandparents – the country way of life has kept them fit, active and young-looking.

Gwen speaks quietly – she is shy and gentle, but gives the impression that her feelings run deep. Sid is fluent, articulate, with a wealth of stories about life between the wars, and particularly about Len Cakebread. The image of the portly Len leaning over his gate at all hours of the day, ready for a chat with whoever was passing, lingers in the minds of all who knew him. Everybody has a 'Len story'; possibly the truth has become embroidered, but only with affection. How he would shoot sparrows with a shotgun from his bedroom window. How, one

Christmas day, he ate three Christmas dinners. How, on ordinary weekdays, he sat down to enough lunch for four. Sid knew him well for years. Indeed it was he who found Len collapsed inside his front door, victim of the stroke which killed him.

'Them and us' on Hawthorn Hill

Sid I was born in Little Bendysh, one of seven – eight, really. My twin sister died just after birth; so I had four sisters and two brothers. We were brought up in a two-up, two-down cottage. We slept head-to-toe in the bed: two at the top and two at the bottom. We had to walk right up to the farm where my father worked for drinking-water. He took two buckets up at five o'clock every morning when he went to milk the cows, filled them at the pump and brought them back breakfast-time. On washdays he'd fill the copper too. When he went back after breakfast he'd fill them again, and bring them back lunchtime. It didn't strike us that it was hard, but it would do now!

We had no electricity, just candles and paraffin lamps. When I was five, in 1938, I started school up at Swanbrooke; I was there until I left school at fourteen. We walked from the council houses in all weathers. The elder ones had pushbikes, and they put the youngsters on the carriers or the crossbars. We left home about quarter past eight and got to school at nine o'clock. We'd mess about on the way, getting soaked and muddy. If you'd got wet feet walking in the stream, you had wet feet for the day. The only heating was a great 'tortoise' stove about four foot high in the middle of one wall, with a big guard round it. We hung our clothes over the guard to dry.

The infants played on the green and the older ones were allowed up into the field behind the church. We played in the bottom of the field, providing Jack Jacobs's cows and the bull weren't in there. Jack provided the milk for the school, in third-of-a-pint bottles. They had cardboard tops with little rings, and you pushed the ring in and put your straw in the top. You had that about ten o'clock in the morning, and you had to drink it. But we all liked it, we were ready for it by then.

Jack was a real 'good old British' character. He was more or less the local dairy farmer – he produced all the milk for Swanbrooke and the biggest part of Bendysh. It was milked by hand, bottled up there as soon as it had gone through the cooler, then delivered all the way round. My sister did the milk round. Jack lived at Moat Farm before he came to Swanbrooke Down, and he remembered seeing the murderer, Samuel Dougal, before they caught up with him. He was officiating at a sports day. One of his earliest memories is of the search for Miss Holland's body.

Jack Jacobs was one of the forty men in Swanbrooke Down who set out to fight in the Great War. Never having gone far from home before, he got lost. However, in the company of four other young men he eventually found his way to Dover, where he trained for four months with the fourth Battalion Royal Fusiliers. He fought alongside his friends in the Battle of the Somme. Two of them fell; Jack was awarded the Military Medal for destroying an enemy machine-gun. He was badly wounded a few days before Armistice day, and spent months in hospital.

Jack bought a little farm up the Gap, and went into dairying. He started the local milk round with his pony and trap; his pony, well known to the children, was called Ginger. He kept a ferocious bull called Benny in the meadow behind the farm. This is one of the very few pieces of meadowland still remaining, with a carpet of cowslips in early spring.

Jack died at the age of ninety and his ramshackle old bungalow was snapped up by a property developer. One Saturday in high summer the fire brigade was called out; Jack's old place was on fire. It was razed to the ground by teatime. The cause of the fire is unknown and there is no evidence to link it to the property developer. Within a week the outbuildings and overgrown garden had gone too. A large modern residence now stands on the site, towering over the village from the crest of the hill.

Sid It was good discipline at school – they didn't think twice about giving you the cane. It really was 'Hold out your hand!' and you daren't drop it; you got about six strokes.

Gwen They gave you severe punishments for trivial things. At the boarding school I went to, if you were caught indoors at playtime you got the cane just for that. I suppose it taught you to do as you were told. But I wasn't naughty, I was very quiet, although I got the cane once or twice.

Sid The caning here was done for good reason. And you daren't go home and tell your parents, because they'd say, 'Well you had the cane for a reason,' and if you didn't watch out you'd get another clip round the ear. But that made sense – school and parents were backing each other up.

Gwen Today so many parents don't bother with their children – they leave it to the school, who don't do it. At home there's most often no discipline whatsoever. Parents let their children run riot. The parents are at work when the children get back from school and a lot seem to want to do their own thing, not stay in and look after the children.

A classic case was the lad next door to us; we always had to lock our door. In a way I felt sorry for him, because he would come home from school and there was nobody in, so he got into mischief. He went on from there, he got worse, and he got very sly in the end. Yet he really could be a very nice polite young man. If someone had just taken notice of him ... But his father never did, he wouldn't let him be responsible for things. You've got to let them learn; they're going to make mistakes, but that's the only way you learn.

Sid It was a very close community, we were all more or less in the same boat, and we enjoyed life because we made our own amusements.

Gwen We didn't have a lot, but we were content, and the children had the countryside to play in. Nowadays you can't scamper in the woods; there aren't many left, and you daren't let them in case there are strangers around.

Sid We used to get up to mischief mind you, but it was straightforward mischief. One of the school lady-governers kept a Jersey cow and a couple of goats. She pegged them along the bank in front of Clarice Penington's cottage. When we came out of school we tore up to these goats, and one would hold the horns, and the other would get hold of the udder, and squirt the milk into his mouth straight out of the udder! We used to dare each other to do it.

We messed about in the village for a while, then we'd go off down the Little Bendysh road, and call at Sam Gapes's house where his mother would give us a cup of water. Every day through the summer, regular as clockwork.

In the winter we would stop in the fields where the men were hedging, clearing out the dead wood for faggots, and burning the scrub. Their bonfires were lovely, so we'd stand and warm our hands. We took faggots back for the village bread oven – one enormous oven which baked bread for all Bendysh. On Mondays they'd bake a 'wash-day pudding' in it, like bread and butter pudding.

Old Tom Crock, who lived at the end of the street, was a short man, he had a massive long beard, and he wore one of these top hats and carried a walking stick. We used to cycle along and he would be walking to Bendysh with his back to us. We'd just clip the top of his hat to knock it off! The following day, if he was coming towards us, we'd have to go up the Haverley road and round the other way, without going past him! But it wasn't badness. And we'd put up with the consequences of our mischief if we were caught.

It was a church school, and we had Bible education every morning first thing, then three hours of reading, writing and 'rithmetic. One afternoon a week we had drawing, and perhaps there'd be some handicrafts, like rugmaking, but for anything like cookery or woodwork we went to Kings Tarrant once a week. The coach picked the children up from the different villages, and the girls would go to cookery and the boys would do woodwork. On the way home, the boys had to go to the back of the bus, to keep them out of the way of the girls. The woodwork master saw you to the back, but once he was out of sight and the girls were on, we would raid what they'd made at cookery class!

Gwen I first set eyes on Swanbrooke Down when we got

married, thirty-three years ago. I didn't know anybody round here, so I did feel rather a foreigner. We were married in March 1954; in August they finished the council houses, and we applied for one. We didn't think we'd get one because we'd only just got married and didn't have children, but they moved some people out of number 9, and that was the first one we lived in. I got to know people fairly quickly – we had to because the boiler burst! We had water gushing all over the house that first Sunday!

Sid People were more neighbourly then. When you moved in someone would be looking out for you, and introduce themselves. There was no feeling of us up here and those down there, because we were nearly all ordinary working people. I already knew several people anyway.

Gwen We had fêtes in the summer, and quite a few regular whist drives. Our children went to Sunday school in the chapel, and there was a little choir.

Sid Every year there was a Sunday school outing to the seaside, a coachload of us from Bendysh, and a coachload from Swanbrooke Down, organised by the vicar. They met at Bendysh, and if the Swanbrooke coach got in front of the Bendysh coach we'd stick our tongues out of the window as we went past, and they would do the same to us.

They hadn't got loos in the old houses, in 1954, whereas up here there were all mod cons. We had running water, hot and cold, in the house. It was luxury for us. They called the cottages 'the slums' and ours were the posh ones. Nowadays it's thought of the other way round.

Gwen We notice a vast difference in the village feeling. Everybody knew everybody else, everybody stopped to talk, everybody shared their problems, everybody helped everybody. We've known it like that, and now everybody seems distant. Nobody ever locked their doors in those days. I would leave the door open for the baker when I went round to my neighbour's for a cup of tea and he would pop the bread in. I lock the door now even when I go upstairs ... it's an unsure feeling, you never know who's around. We are right on the end and there's nobody around in the daytime. If anybody chose to walk in the side gate and in my back door when I was upstairs, what's to stop them?

Sid The old baker, Reg Johns, he took all day to get round. He'd come up from Little Bendysh, go around Swanbrooke

Down, and finish by quarter to seven at night! He liked his drop of whisky, so he'd call in at the pub. Once Reg was delivering to the Cooks' farmhouse. He called, 'Baker's here!' Then he said, 'I've turned the sausages.' Mrs Cook had left the sausages in the pan and they wanted turning, so he turned them for her!

Gwen I don't know whether he ever spoke a cross word, that man. He'd amble around, give the children what we called penny buns – plain bread rolls. He was really lovely.

Sid Len Cakebread was *the* character of the village. You could have written books and books about Len! When we had new neighbours, he said, 'What's your neighbour's name, Sid?' and I said, 'I dunno, I haven't see them yet.' 'Well you're slipping,' he says, 'because the first thing you should do is go round and say, "I'm so and so, and who are you?" I did that,' he said, 'when the people moved into that ruddy big house, the Hall. I knocked on the door and said, 'Good evening, I'm Len Cakebread and what's your name, may I ask, since you're my neighbour?' They took it all right – some people might be offended, but Len could put it over and not be offensive.

Gwen I don't doubt that he might have offended one or two in his time, because he'd say just what he thought. If you didn't like it that was your hard luck. But he was usually to the point.

Sid So was Bertha. When the vicar spoke at her funeral he called her Queen of Swanbrooke. She was a marvellous washerwoman, and she laid people out. She was a midwife originally. She sat in her armchair at the door of Box Cottage with the door open and she could see everyone who went past.

Len told me some tales . . . Once he told me about a chap who did a lot of poaching. He went off poaching when the snow was down, and the police followed him back to his house by his footprints in the snow. He said hard and fast he hadn't been there, but the footprints were there to prove he had. He was to appear in court in Kings Tarrant and when he didn't they came after him. He said the only way he would go was if the copper took him on the crossbar of his bike! There were no cars then, and Len said that was how they got him there!

Most of his tales are a bit too rude, so I can't tell you. He really was scandalous. It made me laugh.

In wartime, the shop was run by an old chap called Mr Young. We went for our sweets rations. He used to cut the sweet-coupons

with an enormous pair of scissors with huge blades ever so long. The coupons were tiny, about an inch square. He used to frighten the life out of us, because if you got up to mischief he'd say, 'I'll cut your ears off with these enormous great scissors." He really was a frightening old man.

I used to go to the Green Man for a drink; I might pop down Sunday lunchtime, but not very regularly. I smoked then, so I used to go in after a packet of cigarettes, and I might have a half-pint. There weren't many ladies in pubs at all then – the odd one or two, but not like today.

We had the 'slate club' at the pub; we paid in a regular sum for medical insurance. Not a lot – our wages were very low. In 1947 I was taking home thirty shillings a week. By the time we got married in 1954 that had doubled. We had the thrift club at the pub, too, for Christmas, and it was a good way to save up. If we needed the money in an emergency we could take it out up to three times a year.

Most people worked on the land, in the village or within spitting distance. We cycled to work. I can't remember anybody having to catch the train when I came here first.

Gwen People here were all related – you might talk about somebody, and it could turn out to be her son or cousin, so you had to be careful what you said! Families stayed in villages, and there were two or three houses perhaps with all the family in them.

Sid I can understand the villagers taking against the newcomers – 'they from London'. I think we were wary of them; why had they come here if they were working in London? We thought if you work somewhere, you live there. You tended to think they were doing something wrong and wanted to get out of London in case anyone was looking for them.

Gwen I think we were suspicious at first because people didn't move in and out of villages in those days. Families continued generation after generation in the village.

Sid But this change gradually grew on us. When the third and the fourth lot moved in you more or less accepted them.

Gwen People don't like change, and things hadn't changed for so many centuries.

Sid Evacuee children came down from London in the Second World War, and quite a few stayed, or came back. Len had some with him, and there were some up at Grinchells Manor. Us children seemed to take to the youngsters more than did the grown ups.

Gwen Children always accept other children, it's adults who don't accept new things. A lot of the men being killed in the war changed things too. And there's so much more money around these days.

Sid I think perhaps it's a good thing those people moved into the cottages, because they saved the buildings. They had the money to spend; otherwise they would have become tumbledown shacks.

Gwen The only thing is though that the younger people have to leave. People who were born here can't stay, they can't afford the houses, not even the council ones, so the continuity is broken.

Sid When they first had the cheese and wine evening it was packed, and then it gradually grew thinner. I can describe it like this: if you had a dozen hens in the bottom of your garden and you went to market and bought three more, those three would go to one end of the run, the other dozen to the other. That's what happened with the cheese and wine party. That's when the community started to fall apart.

Gwen To put it bluntly, 'them and us'. It was a class division. Still is. There are some people who even if they've got money are very nice to us. The other lot just don't want to know you. You might think, 'Oh, a new face', and look at them and want to smile – but they freeze you. So you think, 'I'd better not say anything.'

Sid I think all villages are the same, though. There's usually a bit of a pub clique, the farming lobby and so on. These divisions seem rather pointless to me.

Gwen Why can't everybody just join in and be friends? Why does it matter whether you've got money or not? But you feel that they think, 'I mustn't speak to them, they haven't got money like we have.' Perhaps *they* haven't got the manners they should have. It's money that's divisive, I think, more than breeding or sense. They feel that if they communicate with us too much others with money like them might think, 'Fancy mixing with them', and wouldn't talk to them. They are all keeping up with the Joneses. You see them getting a new car just to keep up with the next person. Whatever do people get out of it? You're continually grabbing things, to be one of the set. Doesn't give you any satisfaction once you've grabbed it, either.

Sid I love making friends; any new people coming in, I'm quite willing to go and talk to them, whoever they are.

Gwen Sometimes I come down to work through the village and I don't see a soul, and if I do it's not the same. When I first went down to the Gawthrops' to work, and rode through the village, it would be 'Good morning!' to everybody.

Sid When I asked Len what changes he had seen, he said, 'The biggest change is the commuters. They're like a lot of rooks. They go out in the morning to work, and come back to sleep.' So if you don't see the people you used to, that's because they're all in their cars, not on bikes or on foot. It took us longer of course, but life was relaxed. Today they're in their metal boxes-on-wheels with a deadline.

Gwen They're all clock-watchers. Even if it takes longer to walk down the post office for your stamps and stop to talk to whoever is about, the village needs that.

Sid Losing the vicar, as well – that's very important. In the past, if you'd got a problem you wanted to talk about you could go to your vicar. You can't now. He used to come round regularly.

Gwen People went to church more in those days, because that was a community activity.

Sid That's one of the biggest things that contributed to the break-up of the village community – losing the vicar.

Gwen The new one hasn't got time any more.

Sid He's just not here. It's the same in all the villages: most of the clergy look after three parishes, like ours does.

Gwen He's in and out of the services and doesn't have time to speak to anybody. If you do have a resident vicar then he can take an interest in the people in the village. You can go to him when you want, if you need him. But now we've got nobody to call on.

Sid The community was held together more when we had a vicar: it's disintegrated since he's gone.

Gwen I used to thoroughly enjoy going to church, but we don't go very often now. It's sad, really. I think we would if there was a Canon Williams around the place. I liked him! He was lovely, a real friendly family man.

Sid He was a vicar you could say anything to – he'd take no offence.

Gwen He'd come out with all sorts of things himself!

Sid I'll tell you a story about him and Len: Len used to bike along the Bendysh Road to work. Now Len used to like to know the arse-end of everything, to put it straight – and so did the vicar. Len was coming up the road on his bike from the fields after potato-picking one day. Canon Williams was going down the other way in his car and his wife was with him. He stopped his car, wound the window down and he said to Len, 'Where have you been, Len?' he said, 'I just want to know where you've been.' And Len stuck his head in the window and he says, 'What the bloody hell's that got to do with you? I never stop *you* in your motor and ask you where you've been! Where I've been is my business.' And Canon Williams's wife said, 'Thank goodness someone's put him in his place at last!' And that's as true as I sit here, Len told me that himself. But I can't really put it over, not like Len. And Canon Williams, you could say things to him you wouldn't dream of saying to any other vicar, and he would take it. He really was a super man.

Gwen He was fun, and yet he was sympathetic. It's a shame really, because there isn't the same religious education nowadays, either. Most of us were brought up going to church and to Sunday school. It was a part of life, a rather beautiful part.

Sid You'd get up Sunday morning, have breakfast, put your best clothes on and go to Sunday school. Then you'd come home, take your best clothes off, put your old playing clothes on, and you were finished for the day – until you had to go with your parents to the evening service. When you left school, you were allowed not to go every Sunday, but while you were at school you had to be there for 6 o'clock service in the evening. It doesn't seem to happen any more, really because the church isn't the central point any more.

Gwen The people in the church don't communicate with you the way they used to. It shows up in vandalism and violence.

It's not the only change, of course. The landscape has altered so much. All the hedges have been taken out, and we have these huge fields. We used to have little meadows, and lovely hedgerows, and Splash Wood . . .

Sid I remember that being taken out. There were ten acres of woodland out there, and we would sit in our kitchen at breakfast and see the rabbits run along into the wood. The wood was sold off in sections; it was measured off, you bought a piece, and it was cut down you could take most of the wood home.

Gwen They tried to save it, but eventually it was bulldozed. There were some rare orchids up there, and there was said to be a passage from the Green Man through to the wood – a quick way to get a drink, perhaps! They say there was a castle up there once.

Sid In the wood there was a great scooped-out part, like a big moat, and us kids used to slide down in to it. They said that's the place where the tunnel ended – whether that's true I don't know.

Gwen We've seen the hedgerows taken out and the ditches filled in. I hate to see those great fields. The wind is terrible, whistling through.

Sid That's why we get flooded so quickly. Those small fields each had a ditch for the water to drain into, and it would come off slowly. Now it's all drained by clay pipes and it just goes through them and pours off into the road.

Gwen You go down to Devon and Cornwall and there's still all these lovely little fields and hedgerows. But here it's really a prairie. And it's all done just to make money.

> Since the Second World War 140,000 miles of hedgerow have been removed from the English countryside – the equivalent of a single hedge stretching six times around the equator, and nearly one quarter of England's hedges. East Anglia was worst affected: Norfolk lost nearly half of its hedges, Huntingdonshire a staggering 90%. In 1980 hedgerows were still being destroyed at an annual rate of 2,000 miles, in the name of agricultural 'improvement', urban and industrial development, and the building of motorways. The

mechanisation of farming gobbled up marginal land essential to the survival of wildlife. Old woodlands like Splash Wood which had taken centuries to evolve their special ecological balance, were felled in a day. Half of England's semi-natural deciduous woodlands have gone since 1947.

A survey in 1974 showed that of the original forty-seven miles of boundary hedges in the parish, thirty-four remained. A quarter of Swanbrooke Down's hedgerows had disappeared since 1945, and since the survey at least another mile has been destroyed. Two hedges in the parish were of extreme antiquity, probably around seven hundred years old. Going by the established measure of one species of shrub or tree per hundred years in a thirty-yard stretch, one hedge was found to harbour wild plum, hazel, ash, hawthorn, field maple, wayfaring tree and willow. The other, one of the boundary hedges of Mumford Hall, contains spindle, hawthorn, sloe, elder, ash, hazel and wild rose.

Gwen Our little grandson loves to see things like that, and I want to show him things. But you have to search now for the wild flowers, so I show him things in the garden – the dandelions, bees and so on. I took him for walks along the road in the summer to show him the few wild flowers there are. 'Can I pick some, Nan, to take home to Mummy?' We spent all our time picking wild flowers when we were children, and learning their names, but now I think 'What can I show him now?'

He loves watching the tractors and combines. We've got a picture up the stairs, of the plough-horse working, and I say, 'That's how they used to do it years ago.' 'Before they had combines?' he says. And I say, 'Yes, before any machinery, the horses went up and down the field, all day long, and they didn't break down!' He said, 'No, they don't, do they! Not like the combines and tractors.' I do like to talk to him about the days before machinery.

Sid Yet they weren't necessarily the 'good old days'. There's times I don't want to go through again, yet there's times I'd like to see again.

Gwen People didn't crave for things; they accepted what they'd got. There was a lot of discomfort, much more cold and damp.

These days everybody seems to grab, and that's not nice. I remember just meandering about, standing and talking, sitting out if it was a nice day. Nowadays barbecues and the rest have to be added. If you go and sit outside with people you've got to have something smart, you can't just sit and talk!'

Hawthorn Hill nowadays is very quiet. Thirty-four years ago it was chock-a-block with children; now there are just three children in eighteen houses.

Sid There's not the community there was when we first came – apart from the people still here from when we came. We still get together.

Gwen A neighbour and I still go round each other's every Thursday afternoon for a cup of tea, just like people used to, for about an hour. I don't see them hardly, otherwise – I'm right on the end and I don't see anybody. But Edith has always done that. We lived next door to her originally, and soon after I got there she said, 'Do you want to come round for a cup of tea?' Everybody went round Edith's for a cup of tea. She was always in and out of our house, too. She'd run out of sugar and she would borrow some. It was lovely. It's part of being next-door neighbours, borrowing. Not many people do that now.

The village isn't the same without the shops. We had two – one was The Stores, run first by Mr Young with the big scissors, then by two sisters, then Mr Stone and his wife. It was a little grocery shop where you could stand and talk. It was lovely.

Sid You could do all your shopping there apart from the meat; the butcher and the fish van came round, and a grocery van, and a fish-and-chip van every Thursday night.

The village shop was run by the copper's wife. The first village copper I remember was old Tardy Nightingale – I don't know what his proper name was – the shoemaker's son. My father mended our shoes, but the only thing he couldn't do was make the hemp, so we had to go to Mr Nightingale for that. It was long strings of very strong fibre and he'd twist it around; then he'd get this wax and hold it in his hand for a while and run this black wax up it, backwards and forwards until it was all coated, and that was what he used for stitching shoes.

The radios used to be run on batteries and charged up by accumulators – there was no electricity. When the accumulator ran down, you'd take it to the other one in the bakehouse at Bendysh, and that'd be charged up. You wouldn't dream of having the radio on all day – it wouldn't last! It came on perhaps six o'clock for the news for my father, and you might be allowed to listen to a half-hour programme in the evening.

Gwen Ours had to last a week, because the firm came out from Kings Tarrant to collect them once a week.

Sid You just switch on and it's there, today, and somebody will pay the bill.

Gwen We take electricity for granted now. When it goes off, do you know it!

Sid Every village had a May king and queen. I never did get to be May King! It broke up just as it got to my age. The Queen's crown was made of hawthorn, the white may, and all the youngsters went May-singing. The whole village got together. The crowning was something to look forward to, and it was an honour to be picked for king and queen. They were given a white prayer book by the vicar.

Gwen They had sports in the villages, too. All the children took part.

Sid The year of the Silver Jubilee the village had a sports day. All the children had a cup for every royal celebration – we've still got two of the children's coronation cups. Jubilee day really was a big do. Teas, sports, and old Mr Vickery had a party for the children up at his house.

Gwen There was a celebration for the wedding of Charles and Diana, and they had races and games in the field. When the children had tea, we thought they would have tables, a sit-down tea with sandwiches. But each one was given a little packet in a box. It really shook me. I thought, is that what they're getting? Is that *it*? I thought they were going to have fun, balloons and that – they could easily have done it in the village hall. I thought, heavens, how mean can we get? So cold, to go off with your little box and sit in a corner. I honestly couldn't believe it. This village doesn't seem to want to *do* things together, nobody seems to want the responsibility of organising things. There's them up at the church, they want money for its upkeep, but you can't just keep contributing *money*. We don't mind helping out with dances and fêtes – that would help bring the village together.

Sid But there isn't anywhere to have a fête now. If we had a recreation field we could do things together.
Gwen We used to, and we would help. It was usually us from Hawthorn Hill doing the washing up, but we enjoyed it because we were part of it. We need something to get the village together. All these new people with money, I suppose they think we're not good enough. They don't bother to get to know us. It doesn't matter to me whether you've got any money. But they judge you on what car you drive and what clothes you wear and don't think about the person underneath. Perhaps they wouldn't want fêtes on the green. But what do they want? There must be something for people to join in.
Sid The rate things have changed these last twenty five years, if it goes on like this goodness knows what lies ahead!
Gwen But there must be a limit. Things will start going back to natural things again. Most things go in circles.

Sid I'll tell you another story about Len: one year he had three Christmas dinners in one day. He had his own at home, early, then he went down the pub and had another about half past two, and then he was invited to Muriel's in the evening! He didn't drink a lot, but Len could eat! Once he had two whole pigeon puddings for lunch, along with fifteen small cauliflowers and twenty-two potatoes. That's as true as I sit here – I saw him sit down to it! He used to shoot the pigeons out of his bedroom window with a 12-bore. The sparrows in his thatch he'd shoot out with a four-ten.

He was an active man. Len didn't move that sharp, but he was always about and he was a big chap. He was always happy and always working.

When he had his first heart attack he weighed about seventeen stone. They put him on a diet in hospital, and they would bring the food in for the other patients, while all Len got was raw carrot and apple. He told me, 'I said to the nurse, my dear,' he says, 'if you bloody well want me to die,' he says, 'you keep bringing me those apples and carrots and I shall be sure to die.' He says, 'Because you'll never get me thin,' he says. 'I'll never lose my weight. If I lose weight,' he says, 'it's because I'm ill and I shall be gone. When your belly-button reaches your backbone,' he told me, 'you've had it!' He was supposed to stay on a diet, but he didn't. He said, 'The quickest way to get me to die is to put me on a diet. I know what I like, and I'm going to have it.' He was seventy eight when he died. He grew all his own veg, apart from potatoes. He got those for nothing from Duncan Vickery. People were always giving him things, but he'd give you things as well.

Gwen We went potato-picking for old Mr Vickery and he was a tight character. He'd come behind you digging out the little potatoes, because he wanted his money's worth. You couldn't go off that field until four o'clock. We would go up with prams and push-chairs with the little ones, and he used to say, in his Scots brogue, 'I can't make it out. These women come on the field, I lift their prams and bags on to the trailers every morning,' he says, 'with all their food in,' he says. 'They eat the food in the day, and at night,' he says, 'their ruddy bags are a damn sight heavier than when they got on.' Full of potatoes you see! He always gave us a box of chocolates, but we really had to work! The women today wouldn't do it; they couldn't. We used to get up, get the children ready, make sandwiches and drinks, and go up the field to start at nine o'clock. We'd work until four, with half an hour for lunch, sometimes in fog, and when it had been raining it was muddy and wet. If it wasn't raining overhead you were up that field no matter what. You'd try to pick your feet up and they just got muddier and muddier. When we got home we'd do the housework and cook a meal. It was a hard life – and that was in the sixties.

HOWARD GAWTHROP

Merchant banker

Mad March hares were frolicking in Darvel field as I made my way along to the Gawthrops' house on a tempestuous day towards the end of the month. It was squally, blustery, and very cold. I found Howard lighting a fire in the living room, kneeling stiffly and slightly breathlessly on one knee. A tall, balding, corpulent man, he heaved himself back into his armchair and began an elaborate ritual of lighting his pipe. A white cyclamen stood on the table beside him, a highly polished three-legged antique piece. A long low table in front of the sofa was covered with huge books, and a handsome oil painting, of an ancestor perhaps, hung over the mantelpiece. Heavy curtains were drawn around the bay window, enhancing the room's plushness and warmth.

Howard is a highly successful merchant banker in the City of London, and although he travels the globe he is frequently in Swanbrooke Down at weekends. He used to commute daily to London, but increased pressures have dictated a small flat in London; thus half of the Gawthrops' life is spent in London, but Swanbrooke Down has prior claims to their affections and they regard it as home.

Howard and his wife Sylvia live in what used to be the blacksmith's place, and the site of the old forge is still plain to see. Over the years they have extended through four cottages to make one big house, with garden and swimming pool at the back. The house has an elegant yet homely feel – book-lined, picture-hung, lamp-lit. Ever since moving to Swanbrooke Down twenty-five years ago the Gawthrops have involved themselves in village activities, in particular with the church, so everybody knows them. They give a Christmas party for the villagers which has become almost an institution, and much enjoyed.

Howard has an emphatic and confident manner; he articulates his views unequivocally. His thoughts on Swanbrooke Down are clearly well-considered, and he had evidently marshalled them.

Commuters have revitalized Swanbrooke Down

Howard We came to this part of the world when commuting to London was much less common than it is today. The railway service between Cambridge and London was unreliable; relatively few people were able to commute, because of the time it took. I don't see village life from the same point of view as Wilf Middle-ditch who remembers this as his ancient native home; to me the striking thing about the changes in Swanbrooke Down is that it has been saved, in the nick of time, from virtually disappearing.

This place came into existence as somewhere for agricultural workers, and those who serviced them, to live. While we've been here employment on the farm has declined, though it wasn't all that great when we came. Rex Vickery will tell you that most of the cottages were condemned as unsuitable for human habitation, and the council wanted to demolish them.

It is a great pity that the council decided to build houses outside the village. I haven't the faintest idea why; I assume they were able to acquire land during the post-war building boom, and had to build as many houses as possible. Perhaps it was speed, efficiency, they were easier to lay out; people liked to build 'estates'. Sadly it did not integrate the houses in among the existing ones. I have a strong belief that a village community can only accept a certain number of new people per annum.

There are fewer and fewer of the old inhabitants. It's not a question of social difference, simply of relative newcomers, of people who do not have ancient roots in this place, and those who do.

We started married life in a London flat, and it wasn't long before we felt that was not what we wanted to live in. It wouldn't be big enough, and we decided to move into the country rather than consider the suburbs. The price of houses here was very modest then compared with central London, and the fare to London was modest as well. The rates were low, and all ways round it was cheap, so that was a factor.

We worked our way down the railway line from Liverpool Street to the station here. We fell in love with Kings Tarrant, looked at this house, and fell in love with it on sight. So it was an accident that we came to Swanbrooke Down – we'd never heard of the place, and I imagine that could be said by a large number of people here.

We quickly found what we believed and still believe to be a remarkably good social mix. There was very little noticeable friction between people. The friction in the village is a recent development. I believe it is because of the arrival of a socio-economic group not present when we first came. Then there were the old villagers, and people who came who had an instinctive understanding of village life.

Swanbrooke Down has recently become much more like an executive housing estate. That is the change I regret, not the change towards commuting. It's difficult to imagine who, apart from commuters, would be able to live here; only retired people or perhaps an author like yourself, which is relatively unusual; there are very few ways to make a living in Swanbrooke Down.

We were never conscious of resentment towards us as commuters. It's fashionable to believe that there is resentment all over the country about the price of property being pushed up and the locals not being able to live in their own village. When we first came a lot of older people had shaken the dust from the dreadful old cottages off their feet and gone to the council houses, which may not look very beautiful but which were palaces compared with these cottages. Down by the bridge stood two very old, unimproved, cottages, and they were mind-bending slums.

This house has been significantly improved. It had always been a cut above the others, because it was the smith's house, and the smith was a relatively prosperous person; a man with his own business. This was originally four cottages. The smith had ceased to operate here a long time before we came. Out in the front is a covered-over well; it's dry now, but it was the village well, and the Middleditches of this world can remember people using it. The forge itself was a barn with an earth floor, with traces of the forge's footings, but it had long been cleared. The house had been improved to an extent, and we have gradually extended and improved it.

A high proportion of the human race are seeking happiness. A lot of people want to feel they *are* somebody in *their* place. Not important or grand or powerful, but known and accepted as individuals. One of the things I dislike about London is the total anonymity. Some people like that; but we, like a lot of others, first of all want the fresh air. If you travel from London by train in the evening, when you get out the other end the difference is extraordinary. The lack of pollution, the quiet and the peace. And the fact that it is a manageable community in which you actually *know* people. After we'd been here three or four years we knew, by sight, or possibly to speak to, virtually everybody in the village. Sadly the turnover has become so rapid we've lost track of it!

The church was much more important in those days. The vicar was a social worker, living full-time in the village. It was a great loss when he went. Canon Williams was an enchanting, dignified priest in his late fifties, much loved here. Also there were two shops in those days – one was pretty modest, but it was a great loss when they went. You had focal meeting points. Fortunately we've retained a pub, which again used to be more popular than it is now. Although it flourishes, it attracts very few village people. When we first came the pub was very old-fashioned, run by a lady and her daughter. The village went into the public bar, visitors into the saloon bar – except on Sundays when by established custom some of the village went into the saloon. No longer.

I think we came because we are both very much *English* people, whose families have lived here for thousands of years. My family come from a rural area in the north of England, Sylvia's from rural East Anglia, so living in the country is more natural to us than living in London.

I don't really know how other people perceive us; it's fair to say that we have been a great deal better off than most people in the village, but we've always wanted not to make it obvious. In any part of the outer suburban ring of London there is a competitive atmosphere and people live a very expensive life-style; we have always felt that would be inappropriate here, and would make anybody who did it profoundly unpopular. Our desire was to fit in as much as possible. All right, live your own life as you want inside your house, but outside fit in and to make no parade of wealth. We both felt anxious to participate in village events, because they bring you into contact with the other people. There isn't much point living in a village if you don't take part in its activities. Might as well live in the suburbs and go to the theatre every night.

It's perhaps as well that there isn't anyone very dominant

trying to take an important role in the village. With some caution Sylvia and I started the Friends of Swanbrooke Church some years ago, because we were asked to by the church. We tried to tackle it so as not to imply that we were trying to gain any preferment. It's a very sensitive thing, the village social community, and it's terribly easy to make mistakes.

Both of us were brought up in the Church of England and it is part of our lives; instinctively we headed straight for the church, and always took part in all the functions in the village hall. I organised the carol-singing, trying to do it in a way which did not imply that one was setting oneself up as anything, but just doing what came naturally, as a pleasure. I was very struck, out carol-singing one night, when a small child walking past here said, 'Oh I can't knock *there*!' I stood back and looked at the house, and suddenly realised that it's enormous compared with the others. It made me wonder how we are perceived.

Every English village traditionally has a squire. Here the squire was up at Mumford Hall. When we came a real 'squire' lived there, but he was a shy man and didn't come into the village much. He wife was more evident, she went to church, and there was still a feeling that Mumford Hall was the 'big house'.

There is room for a squire-figure, and tragically that has gone. Not because there could never be another after Mr Stockbridge –

a squire doesn't need to *own* the village – but unfortunately (or is it fortunate?) the farms around here have been of a relatively modest size, so the farmers have been solid yeoman farmers, not gentlemen farmers. Mumford Hall was farmed until it was sold up in the late 1970s. It would be nice if there were some more obvious leader in the village, and that used to be the vicar.

I find it difficult to define what we felt was our social position. We always felt strongly that in Swanbrooke Down nobody cared a hoot who you were or what your importance might be in the outside world, and to some extent that is still true. For example, Harry Long is managing director of the biggest wines and spirits company in the *world*! It's a massively important company, sales of thousands of millions of dollars in the US alone, but it is typical that he, in Swanbrooke, is just someone you know; something of a natural leader – it would be surprising if he wasn't – but he keeps a modest profile here.

A new socio-economic group has arrived – and it's younger. It is bedevilled through no fault of its own by the problem we suffer increasingly in England as a whole; rootlessness. If you work for a large company or the Inland Revenue, you get shifted around all the time. It's an estate agent's dream-world in which properties constantly change hands. People aren't long enough in a place to become part of the scene.

This new group aren't just to do with money. In a very crude sense they are 'yuppies'; yet upward mobility is a good thing. Britain has always been a socially mobile country. I've never believed it to be as rigidly class-ridden as people think – nothing like as rigid and class-ridden as the French. It is possible for people to change their situation.

This village seems remarkably free of conflict. Some villages, one is well aware, have cliques; people fall out, and there is a bad atmosphere. A lot of places are hideously divided. Fortunately this village has not been prone to that. We have always tried to avoid doing things which would divide the village. You need to be very sensitive; you don't come into a village like this and campaign vociferously for change! It would be easy to create an uproar in Swanbrooke Down if you came in from a middle-class background, and started saying you wanted street lighting, for example.

Take conservation. One has to be sensitive to the conflict of interest between the farmer running a business and the desires of people like us for a slightly utopian existence. The strongest conservation element usually comes from middle-class people who come into a place and want to advocate that line. I'm not against it, I'm for it, but I think that one has to be very gentle about it. And to remember that things happen slowly in the countryside. There is a time, in these things, and there is a speed at which you can go.

The age structure of the population has changed completely in our time. When we first came there were *some* children, but some years before that the school had, sadly, become – in the eyes of the authorities – non-viable. I guess they were right: there were probably about ten children of school age in Swanbrooke Down at that time. The population was ageing, and younger people hadn't moved here because there wasn't anything for them to do. Now there are forty-four children of school age in Swanbrooke Down, an extraordinarily large number. The tragedy is that there is no school, no focal point. I believe however that the playgroup is an important social factor in Swanbrooke, and a very good thing. To maintain the vitality of this community we need focal points, so that although people may have to get their living elsewhere, they can live in a community when they get back here.

This is threatened by modern mobility. But again, without the motor car, who on earth could live here? Public transport is for all practical purposes non-existent. The motor car has been in a sense the saviour of Swanbrooke Down.

This means that people who live here are mobile and able to go all over the place for their pleasures. However, I would argue that perhaps the greatest threat to community life is the television set rather than the motor car. The TV provides permanent in-house entertainment, so people just stay at home. I doubt whether people travel far in the evening for entertainment. I should think the vast majority are *in* Swanbrooke Down. But when we ran the cheese and wine party, at a price designed not to put people off, it attracted only a tiny minority. It is rather disappointing.

It's pretty widespread; it's not just happening in Swanbrooke Down. All sorts of pressures keep people at home in the evening. Increasing numbers of women go out to work, and don't want to go out again. When there was no entertainment in the house, it was presumably very attractive to go to anything communal. The pub has a limited appeal – some people can't afford to go, or just don't like it. There isn't anything else of a regular nature to go to.

Although we have a place in London I regard this place as home. So do the children. Perhaps we're unusual, in that we have lived here for nearly twenty five years, and our children have never known any other home. They were born here. If we have ever toyed with the idea of moving they have always expressed a strong desire not to move. It's not only Swanbrooke that is attractive – there's more to it than that. Kings Tarrant is remarkably attractive – one of England's very lovely towns. It has changed, of course. When we came here, if you spoke with the sort of voice that I do, and bought something in a shop in Kings Tarrant, they would ask whether you would like them to send the bill. Now you have to present your plastic card and they ring up Access to find out whether you are OK. Which is very sad, but inevitable. We have to accept that it is supposedly progress. The old ironmonger in Kings Tarrant, you could buy any one of about three million items from him. He has long disappeared, sadly. But it's still a very attractive town.

A social factor not to be overlooked is, when you come to a place like this, what stage of life you're at. If you have young children, that makes a massive difference. When we first came I didn't meet many people but Sylvia met lots, because of children – children's parties, going to schools, sharing school runs. That was important in making us feel at home relatively quickly. The children still know quite a lot of people around the place.

I'd never really thought about where one fits into a community. I just feel that we live here, and we try to fit in without consciously trying to do very much. It's nice to know as many people as possible. When you see people in the street it's nice to know who they are.

Len was the most charming man, a perfect gentleman of the old English country school. He was born in the house opposite, and he once said that when he was a boy seventeen people lived in that house: four families. He never seemed to resent the fact that times had changed. I never heard him complaining about changes. Frankly, the people who write articles in the *Sunday Times* about villages seem to believe they were utopia. They lived in miserable poverty, in appalling conditions, and it's quite shocking that as late as the 1960s vast numbers of country people had no running water or proper lavatories in their houses. The last two such cottages here, Sam Gapes's and Arthur Bush's, are on their way out.

During that spring and summer I watched the builders at work. Sam and Arthur lived next door to each other in semi-detached, box-shaped cottages. Simple whitewash, slate roof, one central chimney. One window downstairs at front and back, one up: in Arthur's upstairs window sat three old teddy bears, looking towards the fields. The tiny front gardens were lawn and wildness, and at the back they stretch down to Winter Water. The cottages had no central heating, no inside lavatory, no mod-cons. Yet for all that, cosy, homely. Once Sam and Arthur were buried and Arthur's wife had gone to live with her daughter, they became primitive, dank and cheerless.

The builder, a local man, decided to restore rather than demolish them. As the men worked I could see what a piteous condition these old cottages were in; frankly, they were about to fall down. It was quite surprising to me that two old men, one with his wife, were living in an affluent East Anglian village in those conditions in the 1980s.

Howard Len had a very proper sense of social manners – he always called Miss Braybrooke 'Madam'. We used to hear him when he walked up the garden in the morning; he had a very loud carrying voice. Len knew where he fitted in and he was comfortable there; he lived comfortably in his skin, he was quite relaxed. I don't think he would ever have been a socialist, wanting world revolution. He would have disagreed strongly with any rapid, let alone violent, change. He was traditional, a charming and civilised man.

Waldo the Pole was one of the real old characters. I understood that he was a so-called refugee; or he may have been a prisoner-of-war from the Polish army, and ended up here after the war. Anyway his family were in Poland and he was completely alone. Somehow he landed up here and stayed on as a farm labourer at Mumford Hall. He lived a separate life – he spoke little English. He went down the pub every now and again, and high days and holidays he would get gloriously drunk and would be found lying in a heap by his bicycle on the way up to Mumford Hall. He might get drunk in the pub but he was absolutely sweet – nobody could ever disapprove of Waldo! Everybody felt sorry for a man dragged forcibly from his own country and home and put in a foreign land. It was very sad for him, and thank God it never happened to any of us.

Swanbrooke Down dates back to the first Saxon who lived here with a few pigs, and who scratched around in the woods. Then a few more Saxons came, and it probably didn't change a great deal until the 1920s. For hundreds of years the people in Swanbrooke Down would have worked within walking distance. People still live in Swanbrooke Down and work within travelling distance. If it wasn't for them and their motor cars the place would be full of old people.

The number of people employed in agriculture has fallen much lower in England as a proportion of the population than, for example, in France and Germany. Once you have removed that basis for the village, it will literally crumble and the houses disappear. *Or*, other people will come in, retired people or whatever. There have been many gloomy predictions that villages like Swanbrooke Down will become geriatric homes, but in fact Swanbrooke Down probably now has more schoolchildren than ever in its history. It's got a very young population, it is *not* dominated by the elderly. There are people of all ages, and of all kinds of professional backgrounds. And it has never mattered who you are or what you do.

The Hawthorn Hill divide is very unfortunate; I don't know whether it's social or what. It's been keenly felt in the church where it has always been quite difficult to get much of a relationship going. But it's not as rigid as all that. If you were to wave a wand and scatter those houses around the village it wouldn't make much of a social difference.

A vicar, resident or not, could have a bigger role in Swanbrooke Down. That is not necessarily to criticise the present vicar; he has three parishes over a large area, and he suffers, as do others, from the corporate state syndrome. By which I mean that if you have to go to hospital in Swanbrooke Down, you end up in a town about half-an-hour's journey away. And children must travel several miles to school. Everything is pulling village life apart.

A full-time vicar would have more direct personal contact with people in the village, which might do more than increase church attendance. I think the church will retain a residual role; it's the biggest building, dominating the centre of the village. The churchyard is where people want to be buried even if they don't go to church very often. The embers are alight but they are burning low. Congregations have dropped a lot since we came, but it's still meaningful, and Christmas morning church was well-attended. There's not much anyone can do about a village like this – all that is needed is a small number of energetic people interested in encouraging communal activity, who don't want to live a selfish private existence. The people I resent are those who never have anything to do with anybody else. I say, 'Why on earth have you come to a place like this?' I have the impression there are quite a lot of them. Sylvia tells me I'm wrong, that things like the playgroup, the Mothers' Union, the WI, the village hall committee and *Village News* are active, and involve a lot of people.

The problem is the social one of a highly prosperous country. Britain has probably never been as prosperous in all its history. I come back to the TV set, even without a video-recorder. You can have as much entertainment as you want, without bothering to associate with other people. Small children are a restricting influence – people can't go out in the evening because of baby-sitter problems.

Nevertheless, villages like Swanbrooke Down are still centres of a very agreeable way of life, probably the most balanced and settled there is. No crime could be committed in Swanbrooke Down *by* anybody in Swanbrooke Down. Burglars might come from somewhere else, or some poor wretch in Swanbrooke Down might be engaged in burglary elsewhere. 'Small is beautiful' is as true as it has ever been. It's part of why people want to live here. You can live here alone without feeling frightened, threatened or lonely. You feel this is a safe place, everyone's friendly, and if there is a problem, everybody will help everybody out.

It's an agreeable existence, but it would be wrong to attempt to prevent any change. It's perfectly acceptable that there should be one or two new houses built here every year. I would be totally against thirty or forty houses being built all at once, because then the separateness of Hawthorn Hill would be writ large. You would have a group of people from heaven knows where, people with money, who earned their living somewhere else, coming because the estate agent had offered them a house which seemed all right and they could afford it. They would quite likely come and go quickly and would be very unlikely to put down roots in the village. They would live in their house on the estate, not in the village.

The planning people don't seem to be sensitive to the delicacy of the social fabric, which can take only a certain amount of change. If you tried to double the size of Swanbrooke Down, and took thirty years over it, it wouldn't matter. In some ways it would improve it – maybe a shop would be viable, maybe even a school.

One feature of this village is that people don't talk about houses by their names; they talk about them, as was always the custom, by the name of the people who live in them. Your house is Ros's house. It's *people*. Lagden's, among others, was named after the people who lived there. That's because people actually know each other, even if they may not know the house. Ask Pauline the Post. I bet a letter addressed to Howard Gawthrop, Swanbrooke Down, would reach me. You can't do that in many places. People are still more important here than houses.

Perhaps Swanbrooke Down is special because nobody is trying to be something they aren't. People are just themselves, and nobody's trying to impress. I don't think Swanbrooke Down would be easily impressed anyway! You don't get away with things in a small community.

There are certainly people who move here from the towns, possibly to gratify their image of the rural idyll, and continue to live a town life. But I'm relaxed about it. Not everybody is fortunate enough to have been brought up in the country. It's dreadful to despise people because they aren't the same as you, because they are town-dwellers.

Deep in many English people is this desire for roots in the country. Newspapers constantly bemoan the fact that the British don't have the same urge to get rich as the Germans or whoever. It's because we are a much more balanced people, we sincerely do not want to be rich. Time and time again people make successful careers in industrial companies or in the City, and the first thing they do is buy themselves a place like Mumford Hall and set themselves up as country gentlemen! The place is riddled with them. They really want the English squire's life. They can't *do* it, they didn't inherit it and they weren't brought up with it; but they think they can buy it.

When you look at the development of Swanbrooke Down it would be wrong to ignore Kings Tarrant. You go there on a Saturday morning and see chaps in slightly worse-for-wear corduroys and battered shoes and sweaters with holes in the sleeves wandering about, and you wonder who on earth they are. They are highly successful lawyers, stockbrokers, bankers, chartered accountants, who move on a world stage in their business lives. They are walking round Kings Tarrant feeling slightly the worse for wear because they've just got off the overnight plane from New York, and they are there for the therapy of a balanced existence. I have often said to Sylvia that I could never have done my job for the past twenty-five years without a sane, rooted existence in the English countryside. I could not have combined the job with the frenetic London social whirl. I'd have gone mad. Kings Tarrant is still rather a gentle place; slow and peaceful. People see it as a tremendous antidote to the pressures of business life.

Business in the City has changed out of all recognition in the last twenty-five years, and is enormously more pressing. When I first came here, there was a fastish train to London at eight o'clock and another at twenty past. There may have been earlier trains but goodness knows who took them – I never did; it was quite unnecessary. Now I am told that the 6.30 is very full; the 7.30 is probably the main commuter train, and the eight o'clock is half-empty!

SYLVIA GAWTHROP

Banker's wife

A while after talking to Howard I visited the old forge again. It had been raining all night, so hard that one of the low-lying fields in Poor Street, once a meadow and now under the plough, was flooded. Winter Water was swollen and racing. I picked my way through puddles, shading my eyes against the low April sun. Listless trees dripped. Nobody was about. I was relieved to step inside the Gawthrops' warm house, and accepted a cup of tea gladly.

Sylvia had chosen to talk separately from Howard, feeling that their views might be quite different, and that they should each have the chance to air them uninterrupted. She sat opposite me in a huge armchair; neat greying hair, upright bearing, tall, with blue-grey eyes. Ankles and knees together, hands on her lap, she leaned forward as she talked, poised and elegant.

We were in Howard's study this time, a smallish room lined with bookshelves and every surface cluttered with papers and periodicals. Sylvia started speaking with a characteristic reserve, but soon warmed to her subject. We were joined at one stage by Victoria, her fourteen-year-old daughter, and I could not resist asking her what she thought about village life; evidently I did not catch on her on a good day.

The light faded as we sat there, warmed by lamplight and a gas fire, and the greyness of the day faded into darkness. The trees still dripped as night fell.

A balanced and integrated community

Sylvia I have East Anglian roots. Both my father and my grandfather farmed in Cambridgeshire, so as far as I am concerned it's more attractive here than in the Fens! What matters now is not that I'm in East Anglia, but that this has been *home* for nearly twenty five years, so I have spent longer here than anywhere else. This is where my *own* roots are as opposed to where my childhood was.

I'm not sure that one actually *chose* anywhere in particular – to be quite honest we went where we could afford a house. I'm not sure we consciously said, 'We want to live in a village.' This was the first house we were shown in this area, and for almost the same amount of money it seemed infinitely preferable to a town estate.

Before we even signed a contract – this is a sign of a change of the times – the people selling the house asked us to stay for the weekend. They were having a drinks party, and introduced us to thirty people in Swanbrooke Down before we even signed a contract. They also asked Howard's parents and my parents for Sunday lunch so that they could see the house! They were marvellous.

It was quite a contrast for me, moving from London and leaving my job, but there was no feeling of *not* being welcome. I wasn't aware of any anti-commuter feeling. When we had to leave temporarily after three years, Wilf Middleditch said to me that we were really part of the village. We were absolutely delighted. In those days it usually did take a long time to be accepted.

Both of us have been on various village committees. We got involved in village life before we had children. In very early days there was a Conservative association, and I was on a committee. Duncan Vickery, who was on it as well, said, 'Mark my words, girl, this village will be under concrete in twenty years time!' But that association didn't last long – everybody felt you couldn't go canvassing in a small village; it is too small a community to fuss much about whose politics are what.

Howard was on the parochial church council fairly early on, and I felt, 'I must do something here to justify my existence', so – and it was one of the best things that could have happened to me – I co-ordinated meals-on-wheels for about three years. That was marvellous because it introduced me to a whole lot of people of different ages in the nearby villages. I still see quite a few of them.

The WI were always very keen to get younger members, but by

the time I thought I might join, I had small children, and they met at an impossible time. Later on it was in the evenings, but if your husband goes off at a quarter to eight every morning and you don't see him for twelve hours, in those early days the last thing I wanted to do was to go out when he got home.

I was on the parish council for eight years, and for many of those years it was very pleasant and made me feel part of the village. The first time Howard and I just listened in to a parish council meeting we were extremely impressed by the trouble people took over local issues. Whether a house should be added on to or not, for example. Yet planning issues have been the only thing to divide the village. I think generally speaking Swanbrooke Down is a very happy community; now and again there are eruptions, and people get steamed up about problems which are really not very serious. It's fascinating, looking back on it, that it's all to do with feeling threatened. If people feel threatened they get nervous and over-react. The business of Stansted Airport was a threat; a lot of people fought it, most people in the village were against it. The next time round, they couldn't face the same thing again, and there was a great deal of apathy in the village. Maybe the village was more divided than one knew. Whenever there has been a planning problem, it's just that uncomfortable feeling of not quite knowing where people stand. In the early days people were, generally speaking, all on one side.

One thing amused us when Howard was first on the PCC. He would come home tired from the office, and have to go to a meeting. He'd have spent the day signing cheques for hundreds of thousands of pounds; Grace Braybrooke would get up and say that she'd got 12/2¾d in churchyard funds, what should she do with it? There would be quarter-of-a-hour's discussion about it! It was good for him because it kept things in proportion.

We have been quite involved in village activities. I have a feeling that in the past, people supported anybody who did anything. Nowadays people do things, but with a fair lack of support. The wine and cheese party the other night was very poorly supported. The barn dance at Mumford Hall wasn't well supported either. Yet here you all are living in a village together; surely that, even if nothing else, gives you an interest in common.

For years here it didn't matter what you did for a living; when you got back to Swanbrooke Down you were just Howard or

Sylvia or whoever. For years most people probably didn't have a clue what Howard did, and that we liked. Other City people were going back to Surrey or Sussex, to a weekend life with the sort of people they had spent the week with. All keeping up with the Joneses. When we started off we had very little money, but one has never been aware of any problem on that score. We've always been lucky in having Grace Braybrooke next door to us, who is the most amazing person – one of the greatest 'ladies' I have ever come across – as opposed to Lady this or that. It helps to keep one's feet firmly on the ground.

The greatest change for us personally has been the building of a tall house opposite. We didn't argue that there shouldn't be a house there – there was no reason why not – but there was every reason for leaving the hedgerow in front of it just as it was, and the bridge could have been shared. But the District Council ignored everyone who wrote. We now look straight across a concrete bridge to a new house. Before, we looked over an orchard.

When we first came the people who commuted were rather older than us. There weren't many young people round us. Since then a lot of people have come in, from different strata of society, which is healthy because it represents a real slice of the social life of England. Howard has often said, 'These people never contribute anything,' and he's absolutely wrong. There are people on the village hall committee, the bellringers, the people who run the playgroup – there's a lot going on. In a small community like this it is quite easy to get the newcomers involved, whereas as if you plonk an estate of twenty or thirty houses down you'll be lucky if any of these families involve themselves.

The lack of church life has changed things. Talking to people in the past few months, I have felt that quite a lot of people *would* go to church, given a little encouragement. Some make a great effort to go to church somewhere else! They may end up coming here, which would be nice. A lot of it hangs on not having our own vicar.

The other change is the pub; for all the nuisance of the cars parked out here, I would much rather have a good pub, and put up with parking, than a dead, derelict pub. Derek the publican does things for the village and he's super, so I find it difficult to criticise anything to do with the pub.

The shopping has changed of course. When we first came Arthur Stone's shop was still going. When you went in a clanging bell hung one side of the door would carry on ringing until you put your hand up to stop it! He sold flour and sugar and tea – I remember once casually asking for a pound of sugar and a couple of pounds of jam; such was his kindness that instead of saying, 'Actually sugar is sold in two-pound bags,' he disappeared and came back with a specially weighed-out pound!

I feel that the village WI is dying somewhat, although they still organise the pancake race. That's a nice bit of 'old England', as are the Morris dancers. Bearing in mind that the village only has a church, a pub, a village hall and a PO, I don't think it's too bad, all the activities that go on. Generally speaking people pull their weight. The Friends of Swanbrooke Down Church, although it has only been going three or four years, is very encouraging.

The *Village News* helps keep people informed about what's going on, even if they're not involved. It comes out every two months, with contributions from everybody, so it keeps us up-to-date. It's a shame that now the vicar doesn't write a letter every issue, or at least occasionally. Since he doesn't visit newcomers in the parish it would be one way of making them realise he existed!

There's an awful lot of feeling that 'the village isn't what it used to be'. Well, I suppose some of the old people must have been horrified when we came on the scene – but they accepted us and made the best of it! It's up to us to do the same for newcomers now. Nothing stays the same for long. I feel quite happy about Swanbrooke Down so long as it doesn't suddenly get overtaken by a large development. You can't keep the old folk alive for ever – it won't be the same for us when we haven't got Grace. You're always under some sort of threat – life in this house could be made miserable by having the wrong person next door, or the wrong situation in the property behind us which is about to be sold. But we're very lucky that for twenty-five years we have had a good neighbour, and a lovely garden behind us.

People say Swanbrooke Down isn't a place where old people can live because there isn't proper transport, or the internal structure to cope with old people. But you want a balanced community – old people as well as young – and it would be sad if Swanbrooke Down became a place with no one but middle-aged and young people. It's no worse now for old people than it was all those years ago – it's much better, because they've got warmer homes and young, mobile neighbours. As long as you want a peaceful life I can't see what's wrong with Swanbrooke Down. There are still the delivery services. But I would like to see a couple of old people's bungalows down in the village somewhere.

Len spent hours leaning on his shovel chatting. If we had any blockages in the street or the gutters, Len would sort it out. Now if a branch blows down it just sits there – nobody seems to have the *nous* to do anything about it. He was a marvellous character – you have to be able to hear his voice to appreciate him, but I used to love to hear him talking over the fence to 'Miss Braybrooke' – 'Mr Cakebread' – lovely conversations they had. He told a story about the war when the girls stood at the corner waiting for the chaps to come down from Mumford Hall, how they were no better than they ought to be! He told us about the person who hung himself in the shed up the garden here. He remembered when there was a well out the front and everybody had a legal right to draw water from it. He wouldn't let me tape him – I did ask him. There was nothing malicious, ever, in his talk – just amusing stuff. I can see Bertha to this day sitting by the door. She was much older than he was, and was very much stuck indoors – a typical village lady, too vast and well fed to move. A village lady of some stature. Len went out to get all the gossip for her so she never had to move far!

Old Daniel lived in his caravan by the pond which has since been filled in. That was a real old-fashioned caravan; how he managed with his plumbing I just wouldn't know. He lived in the pub a lot of the time. When he died the only thing was to set light to the caravan. What else could you do? He didn't have any surviving relations.

Waldo the Pole lived in a cottage in the Dip; that area has changed enormously, even forgetting the houses behind. The big house on the corner has completely changed that aspect of the village. Although the cottages were probably slums, it's the difference between an old rural scene, however derelict, and a modern suburban estate.

One of my early memories is of seeing an old man lying on the roadside one Sunday, with his bike up on the bank, and saying, 'How awful! We should go up and help that poor old man!' People joked about it, but I didn't realise that this was quite a regular occurrence after Waldo's visit to the pub. There he stayed, slept it off and went home again.

Of course there have been frictions between families from time to time, but in all these years I would say not many. What actually goes on I don't know, but there haven't been, as far as I am aware, wife-swappings or divorces – very little of that. It's a well-balanced, integrated sort of place. Howard has always felt that because he was away working, he hasn't got the strong feeling I have about the place. That's natural, because I've been here all the time. He possibly attaches more importance to it now, having the flat in London; he realises he wants to go to Swanbrooke Down at weekends. If I suggest a weekend in London, he says 'No: London to me is work.'

Living in the same place all this time has given me stability. I wander around the churchyard sometimes, and feel I know everybody. It's not necessarily Swanbrooke Down that's done it; that's just where I have happened to be. My overall feeling is, yes it's changed, but as long as things remain as they are it's a jolly good place to live, with a happy community. It's by no means ideal; the houses are small, with tiny gardens, and there's no countryside to wander in, no recreation field even. Newcomers tend to be very young, often just married; they have to have two cars, therefore they have to be reasonably well-off. In the past newcomers were frequently older couples.

Over the years, any unease has been due to the threat of planning. Some people have felt threatened by farming practices. That's happening everywhere, but I must say the farmers round here seem to have been ruthless, pulling out hedges and filling in ditches. Only a few miles away it looks quite different. For a long time now people here have felt that you have to be very careful where you walk, or someone will shout at you for putting your foot in the wrong part of the field. And you never forget it. The only time I have ever felt threatened, walking on the land, even just off a footpath, was round Swanbrooke Down. Surrounded by such unwelcoming intensive farming, you are frightened to go anywhere other than a public footpath.

Victoria would hate to move; she thinks of the village street as an extension of the garden. We've got a tiny garden like many in the village. She has spent many happy hours playing in the filthy old stream because that's the only place to play! When her sisters were small Darvel meadow out the back was all grass, and although officially private, nobody seemed to mind and there was a footpath across it. There were lovely old willow trees to climb by the stream, and various walks which weren't too muddy. There was the cricket field to play on, too, and when it snowed they could toboggan on the hill behind the church, and down by the Gap. Swanbrooke Down has less space now for children to let off steam than there is in the middle of London! Where can you fly a kite in Swanbrooke Down? The churchyard is the only place now. Seventy children! It's unbelievable. This must be the overriding change, there being so many children. For the children themselves it must be great fun, in and out of each others' houses. Our children didn't have that. It's an invigorating change – it must surely put new life into a village.

VICTORIA GAWTHROP

Schoolgirl

It's not the most frightfully exciting village

Victoria It's all right living in the village, but there's not many people I know, it's all older people. It's not the most frightfully exciting village. They do make an attempt, like the youth club with its table tennis, and this Saturday night they're having a competition, but I still wouldn't feel very happy if I went along. They have a sort of disco and I don't really want to go to that. It's all right if you're horsey, but I don't want to be like that.

We ought to have a shop. You have to go five miles to Kings Tarrant. The bus service? I wouldn't use it for the life of me. And I'm not going to cycle five miles just to get to Kings Tarrant; I wouldn't be able to get much there anyway.

I can't remember how I felt up to the age of nine. I suppose I used to go out on my bike, and play in the stream and use the village a bit like the garden. Then I probably said I wouldn't want to leave Swanbrooke Down, but now I'd be quite happy to live somewhere else. I wouldn't actually want to live in London, although I know lots of people there, because I can't go and see them even if they live down the road! What I get really annoyed about is that I'm not even allowed to go to the bottom of Kensington High Street on my own – I can only get down the street on my own if I buy orange juice for Daddy's breakfast! I'd like to live where there are lots of people I know, perhaps in a village where we had some land – we haven't got a very big garden to do much in.

Mr Whoever-it-was who offered to give a field to the village if he could build a couple of houses by the church – he said we could have a swimming pool. It would be really nice to have a swimming pool for the children, but it still wouldn't *do* much. You're just extending the village which is a bit stupid, because then there's more people to cope with nothing to do.

It's not what you expect, not having anything to do in the village; it's a non-event. I don't see how people want to live here. When Mum and Dad got married they came here; everyone who gets married comes here, in spite of the fact that there's nothing; no one else comes here, because it's really remote. Then they have children and they move again.

If a child wants to get sweets or something, you have to bike all the way to Haverley, which is ridiculous. Then the parents say, 'It's too far, and someone might pop out of the hedge,' you know? You can't even buy sweets in the post office. I'm not surprised she gave up the shop, it's too much bother. There's no one prepared to come here and set up a shop, because now people are dependent on Kings Tarrant.

The church is – well, Mr Mansfield makes it so boring. I quite like to go to church at school – if I'm in the mood for walking 2½ miles there and back! At least the parson there is much more interesting. I never want to go to church here. Can't be bothered to get up early to listen to a boring sermon that's about nothing. Just lecturing himself.

In the village on the way to Kings Tarrant, there's the station, there's a pub – although we've got a pub here – a little station shop where you can get sweets, and it's so much better. I'd be quite happy to cycle to Kings Tarrant from there because it's only two miles. Whenever I've got the enthusiasm to cycle to Kings Tarrant Mummy's got something else she wants me to do. And when I arranged to meet a friend midway we couldn't because of somebody popping out of the hedge.

We're lacking a dog for a start. I hate just going for a walk in the winter – it's the most awful thing on your own. With a dog it's much more fun.

What I'd really like when I'm older is a moped. I don't want a car. Parents' view is that this is a place where you can come back to, once you're mobile, which is peaceful and relaxing – lots of lovely home cooking! But for me it is so difficult to go and see someone – five miles is so ridiculous. Whenever I want to see someone we're doing something! All my life I've regretted not having a sister or brother nearer my age. I was really insulted when my elder sister said, 'You only know about two people.' I thought, well I haven't had the chance to get to know anyone else. I don't know that many fourteen-years-olds – I went to a party the other night and only two of us were fourteen, the rest were all sixteen.

DEREK LAURENCE

Publican

April gives way to May in a typically unsettled manner: days of cloud, wind and rain interspersed with bright, sunny, cold ones.

One fresh and breezy morning, walking back into the village with my dog, I see Derek's Range Rover returning from his regular morning trip to the Haverley shop. I seize the moment.

The pub stands halfway along the village street, a long, low building of brick and timber, with roof of thatch; it is about three hundred years old and has been an inn throughout its history. Derek keeps it immaculately: patios and pavement swept, sunshades crisp, outdoor seats scrubbed. In summer, hanging baskets and tubs of flowers festoon the courtyard. Twice a year the Dog and Duck is host to a troupe of Morris dancers who dance in the street and refresh themselves at the bar. All through traffic is diverted as the villagers throng to watch this ritual English caper.

The pub's dark oak beams are hung with highly polished horse brasses. The lounge bar has comfortable chairs and low tables, the public bar plain wooden tables and chairs. The end room, once stables, is now a restaurant area.

I called to Derek, who responded with his customary geniality. He is well-built, tanned, with thick grey hair swept back off his brow. He gives the impression of being happy in his work, and is always ready with a helping hand, seeing the role of publican as more than innkeeper, as having perhaps an element of the community caretaker. He has become immensely popular in the village for the active concern he shows to the elderly or infirm – he will light their fires or pop around with a meal on a tray, and check that they are all right if there is a power-cut.

Derek has nonetheless contributed to the advancement of suburbia in Swanbrooke Down. The pub attracts people from miles around with its fish and chip night, its olde Englishe evening, and its Sunday roast. Smart cars are parked all along the street; the smell of chips is inescapable. Groups of well-fed people, stillettoed, lipsticked, tightly-belted, handbagged and hairdoed, potter around the village exclaiming at its rustic charm. The one day when the village is spared this scrutiny is Monday; that is cards night for the locals.

To some extent the Dog and Duck is still a 'local': the public bar, traditionally the sanctuary of darts players and farmworkers, still more or less operates as such although its clientèle is more middle-class; green wellies and Barbours have not infrequently been spotted there. However, a hard core of villagers meet regularly, and much village policy is discussed or even decided there.

Derek led me into the public bar – deserted at ten in the morning. He poured me a ginger ale, and a half-pint of beer for himself, and sat opposite me, waistline nudging over his trouser belt, and told me about life as Swanbrooke Down's publican.

Stories to tell, but not telling them!

Derek The spirit in this village is special. It's a tremendous thing, no two ways about that. Especially if somebody's in difficulties, people rally round. Before I came here I had a restaurant in Epping and lived in a village nearby. There was never anything like this spirit in either place.

Swanbrooke Down didn't find me, I very much found Swanbrooke Down. I had my eye on it for a long time. I wanted to buy the Dog and Duck and live in the village. We looked at some of the houses here; the modern house next door came on the market and I came to see it. I went back home and said to my wife, 'I don't want to buy that house, but I'll buy the pub instead.' Totally jocular. I was looking for a new place to run a business anyway, but this pub had just changed hands, so I'd lost it. I was quite upset, and was negotiating for another place I didn't really want, when I happened to ring the brewery manager. I said, 'Have you got anything coming up?'

He said, 'We've only two on our books at the moment, then nothing for six months.'

I said, 'You haven't anything like the Dog and Duck at Swanbrooke Down, have you?'

'It just happens that's one of them,' he said.

Right', I said, 'let's talk business!'

'It'll cost you a lot of money.'

'I don't mind.'

'It's only got small accommodation.'

'I don't mind!'

So that's how it came about.

The living quarters *are* small. When we bought it there was only one bedroom, and the rest upstairs was a mess. But we spent a lot on it and now there are two bedrooms, a living room, a kitchen, and a decent bathroom. The finest thing is living on the job. In Epping Linda and I saw each other on a Monday. I went to the restaurant at eight in the morning, and got back at three or four the next morning. Linda had her boutique. She was asleep when I woke up and asleep when I went to bed. So I closed on Mondays and she took the day off. For eight or nine years that was how we went on. That's not a good life really, so we said, next time we go into catering we live on the premises. Although she's still got her boutique, she really has become interested in the catering business. So she comes home at night and goes into the restaurant, leaving me behind the bar, which is great. There's one in each place, that's what the customers like.

We haven't got many older folk in the village now, but people do look after them. A number of people take the older folks shopping, for example. We go out to old Mrs Francis in the cold weather, make sure she's got the fire lit, and take a meal round. We used to take a meal to the old lady who lived on her own in the Green Man. That's what you get in a real village as opposed to a town. You *know* everybody, you know their problems, and you try to do something about it. It doesn't stop with us, either, it is a general feeling all round the village; people care about these things.

I don't know why it should be so in Swanbrooke Down particularly. The village is at a slight disadvantage in that the two central points ought to be the pub and the church. Well, we've got the pub, but we really haven't got the church life. And I think it ought to be there. I can only talk from when I was a kid in Scotland. We did all sorts of things in the village. There wasn't a pub, and everything was centred round the church; we went to Sunday school, and to church three times on Sunday. You weren't allowed to ride your bicycle on a Sunday, or to have Sunday newspapers! Perhaps that was going too far, but there are lot of things that can go on in the church.

I think every village community is divided. I'm not sure Swanbrooke Down is divided completely, but there are the pub-goers and the churchgoers, and you don't get a lot of mixing. I would say it's about 80 per cent/20 per cent now. I'm not saying that's a bad thing, because we don't run a bad house here! But I wish it was a little bit the other way round, because that's when the mix is right.

It's obvious that without a resident vicar we lack pastoral care – and there's nobody to fill that role. I certainly don't fill it, to any great extent. Yes, if someone's got a problem, I hope to get to them before they have to come to me! But that's just me being me. I'll make time to do whatever I can do to help, it's as simple as that.

The playgroup draws people together, so that everybody knows what's going on, whereas in some villages they don't. We also have a parish council, and that's got a lot to do with the feeling here. Take the stream-cleaning, which it organises. We're out two or three times a year for the benefit of the village, and that brings people closer. There are obviously some people who don't want to get involved, but most, especially those with children, do want to. I think that's why Swanbrooke Down is special.

Four years ago we had to do special fund-raising nights to keep the playgroup going, there were so few children. Now they've got all the money they can use, so the new blood is probably a good thing. As they grow up – *if* they stay, that's the thing – they in turn will become good villagers.

There are two sad things about Swanbrooke Down. One is that most of the old characters have gone, and the other is that houses are so expensive people move in and out rapidly and we're losing a lot of the friendly atmosphere. There have been difficult times when nobody's known who is really living where, they've turned over so fast. I've only been here seven years and in that time perhaps fifty per cent of the houses have changed hands.

The pub is much more of a local now than it was when I came – especially in this bar. I've got two businesses here, my pub and my catering business, which draws people from miles around. They like Swanbrooke Down and they like what we're doing. We do a cards night on Mondays, fish and chips on Tuesdays, olde Englishe on Wednesdays – that's steak and kidney pudding, or a baron of beef style of meal, then *à la carte* for the rest of the week. A special traditional Sunday lunch, and Italian on Sunday evenings.

This bar brings people in from all the local villages, and I'm very pleased to see them! But the public bar reflects this community life, from your now resident 'squire' up at Mumford Hall, right the way down.

The gentleman who owned the pub before I came, Duffy, had vision, and made the pub what it is now. It was doing very little business when he came. It had been owned for forty years by an

Australian guy who didn't fit in at all. He looked after the public bar but neglected the other side. We've increased the turnover more than tenfold. There's little more we can do with it now, so we've just got to keep that going. We've made some improvements on Duffy's work, like building the patio outside, and the barbecue, so the kids can enjoy it in the summer.

I hadn't run a pub before; I've been in the catering trade for twenty-odd years. I don't think I'd like to be a publican on its own, just as after ten years I got bored with being a restaurateur. But the combination, though a little bit exasperating and tiring, is much better for the brain. You don't get cabbage-like – you've got too much to think about. The easiest part is when you're open! The most difficult part is the organisation, the buying and all the rest of it.

I've a little place in a Dorset village probably a quarter of the size of Swanbrooke Down – no pub, no shop, a couple of farms, a few cottages and a chapel. Absolutely marvellous. Every four months I go down for two weeks and learn to sleep and relax, and then think up ideas for this place! Other people take nights off or days off, but I can't do that. I like to be here the whole time I'm here, then to get *away.* I'm very lucky in having Toby Wagstaff behind the bar; he is a real country character. The stories Toby could tell you about this place . . . far more than I can. He's been around here for about seventeen years. He used to work on the Vickerys' farm. He worked in here part-time until I came, now he's full-time. He's sung in the choir, he's worked on the farm, he knows everybody and everybody has great respect for him. There isn't anything he wouldn't do to help anybody, either. They come from miles around at lunchtime because Toby Wagstaff is there and he's a character.

Arthur and Sam I loved very much indeed – that's why we've got the wooden seat outside; we clubbed together and bought it as a memorial to them. Sam had this old bike, 1934 I think he said it was, and he used to cycle to the pub. One day, about a year before he died, he fell off on his way here, and he said, 'I don't mind falling off on the way *back*, but *not* on the way in!' So he parked his bike and that was it, he walked after that. I bought the bike off him and I cycled up and down for a little while until I got too busy. Now Rex Vickery is keeping it as a sort of Swanbrooke Down museum piece!

Arthur was one of the most amazing people you could ever come across. Until his eyes went, he would do the *Times* and *Telegraph* crosswords in about half an hour! And I'm talking about the age of eighty three – he died when he was eighty four. His eyes went rather bad about eighteen months before he died, and he seemed to lose heart – he couldn't do his crosswords. But his wit was still very sharp.

Sam was different altogether, very deep, very countrified. Lots of stories go around about Sam, which the vicar told at his funeral; true stories, but I won't repeat them because I wasn't here when they happened. What a shame to lose a character like that. But he went *his* way. Arthur's wife is living up in Worcestershire with her daughter, but she's getting very old now. She was the quietest of the lot – a tiny little person, but the guvnor! Very quiet, but what Dorothy said, went!

Being in this job means sitting on fences. I was asked to go on the parish council recently; then this situation came up with the building development behind the church. I thought, well the village is totally divided on this, and much as I want to go on the parish council, it makes life too difficult. I would have liked to put back into the village something of what they give me, which is an awful lot, even if it is only putting up with the cars. But with that situation there was no way; I would have had to show my colours.

Robert Stockbridge gave the village a field behind the post office as a play-area, but omitted to carry through the bequest in his will. That land was, inevitably, built on. Then a meadow behind the church was offered by one of the farmers, and used by the cricket team for a couple of generations. The farmer then fell out with the parish council. The meadow was sold off to the property developer who had bought Mumford Hall. He submitted plans to build a couple of dozen houses on it. Knowing that this would stir local feeling, he pleaded that if he were allowed to build the houses, he would also build an 'outdoor sports complex' and an 'adventure playground'. Even, possibly, a swimming pool . . .

Passions ran high. An open meeting was called at which it was evident that the village was divided. A referendum was decided upon, a secret ballot run by the parish council. The results of this hit the development firmly on the head. (words like 'blackmail' were written on some papers) and the plan was withdrawn.

Derek Situations like that don't often occur, but when they do I have to be fairly reserved. There have been a couple of others, like Stansted Airport, but for those I've taken what I feel to be the right direction. I stopped the hunt meeting here, because I didn't agree with it, and it would appear that most villagers – or at least those I've spoken to – have been delighted. I'm not a yes-man, but I do take other people's thoughts into consideration. I could get myself into very deep water if things become divided. The only issue I am firm on is mains drainage. I will fight for it! I'm fed up with my septic tank and so is nearly everybody else.

I feel rather bitter about this new scheme because when that field came up for auction a few years ago I put in a bid for £23,000, to make it into a cricket field and a kids' playground. That was to be given to the village and the village would give me the money back, interest-free, over a period of time. Mine was the only bid. The farmer who was selling, who was on the parish council, got his solicitor to write and say that the bid wasn't high enough and that was the end of it. The next thing I hear is that the owner of Mumford Hall or his organisation had bought it for £24,000. What really narked me was that I could have gone up to £28,000 if I'd been asked, and we would have had a field for the children.

I don't feel bitterness to anybody personally, but it was handled quite the wrong way. But I've carried on without the people involved, or anybody else, knowing my feelings. It's not skilful, it's just *me* – I have no problem steering that kind of course. There are certain things you don't talk about with people. Anything that upsets them I will either say at the time, and that's it, finished, or I won't say it at all.

So there you are, no amusing stories to tell – if I have I'm not telling them! Toby Wagstaff is the one. I see a lot of the village in here, but I don't see a lot of the village, if you see what I mean. Most of the time I'm here I'm working and when I'm not working I'm in Dorset. They come into my house, but I don't get into theirs. I walk the village with Christmas cards, and that shows me the village in toto, but it's difficult to accept invitations to parties and things like that – I go for about half an hour then leave – they don't want me there as well as in here! I'm everybody's friend and nobody's, although I've got some very staunch friends here. The minute I've got a problem I can count on them. It's probably true that they come into my life more than I enter theirs, but I don't think that matters. As long as we're there one way or the other.

The biggest change in my seven years here has been the demise of the real characters. That is the saddest thing. They were straight out of medieval England. Apart from Rex Vickery, say, who was born here, there are so few who can really talk about the history of the village. I can't – I only know what I've read and picked up. People who come here haven't got much of the country person's viewpoint – that's probably putting it the right way rather than kindly or unkindly. Most are willing to learn, after all they chose to come here.

It'll be a long time before you get a Swanbrooke Down 'character' again. You can almost say Toby's going to be one, and Rex Vickery. There's Mrs Penington – she's a character! Where you go from there I don't know. Jack Jacobs was quite a character. The day his house burned down was quite emotional. Sad it should go in that way. It had to be done, but knocked down, not burned down, there was something shocking about that. All because the new owner was in a hurry to get a new house up. I don't know how it happened. I got a phone call from Haverley, from somebody who saw great palls of smoke. He said, 'There's a great fire down there, go and see what's going on.' So I went rushing down just as the fire engines arrived. A house doesn't just catch fire like that, with a spark – it looked as if petrol had been poured along the floors. It was under control, but it was sad to see an old man's history go up in flames, and all the rubbish cleared.

It's a bit the same with Arthur's and Sam's cottages, although it's being done in a much nicer way. You could see the teddies in the window every time you walked past, and the number of times I've been in that house ... If they wanted a light bulb changed or anything like that, Toby or I would go round. It was so nice in there! And then suddenly it's not there any more. I used to take them meals too. I'd take them to anybody who was ill – it's no problem, just a question of knowing when they want it or when they don't, when you're being a nuisance or when you're a help.

These older people they were so independent – it was quite difficult to say, 'Well hey! what'll you have?'

'Baked beans on toast, something like that.'

'Oh, no you're not. I'm going to bring you a roast.'

'No you mustn't do that!'

'I'm going to anyway. Have your baked beans as well by all means!'

But not too often – that would be an intrusion on their independence.

The pub is the pivot of the village. The pub, not me personally. I don't think I should be, that would be wrong. I happen to be the sort of person who provides a situation for everybody to meet here, yes. I enjoy doing it; but I am not the pivot. A tremendous number of people, especially the parish council, have done fantastic things for the village, far far more than I do – I'm just *here*, and it's as simple as that.

TOBY WAGSTAFF

Bartender

When he told me he had once been a shepherd it came as no surprise. Toby Wagstaff has that timeless quality which invites rustic literary clichés: the twinkling eye, kindliness of manner, genuine humility, jovial friendliness and ruddiness of cheek that feature in fiction because they exist occasionally in reality, and because they evoke the ideal simplicity of country folk at its most appealing. Everyone likes Toby, and indeed everyone would benefit from knowing a Toby. He takes no lasting exception to people, or if he does he doesn't show it. He has had unenviable problems to contend with, but they have left no visible sign of bitterness. Perhaps he just takes life as it comes, perhaps he is truly content with his lot.

Middle-aged, tall, with receding brown hair and a weather-tanned skin, Toby has been serving at the Dog and Duck for twenty years. Along with the half-timbered rooms, the open log fires and the 'olde-worlde' atmosphere, he is one of the main attractions. People come to enjoy his company; always ready for a chat or a joke, or to be a listening ear, Toby is the mainstay of the bar, and a valuable business asset.

It was midday in mid-May: cow-parsley was hand-high along the stream. The grass was lush beneath its tracery, the trees in new leaf. Between the village and Mumford Hall a blue mist lay lightly over fields of yellow-bright rape. The cuckoo's song echoed across the valley. I had woken early and listened to the dawn chorus, a spilling of sound at full throttle as the moon surrendered its silver shadows to the morning. The crisp dawn gave way to an irridescent day; England at its most beautiful.

Derek had given me permission to drag Toby away from his lunchtime duties that Monday, their quiet day. We sat in a corner of the lounge bar sipping soft drinks while he told me about his life and about the characters who had coloured the 'local' over the years. Some of them were leaning up against the bar as we talked, eyeing us quizzically as they downed their pints. Toby spoke – surprisingly – quite nervously, flitting from one subject to another – but then there was so much to tell. How to get it all into the hour? For he had to clear up at closing-time. And how to select? Undoubtedly the tape-recorder was inhibiting – without it I might have unleashed a torrent of unprintable memoirs.

A shepherd's tale

Toby I started farming in 1943, and was a herdsman for about twenty-five years, working with pedigree Jerseys. I come from a broken family; I left home and went my way, into farming. When I got married, I thought, 'I've got to specialise', so I went into Jerseys. All farming during the war was mixed farming, a little bit of everything. So I got to know what it was all about – I even thatched a stack once! And I've built two or three haystacks. I'm pleased to say that I have, now that these things are non-existent.

When I packed up dairying I came to work for Rex Vickery. Dairying was getting a bit precarious, which it is again now. I left it in the nick of time. There is a vast difference between dairying and arable farming – the difference between working with something alive and something not alive. It was interesting and I thoroughly enjoyed myself, ploughing and all that, but it's not the same. When I left arable farming in 1977 I was glad to get out of that too. Dangerous business, once the big machines came in. There was a case in the thirties in Swanbrooke Down when a farm labourer accidentally stepped into a threshing drum and was torn to pieces. His widow, who was left with two children, was compensated with between five and six hundred pounds.

I used to live in one of Rex Vickery's farmworkers' cottages in Elmshaw Lane, which were built in the 1940s. I got the sack from him while I was living there. That was rather disagreeable, but I'm not bothered now. All the water's under the bridge, and we're still good friends. I don't bear anybody any malice. I was told, at the end of a working day, that I could either finish the job, or pack up and go. Well, after five o'clock my time's my own, even though I was living in a tied house. I said to him, I'm not going to have a row with you, you do what you do, so he did. I happened to belong to the Farmworker's Union, fortunately; we went to court for unfair dismissal, and I won. Yet Rex Vickery gave me a reference in court that would have got me a job anywhere! We had to go up to London to the court, and the presiding judge said he didn't know why the case had been brought, he'd given me such a character reference! It was a silly thing, really, but it meant that I was evicted, and that's why I'm living at Elmshaw.

So I was quite glad to leave farming – especially the dairying. There used to be about six working in the cowshed, and gradually the numbers went down until it was just me plus somebody else – if they could get them. Once keeping Jersey herds became less economic – and for some of the gentry it was just a hobby for the lady – they phased them out. You either went into it in a big way, or you got out of it.

I've seen the countryside go from small fields to prairies. As the machines got bigger they knocked the hedges down. Now they're beginning to regret it, especially up in Norfolk and the Fens. It seemed a good idea at the time, but it was short-term policy. Nature has a way of hitting back. Everything's there for a purpose; I worked with one old boy who said, 'Even if it makes you swear at it, it's there for a purpose!'

Old Daniel Nottage was a steam-engine driver. He had been in the First World War, and also, I believe, he had been jilted. He never got himself attached again and he lived a lonely life. Alone, not lonely. Before he moved into his caravan, he lived in this old shepherd's hut, one with two doors, front and back, and he had everything in there, a burner, the old black range, and a place to keep his food. He was black as the ace of spades. He was a strange old boy, he would come down to the pub, and always leave his stick outside. He and Sam Gapes, so they tell me, used always to stand up for a lady customer. Always smoked a clay pipe, did Daniel Nottage. When Mr Duff was landlord here he would see that he had a clay pipe for his birthday, plus two ounces of Condor. Daniel was never known to say thank you – you knew he appreciated it, but he'd never really thank you. He was a man of few words unless you were on a subject like draining the fields – he knew every drain round here. He'd hear somebody talking and say, 'Nah! I know where that bloody drain comes down' – and he'd name the bush where it came down! If you don't take their knowledge from these old boys, it's gone – and those things are useful to know, like where the drains were when the fields were small.

You could set your watch by him – if he didn't come down for his drink there was something wrong. Nobody minded the caravan there and nobody took much notice of him. He came out with some really droll old sayings; the one everybody remembers was when somebody was talking about washing. He mumbled into his beer, 'Oi washes my feet once a month whether they needs it or not!' We've often laughed at that.

If he didn't turn up for a couple of days there was definitely something wrong, and somebody would go up to see him – myself sometimes. People gave him things like soup. If he was ill we'd get him any bits and pieces he wanted. We had the village shop then so he did his own shopping mostly, but people would get things for him. One day I took him to a once-a-year do of old engines and machinery. People were a bit reluctant to take him places because he was so dirty-looking. But he enjoyed himself. After all, one day who knows, there but for the grace of God go I. You don't know, do you, in this day and age.

He had a ginger cat that was like a dog. It sat at that door and if you went towards it it swore at you. I went up one day to give him some lunch and the old cat jumped out at me; it fell on some barbed wire and we didn't see it for a day or so. Then Daniel says to me, 'Like to sweep my chimney for me?' So I said, 'All right, have you got a brush?' And he says, 'No but I've got a stick with all bits and pieces on it, and there's a ladder round there.' So I went up the ladder and his chimney was one of those like a drain-pipe, with only a tiny hole which was thick with soot, and he said, 'If you push that down, it's only bunged at the top.' I said, 'You've got the fire alight!' and he said, 'That don't bloody matter.' He was just standing there and there was soot going on to the lighted fire! He was just lighting his pipe, never coughed or anything – smoke coming out both doors!

The vicar used to set him on doing bits and pieces – most of the vicars did – working on the churchyard. Then when he was taken ill, Duffy made arrangements for him to go into hospital, and the funny thing was that when people went to see him they had to look round the ward twice to find him, because he'd been cleaned up. He never did come out again – he went into a home and stayed there until he died about three years later. He was quite an old man – eighty something; after all he'd been in the First World War.

I used to work part-time here. I came in 1968 when Duffy took over, and he was here fourteen years. I had never done anything like this before. I came before he started the restaurant; where the restaurant is now was the stables – we've still got the stable separ-ations. The loft was a hayloft – there is still a flap to put hay into it. You can see the fastenings for the doors where they used to stick the hay through for the horses. The pub had a brick floor then, and there were spitoons dotted around because the men chewed tobacco. Sam Gapes used to talk about the fair which was held next door before the new house was built. That must have been in the early 1900s I suppose.

Although the fair no longer comes to the Dog and Duck, Morris dancers still dance there every summer, and always on the first Saturday in June. The senior Morris men, tall and fine in their white costumes, with bells tied to their leggings, lead a ritual baton-dance, leaping, turning, skipping in formation. A fiddler accompanies them, a blue-jeaned teenager who inherited the job from his father who inherited the job from his father ... The strains of the fiddle are curiously insistent, wistful, haunting. The men dance straight-backed, their steps measured.

An ancient member of the group emerges, in a long black shirt, carrying a black umbrella. He looks about a hundred years old. Next to him, in a jester's red-and-white chequered shirt, is half-man, half-horse. The youngest, a village idiot by the look of him, holds a triangle that rings its thin music in time to the fiddler. The village gathers around to watch, fascinated, entertained, blocking the traffic in the street. It is a busy day behind the bar.

Toby I used to come down on a Friday night. There was just one bar then, and they did some food. We had a hatch between the kitchen and the bar, and we did three joints, plus sandwiches. When the restaurant got going in about 1970 that arrangement was bashed on the head.

Our fish and chips night started oddly. Duffy said that on Mondays, Tuesdays and Wednesdays the pub was ghostly. So Tuesday was made fish and chip night. We started cooking them at the bottom of the stairs – it must have looked very odd! In the end they couldn't stand the smell upstairs, so the cooking got banished to the back. Then we did *à la carte* Fridays and Saturdays, and everything in between. I've got a feeling Duffy started the olde Englishe night as well.

This is only hearsay, from talking to the old boys, but this used to be one of the best 'weekend pubs', in conjunction with the Green Man. When the one shut they went to the other! Ever since the Dog and Duck has done food it's drawn people from Kings Tarrant and beyond. You used to be able to count the local people who patronised it on your hand. But you see different changes in a pub, inasmuch as the young people grow up. When I started, a group of young men would come here, courting, on Friday nights. Now young farmers come in, and you see a repetition – a little bit different, but basically the same. As they get married off another set takes over.

It's actually a cycle, isn't it. A couple of blokes here were talking about children, saying that today it's a replica of our grandmothers' day, except you're doing things in the modern idiom. You tell your children they must not do things; when you were a child you were told exactly the same, but you did them. Nothing really changes, yet everything does because you're in a modern idiom. Today they don't take so much notice of their parents, but when they get to a certain age, past adolescence, they go back to what their parents said.

Times change in other ways, though. Take crime; in the sixteenth century there were three cases tried of horse-thieves in the village. They were all executed for stealing a horse! The penalty for stealing anything worth more than a shilling was death, hence the saying, 'you might as well be hung for a sheep as a lamb'. There's a piece in the archives about 'sturdy beggars' being 'whipped and branded'; you don't see beggars here any more, that's for sure.

There have been one or two other cases of 'misdemeanours' in Swanbrooke Down, mostly poaching. Once, right at the end of the last century, the policeman stopped two men he suspected of coming off somebody else's land. They kicked him all over his arms and legs, and left him unconscious. He was in a serious condition for a time.

Robert Stockbridge built the policeman's cottage in 1913, to house an officer of the law to protect him personally from 'Kaiser Bill'. Police Cottage, next door to Holly Cottage, was timber-framed and faced with bricks hand-made at Mumford Hall. A series of policemen lived there over the next fourteen years, keeping a sharp eye on opening and closing hours at the three pubs. They had a busy time with poachers, too; when chickens went missing they would snoop around the local bonfires to see if they could smell feathers burning. The odd dispute between neighbours, occasionally violent, was sorted out by the village bobby, but after 1928 his job was deemed unnecessary, and the police headquarters moved to Haverley.

Toby We call our old people the Committee – they call that the Committee room! There's five of them, Mr Colbrooke and his friends, and they have a daily chat in there. We have a joke; 'What's on the agenda today? Have we anything to put in the minutes?' It's good fun. But you see, this again is how it changes. It used to be Sam, Horace, Muriel's father, and Arthur around that middle table, Friday nights – spade-nap night. The young people have taken over the middle table now. The old people have been replaced. They're all different, yet it's the same. It's nice that it carries on, because there was a time when there was just Sam and Arthur. But since Derek's been here that bar has really picked up.

Sam and Arthur were very different. Arthur was very intelligent – he could do the *Times* crossword. He had many a heated argument with Clarice Penington's husband and his BBC friends!

Arthur and Sam got on very well almost all the time, but they had their arguments! It was great. We used to get a lady from Mouse Hill, she was a character too – she really hit the bottle! We had a tremendous flood one night, when the water came right up to the pub. She came down Mouse Hill, got through the first ford, then got stuck in the next one. She was shouting and the water was going right through her car. 'I'm bloody well wet up to my knickers!'

There was a Lagden up on Mouse Hill, known as a 'higgler'. Now the only way I can work out what a 'higgler' was, is that he was a 'haggler'. He went wheeling and dealing around with his horse and cart, went to market and haggled, selling bits and pieces: some say it applies to people selling eggs: a 'heggler'.

Arthur was very droll. He came out with some witty sayings. He used to help down here, bottling up and lighting the fires. Duffy gave him little jobs and he loved it. When he'd finished he'd sit down and light his pipe and talk to Duffy's dogs – they knew somehow when he'd finished, and they'd come downstairs. He'd give them a biscuit, much against the owner's wishes!

Sam had his own sort of humour: I was often amazed at Sam. He had worked on farms, and you'd have thought he'd have an axe to grind. I know politics are taboo in pubs, but the others would be arguing and old Sam would be rolling his fag and he'd say, 'Well we're a bloody sight better off now than what we used to be, whatever you say!' He wouldn't look at anybody, he'd be rolling his fag and he'd say, 'I'm a damn sight better off, we all are if you stop to think about it.' It used to stop the argument! A wise old fellow, I suppose. There were tales about him not being a worker, but that used to be the thing – people were called bone idle for no reason. Just because they weren't seen to be doing anything didn't mean they didn't. But he was well thought of in the village – he did some gardening for the old people, pottering about.

I suppose there is a new group of young, 'upwardly mobile' people who are making money. If you care to bunch people together and label them. I've noticed that in this pub it doesn't matter what social standing anyone is, nobody sits here without somebody speaking to them sometime. They do get on well, whichever side they come in to, because they are not distinctly 'public bar' and 'snug'. But there is that group I suppose, who are semi-business, the upper-class business if you like, as opposed to the farmworker type that used to be here.

One village superstition has been disproved recently, about Darvel meadow. They said that if that was ever all one crop, somebody at the big house would die; and it was true in the past. Well, the farmer from Haverley who bought the land has it all under one crop, and I never heard of anybody dying. We all say we're not superstitious, but we are! I am on two things: if somebody gives me a knife, or gloves, I'll take a coin and pay for them, because things have happened with me. I'm not going to say it *is* because of that, but the two things tied in. I come from a broken home, and the people I came to live with treated me like their own. The year before I got married I had some gloves posted to me, and within a short time I had to leave my new home. I stayed as long as I could, but I was in rented rooms and couldn't afford the rent, so I had to leave. All within twelve months. Also, a knife cuts friendship. Thirteen doesn't worry me – I live in number 13. Friday 13th comes more often than any other date in the calendar! That is from the *Mathematical Gazette* – when people say 'prove it' I've got the page to show them.

Len came down the pub very seldom – he wasn't a drinking man. I think I've only seen him in here probably three times. Len had a wealth of knowledge of the village – he used to be roadman, and everything was done right. We all take the mickey out of council workers, and probably Len was as bad as the rest, but he was *village*, and he did look after those verges. People used to say, 'Ooh, he's a crafty old devil!' He was sure to be nearby Mumford Hall, the Cooks' farm, and the big house on the hill by Long Lane where rich people lived round about Christmas time, making sure the roads were clean and tidy. He did very well for himself; but he knew where the money was coming from, it was just one of his characteristics. We've all done things which could be called crafty, even if you didn't think they were yourself.

Women come into pubs much more now. When I was courting the women used to come in but every one sat down at a table – they didn't come up to the bar. You can still pick those out today. The ones who come up to the bar were brought up later, in the sixties. Also the drinks have changed; all the ladies had a gin and orange, or brown and mild. Now they're drinking all sorts. Dry martini and lemonade is probably the most popular, and a lot of ladies drink wine. Wine has come in because of overseas holidays. The men still drink their bitter. I don't think they've changed a lot; probably not so many drink shandy.

I have to be very diplomatic. I've never yet regretted saying something. I've often wanted to say something, and stopped just in time! If someone has a bit of sadness or something that you don't know about and you say something wrong, you feel mighty small. You've got to be diplomatic. I'll give you an instance from the days when the gentlemen came up to the bar. A regular customer – we'll call him Jo – came in. Duffy was cook then, and he used to have his Guinness at the bar before closing time. In came Jo with a woman – not his wife – and he said to Duffy, 'Could you do two meals?'

'You'll have to be quick,' he says, 'because I'm just about to shut up shop.'

So Jo ordered his meal and sat down. After a while, Duffy said, 'It's ready.' Jo got to the top of the step and froze:

'Bloody hell,' he said, 'my missus is down there.'

So we thought, Oh dear! – and of course Duffy always called them when the meal was actually on the table! Well, we've got two horse-dividers in the restaurant, and one made a single box – we called it our 'confessional'.

So Duffy said, 'We'll get you down there if you still want to come down.'

The food was on the table and Jo didn't want to pay for it and not eat it! So Duffy got a newspaper and said, 'When I go to the table, nip into this confessional,' and he made a kind of walking screen with this newspaper. Now this chap was a great talker and had a very loud voice. I should think that was the most awful meal he ever had. I should have loved to have been a fly on the wall. That was one of the funniest things that has happened here – but I had to be diplomatic and not mention names. Lots of customers knew these things went on, but you have to shut your eyes. It could be quite innocent, nine times out of ten it is, perhaps it's a secretary or assistant and there's nothing in it. But one mustn't ever see these things.

You try to avoid talking about things which divide the village. Planning issues seem to be the only thing that really do. I try not to get in those arguments. Fortunately when you're behind the bar you haven't time to talk a lot, so you can't participate. The biggest thing was Stansted Airport. I was for it, I've always said that Stansted was put on us many years back, just after the war; the airport authority bought all the farms round about it. One super little woman, a great organiser, raised lots of money for the protest. I once said to her, 'I wonder where all that money's gone? What on earth have the solicitors done with it?' I'd still like to know.

We had a big meeting in the village hall, and of all of us who worked on the farms, the Vickerys and me were the only ones for the airport. But it didn't deter people from coming to the pub. There was just a bit of hassle for a while between those against it and us who were all for it. I'm absolutely certain it was already sealed and signed. I say, it doesn't matter what you do, all this money is going to be wasted. And I'm certain it was. A lot of solicitors got rich out of it, unfortunately. People are so gullible. You can be anti, but it's no good, you've already lost. It's no good taking sides. Yet we can still voice our opinions, it's still a democracy. That was the only big situation I could have got into trouble with. It's often been talked about in an amiable way, but no heated discussions.

Waldo the Pole was as strong as an ox, and a great worker. He used to work at the Vickerys' farm, but when I came here he was up at Mumford Hall. The owner looked after him, always made sure he'd got a job. He was a great one for cutting and laying hedges. You can still see, when they're without leaves, how the wood was laid when it was done properly, before machines. He would work like an ox, sawing up logs. He had a heavy hand though; you really felt it if he patted you on the back!

Waldo would come in the bar, and Horace and Sam would be at the long table there, and Horace would say 'Hold tight! Here comes Waldo!' 'I'll have a whisky,' says Waldo, and pours it into his pint. 'I'll have two more,' he says. And in they'd go. He turns round and says to Horace, 'You'll have a drink?' and Horace would say, 'No no no, I've got one, I'm fine.' He bought them one, but Sam shifted his glass, and of course it went into Waldo's own drink! But next time, he never thought it, Sam did, but in that mirror behind the bar Waldo saw him shifting it, so he says, 'This time you'll have it!' Bonk! In it went! He'd more or less force you to have a drink on him! He was terrible – he'd pour you out a gin and it would be half a tankard! Just neat gin and he'd expect you to drink it!

It's a sad story really. He couldn't go back to his own country. I believe he's got a daughter somewhere in Poland, but I don't know whether she ever came over to see him. I've never known him have anybody really. Waldo used to get really aggressive with this other Pole on the farm – they were different as chalk and cheese – and he really used to upset this other chap.

He often didn't make it back home – he wasn't nice to be around when he got drunk like that. He walked and walked, and went to Kings Tarrant on his bike. He often fell off. He played the fruit machine quite a bit, and won a bit of money; once he bought four bottles to take home, went round the corner and fell off his bike. He never broke a bottle! He cut himself, but not a bottle was broken!

I've only been here since 1968 so I'm a newcomer! But I've never felt like a newcomer here. I've lived in many other places, but in this village people made you welcome, right from the word go. It is partly the trend; it wouldn't have happened in Sam's time because they were all family, and all newcomers were strangers. But with the advent of the motor car, it's a small world. That reminds me; when the restaurant first opened we had a little Australian lady in here who said, 'You won't guess where I got this from – it was in Sidney airport!' It was our brochure. This is to do with Stansted. We get a lot of them in, on Tuesday nights especially – the 'airport night'.

People move so much nowadays – you've got northerners here, and I'm a Kent man myself. People's circumstances depend on their jobs, whether they go north or south; most go south at the moment because of the jobs. Nowhere is out of reach.

PAULINE WALKER

Postmistress

She walks briskly with short, quick steps every morning except Sundays, delivering post to the hundred or so houses in the village. She carries the letters in a wicker basket, and usually wears a dark-coloured tracksuit. Pauline is small, trim from all the walking, and has Welsh blood in her. That is apparent as soon as she speaks. The Celtic strain emerges as you get to know her: decided, forceful. Her strong views on life extend to her opinions about village people; some of them feel it advisable to stay on the right side of her.

There are two places to hear the gossip in Swanbrooke Down: the pub and the post office. Usually it is quite gentle – who is ill, who has just had a baby, what is happening about a new recreation field or who went to the barn dance (and with whom). Pauline absorbs it all and dispenses it judiciously, perfectly aware of her role. It frequently takes a good twenty minutes to buy a couple of stamps; but this is the essence of village life, and Swanbrooke Down can be thankful it has a healthy source to nourish its craving for 'news'. And villagers can always buy stamps elsewhere, anonymously. Some do.

May surrenders to June as we talk in Pauline's neat sitting room at the back of the house behind the post office itself. Its picture-windows look over a semi-wild garden to the ripening corn. There was a feeling of bursting growth; weeds pushed through thick grass under the hawthorn tree, splashed with the first buttercups of summer. Heady-scented may-blossom hung in garlands, creamy-white. Three trees stand in her back hedge: a young oak, ochre-green; a silver-blue birch, and a beech tree through whose silky translucent leaves sunlight filtered on to bluebells. Speedwell and other wild flowers scrambled into the hedge, and through the open window came an inhalation, a freshness and energy that spell high summer in England. June, month of fragrances, lay ahead; roses over the gate, pinks basking in midday sun under the thatch, honeysuckle and night-scented stocks at evening.

Behind the post office counter

Pauline There's lots of communal activity here, but nothing for the teenagers. We were talking about the vicar the other day, saying there ought to be more for young people to do within the church, and more ought to come via the vicar. But I said, 'Actually he's got a very difficult task.' Mick and I organise the table-tennis on a Tuesday, and although the youngsters like table-tennis and darts, we don't get all of them. To me that's quite interesting; if they're not going to come to a fun thing like that, no way is Maurice Mansfield going to get them into church. Perhaps once they've got into the communal spirit of something like table-tennis, the next step might be something communal within the church.

When I came here Canon Williams was vicar; it was his last parish before he retired, and he was very relaxed about it. He was a very nice chap, he would come along at any time and if you were gardening, with the washing on the line, you just pulled your gardening gloves off and sat in the garden with him. With some people you would have felt, 'Oh dear, I did so want to finish the gardening!' You never did with him. He was so interesting, and he had all the time in the world because he didn't have two other parishes. I'm not a churchgoer, but I should think a lot of people like myself used to go to church just to support him! We went to find out what he was like, rather than for what we believed in. And he came to visit us; Maurice doesn't have time. A lot more people went to church then. He *chatted* from the pulpit, he had such a way with him. Even if he had had three parishes he would have had that way with him. Maurice is more of an intellectual than a pastoral man. And Mrs Williams hadn't a family at home so she had more time for the parish.

We have been here fourteen years. We were welcomed with open arms because we had children, and there weren't many in the village then. There was a knock on the door immediately; it was Rex Vickery. 'Can your boys help out? We've got a shoot and we need beaters.' I told the boys what it meant – they were ten and twelve at the time – and that they would be given £1. The pound won and the birds lost. I thought, well, they can suss out for themselves how they feel about shooting. I warned them they might feel a bit sick. Dylan, the eldest, never went again, but Richard did. That was the first call. Then, because papers weren't being delivered in the village, Richard started doing the morning paper round for Mr Colbrooke at Haverley shop. So we settled in pretty quickly.

I wanted to get to know the area before buying a house, so we sold our house in Wiltshire, put the furniture into store, and rented a house in Harlow. We also wanted to see if the children wanted to live in a town. Having lived in Harlow . . . well, there are some things I will do for my children, but I couldn't live in a town again.

We were in Harlow for six months, negotiating for this house. We found it in June, and grass was growing all over what you could see had been a nice garden. I said to the agent, can I go along and cut the grass, otherwise there'll be an awful lot of work when we move in. He said, 'Yes, but be it on your own head; it will be work done for nothing if the contract doesn't go through.' I got to know more people just coming here to cut the grass than I did in the whole six months in Harlow.

I didn't have anything to do there; a gardener went with the rent. So I would drive off in the morning with a flask of coffee, scouting around. I said to Mick, 'Ooh! I've found a house in Swanbrooke Down – an empty, grotty, house,' I said, 'but what you look out on is nice: thatched cottages, pretty. But,' I said, 'it's nineteen miles from Cambridge,' which for Mick was a long way from work. On every house-description we had from the agent was how long it took to get to Liverpool Street. We thought, 'They couldn't possibly be going every day!' We lived three miles from work, or ten miles at the most. Nineteen was stretching it. Anyway, the boys' school wasn't working out, so we started looking at schools rather than houses. We went to Lillingford school, and the headmaster said, 'If you buy a house in the catchment area we shall have to take them, whatever!' So I said, 'I know of a house three miles from here.' Which is how we came. I said to Mick, 'It's easier for you to travel to work than for the boys to travel to school!'

We bought this as a private house. The previous postmaster had a heart attack over the post office counter. His widow ran it with the shop for a while, but never having done the post office side before she found it very difficult. The shop had been started in the early thirties, after Mr Stockbridge died; the reading room was converted into a shop. The agents told her she'd never sell it as a business, she'd do better closing the shop and selling it with an extra sitting room.

The counter and everything was still in the shop, so we stuck our excess furniture in there, and thought about it. Mick's father was ill, so there was much tripping back and forth to London. After he died, we decided to open it up as a grocer's.

The first day, looking back, how sparse the shelves were! We didn't buy much in; we decided to wait until people told us what they would want. If we had baked beans and they wanted kidney beans, it would be hopeless.

Our shop ran for two or three years before we took over the post office side. That came in unhappy circumstances, when Toby Wagstaff was evicted. His wife had taken over the post office in the interim, but they had to move away. We ran it with the grocery shop, which was financially viable because people were supportive, and glad of it, having not had a shop for a while. The people that could bought everything here, yet there were some you never saw at all, who had got into the habit of going to the supermarket.

The idea was to run a family concern. In the evenings one child would count the shop till, another the post office till. My daughter would top up the crisps and lemonade, and Mick would top up the main shelves while I cooked a meal. You can't throw beans on the table every evening! But the family dropped by the wayside after a few years and I was left with it all. I'd be lucky if I saw the ten o'clock news, by the time I'd got a meal, cleared it away, ironed hundreds of shirts – I reckoned twenty-eight a week! I decided there must be more to life than that, so, we closed the shop.

It was sad, because it was a focal point for the village. I felt awful, because of the older ones. People still ask, 'Do you think you will ever open a grocer's shop?', because they want to know if they can retire here. There are so many villages without a shop; that's the way things are going.

Talking to people gave me an inside view of the village. It was quite amusing; people would come in 'just for a bag of sugar'. It was obvious that they didn't want any shopping, they wanted a chat. Or they'd say, 'I feel ever so depressed today so I thought I'd have a chat with you!' For others it was somewhere to ask the way, or to get the things they had forgotten in town; somewhere to get change or cash a cheque, somewhere to call on an afternoon walk, somewhere to send the children to get them out of the kitchen – or just somewhere to discuss what to have for tea.

Len Cakebread often came in and sat down. If I had anything on the stove I'd switch it off. He never moaned, he was always lively and full of stories. He'd go, 'Oh, tired of me gardening for a little while me dear, thought I'd come and see you!' He'd admit to not wanting anything, just coming in for a sit-down. He told me something early on, which I will never forget. 'You do know,' he says, 'that you can do things right in the shop for thirty years, but if you do one thing wrong, that's what people will remember.' He was quite right. You don't get thanks for doing it *right* all the time, you just get told off for the once you get it wrong. You get the odd wrong loaf of bread, and people will not adapt. For weeks they'd get the right loaf, but one week they don't, and I get torn off a strip!

One lady was very rude to me – she didn't live in the village and she isn't in the area any more. I'm afraid I did turn round to her and say, 'Well, I expect it is *my fault!*' She didn't expect that. 'My fault,' I said, 'for putting myself in this vulnerable position behind the counter, and having to take rudeness from people like you!' I didn't care whether she ever came in again – I didn't want her to! 'Perhaps,' I said, 'I shouldn't do this job if I can't take it, and obviously this morning I can't take it.' Mick came home that evening and in his usual way said, 'Had a good day?' and I said, 'No. I've been rude to a customer today. I've lost a very good customer.'

But she came back and was always very nice, and stayed on. We had a repartee after that; we had both put our cards on the table, and it cleared the air.

It worried me that this position was vulnerable, delicate. When people told me things in confidence, I wished they wouldn't in case it leaked out. I wouldn't even tell Mick. He would come back from the pub with a 'Did you know . . .?' and of course I had known for weeks. He'd tell me, then say, 'You knew anyway, didn't you!' He could never understand why I hadn't told him. I said, 'Well, it has leaked out in the pub, and I hope that the person who told me doesn't think it came from me!' It does put you in a spot.

There is only one person I wish wouldn't come in to the post office. I deal with her by acting the post office lady, very efficient, serve her correctly, pass the time of day properly, am professional, and do nothing wrong, because I know she would report me. Which is why I was afraid of her. As she came in there would be a cold feeling down my back. In the end she took her family allowance elsewhere. I was hoping she would, which is awful really. I have got to know her since, elsewhere, and my feelings are gradually changing. But I am still wary. She comes in occasionally, and I feel better towards her now, but I was quite scared of her. She reported me a couple of times to the main post office in Cambridge, about her delivery. Instead of coming to me and discussing it, she went straight to Cambridge. They said, 'You've got a funny person in this village. Don't worry; there's one on every patch!' They would go along with her complaint, and investigate, but they always saw my side of the argument. A lot of people have come across her in the same way. If she is discussed it's always, 'Oh, is she the one who complains?'

There's not a lot of malicious gossip. Some people think the village is a bit cliquey, but I've never found that. Whatever community you are in, you are bound to find people that get on better together than others. I think it's a very good community – if anyone needs help in Swanbrooke Down, someone will give it. Any elderly person will be covered as necessary. Perhaps people up one end of the village have drinks or coffee together more than with people down the other end, but I don't think that's cliquey.

Old Mrs Thake was still alive when we came – she must have been about a hundred when she died! She remembered the days at the beginning of the century when the postman walked from Lillingford, three miles there and three miles back. He would stop at Sparrows Farm to sort the letters. Mr Roberts lived there then, who was the village carrier. He would hire out his donkey cart for half-a-crown a day to go to Kings Tarrant. He borrowed a larger cart from Mumford Hall once a week, to fetch coal from Cambridge, which he sold on to the villagers.

I came on delivering the post purely by chance – an example of this community spirit at work. The postman was a young man who lived with his wife and two tiny children in Elmshaw Lane. After delivering the mail he would hare off on his motorbike to work. That's how he got killed. This was in June, and Dylan had just finished his A levels, so he did the mail all summer because he wasn't off to university until October. The widow, Lucy, was contemplating whether she should do the mail to have an income. Obviously she couldn't do it immediately. In the autumn she still wasn't sure; normally she was very decisive. So I said, 'Don't worry. I'll do it until you decide.' After about a month she decided she wouldn't take it on. I thought, 'It's quite nice being up first thing in the morning, it really gets me going.' So I have done it ever since.

Apart from the getting up, delivering letters can be quite interesting. You have to sort out the intricacies of the letter boxes: the ones that pinch your fingers, the nice old type that flap easily, lovely brass ones, ones so low you have to be a contortionist – and ones that aren't there at all! You soon learn where not to linger in case the dog gets your fingers, and not to vault over the gate tied with rope, or you end up in a flock of geese. There's that look of anticipation on people's faces, wishing I had something nice to deliver instead of a buff-coloured envelope. The round doesn't take long. I go up and down the street first, then up Hawthorn Hill, round by Grimstone Hall to Mouse Hill, back down to Mumford Hall and along to the farm on the Bendysh Road. I get back home as warm as toast and eat a really good breakfast. It's a good way to start the day.

When Lucy was on her own, her feeling about the village was that she had a large family around her. She said it helped her enormously, and I think that's when Swanbrooke Down comes into its own. Lucy was very brave; it would have been easy to have stayed, to have had all this support. But she went to Cambridge because she thought it would be better for the children to grow up where they would have to be more self-sufficient early on, like town children are. She has made a marvellous job of bringing up the children.

I think it has this extended family feeling, this friendliness, because it's a small village. It doesn't happen so much in Haverley. Perhaps Swanbrooke Down is just the right size. The friendliness is not intrusive, it's special. We have people here for bed and breakfast, and sometimes they come back and say, 'Are you coming for a drink in the pub?' They all wish they could afford to buy a house here – they say they have never known anything like the atmosphere.

Yet there are no houses for first-time buyers. Prices have gone right up, so a new social group has moved in. Shall I use the word 'yuppies'? They are upwardly-mobile – no bad thing perhaps – but the sad thing is that they come and go. Not that they are out to make a profit on their homes; they are on an upward trend in their jobs, and promotion will make them move. You've still got a strong nucleus who don't move on, though. One or two who have always been here say, 'All this coming and going is no good for the village; why do they come if they don't want to stay?' But only a few families move on quickly.

I don't know whether everyone would agree that the village accepts you for what you are. The people up Hawthorn Hill feel the social distance. One old chap, an architect, used to come into the shop and say, 'Those houses ought to have been put in individually, among the rest,' which is right. I hear complaints from Hawthorn Hill that they can't mix, but they don't mix much amongst themselves. I used to belong to the WI, and I persuaded one or two from Hawthorn Hill to come with me. There was a girl up there who didn't know anyone, and I had to introduce her to three women who lived virtually next door to her!

If you don't want to mix you needn't. One family makes it known that they don't mix – they are a unit on their own, and that's that. So it's not necessarily a Hawthorn Hill divide, it's perhaps more of a working-class divide. There is certainly a division between public school families and those who go to state schools. I never thought so until I talked to my younger son, years later, about his view of the village after having left it. He would say that there is a difference between the two sets of families, which he noticed as a child, but felt that it just had to be accepted. I didn't notice at the time, but I see it now.

We need a recreation field. There used to be an 'open day', a real fête with donkey rides, with horse-and-cart rides up to Mouse Hill. We have lost a lot, partly because of not having a field. There's not so much being done amongst the villagers these days.

If it wasn't for the village hall committee there wouldn't *be* many activities. There were fewer people this year at the barn dance, and at the cheese and wine party. It is very disheartening. I suppose people have other things to do; perhaps they don't feel well enough integrated into the community to attend these things.

It's beneath some people – they are quite scornful – to go to a Hallowe'en party dressed up is not their scene. I love the Hallowe'en evening, because it's so unsophisticated. It is – 'Shall we have a game?' – 'Oh yes, what game?' I am always made to sit under a blanket and people have to guess who I am. You wouldn't get anything simple like that in a town.

I'm not sure I've ever heard farming discussed in Swanbrooke Down. There's a farming report in the village magazine, and if anything happens to the hedges, that's quickly brought up. I do remember once when Lucy's little boy was going out to the garden to get an apple from their tree, Lucy said 'Aren't you worried about the spraying in the field at the back?' It had never occurred to me to be careful so close to home! She was worried about the type of farming going on.

I expect Rex Vickery talks about farming in the pub. He is very good to the village; he's the one out there cutting the edges along the stream, collecting the rubbish when we've all cut it, or anything that needs doing. He's got the equipment and he does it. I think he does a lot without people knowing. For years he's had one of the men cut the green, and the edges of the stream along by Clarice's cottage. He used to cut around the graveyard as well, but I think they've got a rota for that now. I don't think anyone knows that he organises it.

Derek does a lot, and contributes a lot financially through fund-raising in the pub. If there's a patch of bad weather or a power-cut he'll check with Mrs Francis that she's got a hot meal. Margery Colthorpe is very good in her official capacity of looking after the over-sixties; you can always call on her to help. She came here after a very busy life, and continues to do things. She could never completely retire.

Vickery Senior did an awful lot for the village – on his seventieth birthday he had a party in his garden. He is very generous. In their younger days, whoever came into the village was there for supper, quite soon, with another couple, and it would roll on from there. Quite the squire, he was, although I don't think he put himself in that bracket. He just liked to make people feel at home.

Eight or nine years ago there were seven consecutive big fires in the Vickery's barns. The fire-raisers set a fire somewhere else to distract attention, and lit big ones here. They never did find out who it was, but they think it was someone who *had* lived in Swanbrooke Down, and had moved away. Somebody who had a grudge against the Vickerys. It was awful, because nobody thought it could happen to them at any time. Once the thatches start going up, its round the village. The first one was the old barn, which was enormous. The fire brigade was at the church green spraying the thatches there, even though the barn was right the other side of the farmyard. It happened over three or four months, and police lay in wait for weeks, waiting for the next fire, to catch the fire-raiser.

Recently there's been nothing like that, and one can't imagine it. There are burglaries now and then but that's definitely somebody out of the village.

Waldo the Pole was a sad character. He never learned English, so he led a lonely life. If you persevered, and listened hard, you could understand him; he'd talk about the war and how he came to leave Poland. He was taken prisoner by the Russians while serving in the Polish army. Then he became a prisoner of war in this country. They were based in Lillingford, in Nissen huts. Waldo never forgot. His gravestone is inscribed, 'A Veteran of Monte Cassino'. He was a wonderful hedger, a fantastic worker, as strong as an ox. He couldn't have been all that short of money, but it was inbred in him to live as he had in Poland, on very little. When he moved to the tied cottage at Mumford Hall, he had lots of offers of help but he carried everything across himself. He even moved the path! He had a little path of bricks and slates, and he picked it all up and moved it. He had *wood* to last him for years. He spent his life cutting this wood – he had to be warm! He had quite a spartan way of life, and it was definitely a house with just a man living in it! We all remember him as a jolly, red-faced man on a wobbly bike.

He grew all his vegetables, he was a wonderful gardener, and a bed of dahlias. He kept me in vegetables – he was very kind to me. He never came for his pension without something in his hand during the gardening season. I felt awful, as if he felt he *had* to bring something for his pension – but it wasn't that at all. He'd say, 'Perhaps you could stop up mine in the morning,' and it was because he had half a hundredweight of potatoes! I would say, 'Right Waldo, why don't I take them to the market for you?' because he always had too many things ready at the same time. 'Or Haverley shop, and I'll sell it for you.' 'Oh I don't want money! I do it because I like to!' You couldn't go away without him giving you something – even if it was a thick head . . .

He had a harmonica, which he played in the pub. In latter years he was banned from the pub because he drank much too much. It was the best thing that could have happened to him, because he was living on his pension and couldn't afford that much whisky.

He had very high blood pressure, and one morning, just before he died, he came into the shop looking completely drunk. His cap was skew-whiff, his pullover wasn't on properly, and his coat was funny. Effie Lagden was in, and we looked at one another and I went round the counter, but there was no smell of drink on him. I said, 'Sit down, sit down,' but he could hardly talk. Then Wilf Middleditch came in and drove him home. I rang the doctor, and the ambulance came. Waldo would insist on walking round his house to check things over; I wanted him to sit down, because I was afraid he was going to have another stroke. But you couldn't get him to sit down. The last thing he did was to get a can of beer each for the ambulance man. Even they couldn't go out without something in their hands! Then he saw me, and had to go back again. He couldn't find a beer so he gave me a can of stout, which I've still got. I've never opened it.

The only thing I found sad in Waldo was that he always hoped to win either on the bingo or the football pools – the big money. Which suggested to me that he wasn't that contented with life.

Whereas Len Cakebread, he reckoned he'd got everything. 'I've got *everything*,' he said, and I said, 'How do you mean, Len?' He hadn't a phone, or a car, he couldn't get out much; but he was quite contented. 'I can have *any* food I want!' Which was his thing – I mean he was *huge*! He'd cook beautiful meals for himself, on a Raeburn. It was always warm in there. I called every morning to warm my toes. If the post was early, I would go, 'Ooh, I can't go out now, it's too early for Len!' He did a coupon every week, just for the fun of it, because everybody else went there to do their coupons, so it meant company. The door was always on the latch; You just knocked and went in. He watched sport on the television, he loved that.

He got on well with Miss Braybrooke; if they were in the garden he spoke very loudly. I would say, 'For God's sake, Len, I am *not* hard of hearing! And does the whole village want to hear you, at this time in the morning?' Although he and Miss Braybrooke are a completely different kettle of fish, they looked after one another. If she wanted to talk to him he was always there in the garden. But if he wanted to chat to her, and she wasn't in a receptive mood, she would pretend not to hear and go in again! That was her way of coping with Len, obviously! But they got on very well. She worried about him, and he was concerned about her. They were good to one another.

The morning he died I went along as usual and the curtain was still drawn, so I thought, 'I'll call on my way back, obviously he's up late this morning.' I called on my way back and by that time Sid Pilgrim had called. Fortunately it was he who found him behind the door. Even Sid couldn't move him on his own so he got the chap from across the road. He'd been on the floor all night, and he was still alive, vaguely aware of what was going on. It was a great loss to us all when he died.

Arthur and Sam were characters too, but they didn't keep open house the way Len did. He loved people, and in the summertime he was out leaning on the fence waiting for people – if no one was going to come in he would go out to them. He and Mrs Thake had long chats over the gate. Arthur and Sam were more for the pub. Len never went, he wasn't a drinker. It was quite a thing for him to bring out the sherry; high days and holidays only. He would have the same bottle for years! The pub was Sam's lifeline – he was no cook, and the goodness in the beer kept him going.

Arthur played the piano. He played in concert halls in his early days, and he had been quite a social man. He was clever, with a wonderful vocabulary, and a great memory for jokes as well as other things. They miss him in the pub. His wife Dorothy used to be in the catering trade, so she made him wonderful meals. She used to buy up the shop – you'd think there was a family of six in there!

Sam was keen on the horses, quite a gambler. He came with us to Newmarket and I would watch him rather than the tic-tac men to see who to put my money on. Not a flicker. He would never give you a tip in case he was wrong! He bought a car once with his winnings.

I don't know who you would call characters today. Millie Lagden left last Tuesday, the last of her generation to be born and bred here. Mr Colbrooke, he's up the pub every lunchtime. But there's nobody to replace Len or Arthur; you could sit and let them talk and reminisce for hours.

At one time there were three very old men in the village, who were the best of friends. Fred Rush was one; his wife use to turn him out of his house for a smoke. Even when she was well into her eighties she caught the Thursday bus into Kings Tarrant to do her shopping, and you'd see her carrying it all back. Arthur Bush often had Fred over for a cup of tea so that he could have a cigarette; and old Mr Thake. They'd all three get together and drink tea. I'll always remember one day watching them walking slowly up Hawthorn Hill, each leaning on a stick and with the other hand folded behind their backs. It is a picture I shall remember.

REX VICKERY

Farmer

The sound of lawnmowers heralded the weekend; sweetness of new-mown grass hung in the air as I walked towards Rex Vickery's farm on a sunny June Saturday. Behind the street blue-green wheatfields, elbow-high, undulated to the horizon. A lark hovered over her nest, singing her heart out. Beyond the church, beanfields in blossom gave out their heady fragrance, and a mackerel sky stretched over the sundrenched valley.

I walked over church green, up towards Pebblegate Farm, a solid Victorian mansion built on the site of one of Swanbrooke Down's Domesday manor houses. The village school, now demolished, used to stand in their front garden, which indicates both the impressive scale of the lawn and the diminutive size of the school. Crunching up the gravel drive, I found Rex waiting – possibly apprehensively – in the hall. With little preamble he sat me by a wide sash window overlooking the side garden and what had been the farmyard; the Dip.

Rex is florid, in his late forties, tallish and balding. Small greyish eyes, sharp; he is a shrewd man. Charming, too, when he wants to be. Not a man to be tampered with, possibly; a member of the parish council and a successful businessman. He is married to a Frenchwoman, and they have a son who works on the farm, and a daughter still at school.

Rex's father moved to the village from the Scottish borders in 1936. Now an old man, turning deaf and often unwell, he says it took him five years to be accepted; but the war years brought everybody together and since then Duncan Vickery has been a central figure in the village. I had met him in the street the previous week, and he told me with vehemence that Swanbrooke Down was nothing like it used to be. The rot had started during the war, he said, when the townies bought their rustic nooks, and sat in the pub while he and his mates were out home-guarding. 'I could have killed them,' he muttered in his thick Scots brogue, prodding his walking-stick hard into the road. 'They were so artificial; arriving here and pretending to know everything about the countryside, broadcasting and writing articles and what-not. They pretended to speak like country people –

that really got up my nose; they hardly knew a horse from a donkey. They treated us like yokels and peasants. But they were the peasants and *we* were the aristocracy.'

Now, in what was his farmyard, stand three executive-style residences, double-garaged and mod-conned. The Vickerys have chosen to attract to the village the urbanites they despise. Rex has inherited his father's forcefulness and shares to some extent his views on the invasion of 'townies', with their ideas on conservation and their media-fed theories of farming practice.

A movement afoot for change

Rex I was born here, in the sitting room, during the war. My father came from Cumberland; he farmed there until 1936, when he moved to Swanbrooke Down. I became a partner with my father after a while, and my son is a partner now. The business is a family partnership. It may seem quiet, but agriculture is still quite a force, though it might seem to be a dying trade at the moment! Ten people in Swanbrooke Down used to live off this farm. I was the biggest employer in the village, on the quiet. People don't realise that. Also I'm responsible for old Granny Spooner who lives in a subsidised cottage. When her husband retired, then died, I said to her, 'That's yours for life.' They gave us thirty years' service, so you can't do any other.

My first memories of the farm are of riding on the cart when it was going to get mangolds for the cows. I remember when we had two horses here, and a cart, although we got a couple of tractors in the war. We still had a horse until about 1950, when it died. It was a mixed farm then – we had a lot of cattle, milking cows and beef; the milk was phased out in the sixties, then we kept pigs and beef cattle; we phased them out as the prices dropped.

When Rex's father moved to the farm it was, as were so many all over the country, in a bad state of husbandry. The Depression had left its mark, and at least one-third of its acreage had not been cultivated for years. Some fields were covered in brambles, blackthorn and rubbish, and the place was running with rabbits.

On the outbreak of war the demand for food increased, so the countryside began to be cleaned up. By 1943 Pebblegate

Farm was producing wheat, barley and potato crops; and mangolds, kale and hay for the cattle. Wheat made 65/3d a quarter, barley 110/-. Wages were £2.12/6 per week. All over England the last of the great cart horses were put into retirement as tractors took control.

By 1948 eight men were working on the farm, on a weekly wage of £4.5/2d. There were forty milking cows, heifers and calves. In 1949 the first combine-harvester was bought for the farm; out went the reaper-binders, cornstacks and threshing tackle. Slowly, the need for hand-labour declined, and the 'old-timers' were replaced by bigger and faster machines. In the fifties and sixties, fields became larger, hedgerows were bulldozed, grassland was put to the plough and the farmyard emptied of its dairy cattle. Today all the animals have gone, and the workforce is down to two full-timers.

Rex There were five farmers in Swanbrooke Down and every farm had cattle. You didn't put all your eggs in one basket; you had a little bit of corn, a little bit of arable, and a field under lay, and you had a bit of kale and a few cows and a pig or two. I'm the only family farmer left here.

The fifties were the best farming days – things really took off after the war. It was difficult to get men in the war; we had just one stockman, and the farmer; only the old or middle-aged were allowed to stay. In '48 Father started employing more people – it went from four men to seven or eight. Prices went up, wheat went from 60 shillings a quarter to £5 or £6 in one year.

We had 30-40 acres of grassland for the cattle out of about 240 acres. We grew everything that went with cattle – mangolds and kale and sugar beet. That took up about another 20 or 30 acres. Nowadays it's just wheat and barley everywhere. We do grow potatoes and beans – we're one of the few who do. Most of our neighbours just grow rape or wheat. I grow barley, wheat, beans and potatoes and other root crops. We have 300 acres now – we bought some and sold a bit along the way, where it suited us.

I went to Swanbrooke Down school for one term, in 1948. It was very good fun – best school I ever went to! I could sit there and watch my mother working in the garden! But it was a nice school – village schools are really good. It's such a shame they went, but there just weren't the children. It got down to half a classroom. So I went to boarding school, only nine miles away, and I did enjoy myself. I had a great bunch of friends there; I couldn't get that in Swanbrooke Down. There were only half-a-dozen children in the village, latterly. Now it's gone back to where it was before.

They were quite good teachers – they were very strict, and the discipline was good. It was a church school, at the end of our lawn there, on a tiny piece of land, a horse meadow, with two ponds on it. We used to get the old maypole out on the green and dance round that; learned to swim on the green, we did.

The vicar was a force to be reckoned with, up until the war. After that they declined, until we get to what we have today. I'm not saying anything against our vicar but it's nothing compared to what it was. The vicar ruled the village; he walked up and down and if there was any kid doing wrong, he'd administer punishment. He was called to the school if there were misdemeanours by little boys, and he doled out the punishments. He was involved with all the families. It was far better for the vicar to take a brat who had done something horrible by the ear and go straight over to his mum and dad and have it out with them as well. There was no more mucking around. The boy never did it again. He probably remembered that all his life and didn't become a little criminal! I'm a believer in that; I think we're missing it.

Essentially we don't have a vicar here any more. The village needs a vicar doing his social work. This one told me when he came, 'If you don't come to church regularly I don't come to visit.' I say he's got it wrong; if I don't come to church he should come to find out why I don't. 'That's not my way,' he said.

I'm a believer in the church; I go now and again. I wouldn't like to see it done away with. But I think we've got to have a more powerful vicar. I wouldn't call myself a particularly religious man, but I'm not an atheist. You can be a Christian without going to church at all. I believe in the values and the laws of the church. If everybody led their lives according to the laws of the church the world would be a better place. We need a vicar to administer those laws.

When there was evensong in the old days, there'd be three dozen people in church and a couple of dozen at the chapel. Half the village was represented one way or another. Now there's more people in chapel than in the church – and that's only a handful.

When I left school I came on to the farm straight away. To start with I got up about half-past-five to do the stock with Walter Spooner, who was stockman. We had a lot of cattle to feed and clean out and milk, and then general farm work in the daytime. It was all hand-work of course. We still used a baler when I was young, to make a bit of thatching straw. That was one way of storing corn, in sheaves and stacks rather than piled in a building. We had a threshing drum, too.

We still had a horse and cart, although we had tractors for ploughing and heavy work. We hoed by hand to clean the beet and potatoes and kale, because we didn't use sprays. The sugar beet was lifted by machine and left lying loose, and we chopped the tops off with a beet-knife. Then you put them in piles, came along with a trailer and chucked them in. Work! We worked Saturday mornings, so it was a five and a half-day week. It must have been a nine-hour day. Farm labourers got about £2.1/6 a week, stockmen about £3. I often wonder what would have happened if the Farmworkers' Union had had a leader like Arthur Scargill thirty years ago! It was hard work; when the corn was threshed it was put into sacks, the wheat into 18-stone, and barley in 16-stone sacks, and they were all lifted and carried about.

You're not allowed to lift anything over fifty kilos now! If women are lifting potatoes they've got to be half-hundredweight bags – fair enough. But there's a lot more people ill and off work with bad backs today. They don't do any lifting! I can remember the old boy Daniel Nottage at the threshing machine, lifting sacks onto his back, walking across the yard to stack them in the shed. They all worked until they were sixty-five, some of them until they were seventy. Then they lived for another five or ten years perhaps, and looked after people's gardens. They were fit! People are very weak now; the machines do all the work. And I don't just mean physically weak – I mean weak in that they don't want to do the work. They'd rather sit and drive a tractor than hump things around. My men are loath to and I can't blame them – they couldn't do it anyway.

Mechanisation has been important for us, because after the war we had all this intensive hand-labour. The machines were invented because people were leaving agriculture rapidly. The young men were leaving in droves to the towns. You can see it in the wages book; suddenly they all drifted away. We used to have to advertise for workers, and they were coming from Norfolk. Nobody round here would work on the farm, so they were coming from the real agricultural areas. This area was beginning to feel an influence from London, and the youngsters could see there was a better life than working on the farm. No future in it, and the wages weren't good. Now you've got one man running 500 or 1000 acres. He's got the equipment in the barn; great big tackle.

A friend in the tractor business was telling me that the day of the big machines is on the decline. The figures for last year have gone right down, because of the finances of agriculture for a start; the money isn't there to buy the machinery. Plus farmers realise that you can't keep growing wheat on great tracts of land because it's not financially viable. So he's selling smaller tractors now, and that'll help the environment – smaller fields will be viable again.

Farmers have realised that their shooting isn't so good as it was, and they are putting tree-cover back. People who shoot are great conservationists, whether you believe in blood sports or not. There's a terrific movement afoot now in the agricultural world for change. Alternatives are coming up – we grow more beans, for example, rather than wheat, and we're trying to grow more potatoes except they won't let us! We're always looking for something different. I don't grow intervention corn for the EEC, I send all my stuff to the open market – milling wheat and malting barley. We keep off the intervention because the terms aren't all that good. You don't get paid for 130 days after you've sold your corn; you've been growing it for a year, you sell in October, and you've to wait two months after the harvest – it's not on. The cash flow doesn't flow! I get paid within 28 days on the open market.

They're talking of cereal quotas but I don't think they'll bring them in yet; the wheat tonnage has gone right down in the stores, and I don't think it's going to be a very good harvest this year either, with all this wet. That might not be a bad thing, to get rid of the surplus.

There's no doubt that cereal farmers are going to have to cut their cloth – quite a few have gone to the wall already, and one or two of my friends are not all that well off, where they've two or three brothers on 200 or 300 acres. Their living standards are going to have to come right down. They've had it good for a long while.

Rex was touching on what was, that summer, a lively public debate about farming surpluses. Farmers had produced so much food during the seventies and eighties that there was a 'milk lake' and a 'cereal mountain'. All over arable England silos were stored high with unusable grain. Milk quotas had already been introduced, and there was talk of cereal quotas. The government were looking at the possibility of putting arable land to alternative uses so that the farmers did not suffer too drastically financially.

Public feeling was running high. Intensive farming had produced an anomalous situation in which farmers were subsidised by the taxpayer to produce food that nobody could eat; it was not even good for export. Moreover, intensive methods had radically changed the face of the countryside, in East Anglia in particular. Conservation was a hot issue just before the 'greening' dawn broke. Like many farmers, Rex was sensitive on the subject.

Rex As far as intensive farming goes, and the question of the environment, it always did have a chance. Let me give you an example. Everybody was against Stansted Airport, only because they don't want the noise. But the convenience is tremendous; everybody uses it. There's a lot of hypocrisy. Then pylons were put up, and they are unsightly. If the farmers had said, 'No, put them under the road like in the towns', we wouldn't have these horrible poles everywhere. Nobody objected because they thought it would benefit them. Then the M11 came along, nobody objected to that, but it's the biggest eyesore out as far as I am concerned. I don't want it, it's no good to me. For every mile, twenty or thirty acres of land gone. And the noise! That's done more damage than any farmer around Swanbrooke Down.

In this area I don't think the countryside will get spoilt any more. It'll get better. There's more trees around now than when I was young, apart from the elms lost through Dutch elm disease. When my father came some fields were just blackthorn and brambles. Because of the Depression they couldn't afford to keep the fields under cultivation. The prices for corn weren't there, and the ground was a rubbish heap, full of wire and tins and rabbits. You couldn't put stock on it. One-third of this farm wasn't kept well.

Children in that era were poor and didn't know where the next meal was coming from. Yet it must have been great fun to play in a village like this, with all the open space and scrubby land. They think, 'I remember when the hedges were up over the road.' But that was only because the farmers couldn't afford to keep them tidy. If you look back, not very far back, to any time when agriculture was on a high, hedges would be well kept, laid and trimmed. I suppose we've lost quite a lot of hedges; some people pull out quite big old hedges – I know one or two farmers who have, even parish-boundary hedges. That is a pity, because often they're old woodland edge. But up here they were enclosure hedges mostly, not that old – just hawthorn, a straight line with a ditch, and not particularly pretty. I like to see a few curves in them.

It's true that there's nowhere for children to scamper, now, in the countryside, which is sad. The meadows have gone. A recreation ground for Swanbrooke Down wants looking into. We played football on the field along Elmshaw Lane, and cricket up at Darvel meadow. We spent a lot of time in Splash Wood, but we never saw the secret passage! There's nothing like that left.

I blame that on domineering people who say, 'We want this, and this is our right.' As soon as people say that, forget it! I've never turned anybody off my farm because they don't really do damage, unless it's a couple of weeks before harvest and they're thrashing about in the corn – they're liable to knock a few ears off. I'm all for people being in the countryside as long as it's not abused. But people will abuse it. One or two put your back up, and you say, 'I'm not interested' to the rest. Mainly people with dogs; they chase the pheasants and kill the chickens. But you see a lot of people walking about and I let them get on with it.

People have their rights, yes, but there was a period when the footpaths weren't used and that's why they've got into a bit of a state. When I was younger the farm workers used them for what they were designed for, getting from A to B. One went over the hill to the farmyard here, and a couple of hands at Grimstone Hall Farm walked it every day there and back. Sometimes they'd come back at dinner time, too. But when those people got cars the use of footpaths declined rapidly; nobody walked on them for years. Now it's come full circle and people want to walk them again, which is fair enough. They are rights of way.

I think most farmers are approachable, but they resent people going behind their backs. I resent it when people come into the village and try to dominate over an issue like footpaths, without talking to me first.

The change in Swanbrooke Down, from agricultural village to commuter village, is good in some ways because life is more interesting. When I was a little lad I could call in on every house. The old girls leant over their gates on a summer's evening and said, 'Come and have a biscuit, boy!', or 'I'll give you a sweet.' One old boy made mead and he'd give me a sip! But when it came to cricket, there were only three of us. We'd just sit on the bridge and wait for a car. We played hopscotch and things like that. You never got disturbed, because there weren't any cars.

I suppose it seemed idyllic to townspeople, but it got boring to me as I grew up. We had a few commuters of course so I was brought up with them as well. Then as more and more people came in we got to know them, and went to more parties, and got friendly with these people. It's been a slow mix, really; because it was gradual I didn't really notice it. The only thing you notice is that there's not the old Swanbrooke Down families any more – the Cakebreads, the Gapeses and the Thakes.

The thing I don't like is those people who move off after only four or five years – even though I like some of the people who have done it. I don't think it helps the community. Since last June thirty people have left Swanbrooke Down. Their jobs move them, obviously, and I think the price of houses has made them think, 'Well, if I move now to Peterborough I can buy a house at half the price and have £50,000 in the bank.' In the meantime they've built a house in their garden, or put a massive flat-roof extension on their thatched cottage. There's only about four untouched, and that's something I get cross about. We're a conservation area, with listed buildings, and you're not allowed to build outside the village boundary, yet anyone can build a house in their garden, any extension, with full planning permission. The doctor has doubled the size of his cottage; that, to me, is not on. There's no point in having a preservation order on that house if he can do that. We've got a conservation order so that people can see what it's been like for five hundred years.

I don't think there will be development in the village, just because of Stansted; Swanbrooke Down has a sort of aura about it, and a cottage here costs more than in the next-door village, or Cambridgeshire, and people know there will always be opposition to building. Most people would like to leave the village roughly as it is. I don't think you'll get any big extension of the village. I wouldn't want them to put five hundred houses on the edge of the village to service Stansted; even though it would be on my land. This part of the country is really pretty – I love it. It has character, and it's irresponsible to muck about with it.

I think they should put a few houses in each village where appropriate, rather than build a new town or huge estates. Wherever you put all new houses together it doesn't work. You get more crime, you get more traffic in one concentration, they have to build better roads to service that area, more electricity, more everything, and it's suburbia. A few more houses in each village will increase the traffic a little, obviously, but you wouldn't have to increase the services.

There's definitely not so much community spirit as there used to be. It's a funny term, 'community spirit'. The Best-kept Village competition always gives us nine out of ten for community spirit, but how a couple of blokes measure community spirit I don't know! A handful of people do a lot for Swanbrooke Down, always the same ones – about two per cent of the village. You say there's a lot of community spirit? I wouldn't. It's friendly, yes, but that's not the same thing. The reciprocation between families is quite good – no massive arguments. But when I was younger it was all voluntary to do things. We cut the churchyard once a year with scythes and hooks; it took us two nights, and half the men in the village would turn out. That was one big event us children looked forward to; the men brought a crate of beer and we were allowed a sip. If you called for that now I doubt if more than six would turn out. We had fêtes, and a maypole on the green. The vicar had lovely rose gardens and we had a fête on the lawn every year. On Coronation day the whole village joined in for a party – there were committees and subcommittees all to make it a great day. Now you'd only get the old stalwarts turn up.

The worst thing they did was to build the council houses up the hill. The people up there feel it's a big divide – they all lived in the village at one time. I've known them all since I was so high, so I know how they feel. It was a bright idea, to build this Utopia after the war, everybody to have a decent house. But not up there. Now half of the folk are retired, and they have to walk down here even to get a postage stamp. The houses should have been built along the valley, or integrated in the village.

I don't think there are any other social divisions. At parties around the village you meet people from up the hill, and somebody from down the road; most people do muck in.

When there were older people here, not so many children, people moved in expecting to find paradise. The first thing one of them did, when he moved in next to the post office, was to complain to Pauline about the shop bell ringing! Lots of people complained about little things – they'd found their Utopia and nothing was to disturb it. So there'd be complaints about the tractors going down the village, 'What is all this noise at seven in the morning?' And we'd say, 'Oh, who are you?' and they'd say, 'We've just moved in. I can't put up with these tractors in the morning. I've come here to retire.' You'd get the odd person move in near the pub complaining about people hooting when they left at half-past ten at night. If you don't want that you don't go and live near a pub, do you!

For Father and me the end of the agricultural village came one time when we were carting muck. When we had cattle we would cart it out of the yards at the end of the week, and take it to the muck heap down at the chalk pit to spread on the fields. One day a big lump fell off the trailer right outside one of the cottages. The lady who lived there promptly got on the phone. 'This heap of muck is disgusting, I'm going to ring the health authorities.' And I said,

'All right, we'll come and pick it up!' I mean, to make a fuss about that . . . By the time we got there, everybody had rushed out with wheelbarrows and it was all over everybody's roses! Father said to me then, 'I dunno,' he said, 'I reckon that's the end of Swanbrooke Down as an agricultural village.'

That's country life isn't it – OK it's not very hygienic. Quite a few people who have come here from Harlow for example, or suburban Hertfordshire, have admitted to me that it's not really what they had expected. A lot find it *too* quiet. I know two families who moved away because the wife found it too quiet.

We had an idea who set fire to the barns. A chap who was living in one of our cottages was a bit funny in the head, had trouble with his wife, and they reckon he had a lot of psychological problems. Three fires exactly on the full moon – people say it can make you a bit lunatic! Then two or three more after that. Then people got nasty phone calls, and somebody tried to set fire to the house next door, burnt the back door in. So it wasn't just us. The trouble is farmers are so vulnerable, with all the straw. Only needs one match. We'd had fire-raisers before. One lad used to play truant from school and we kept getting fires between Swanbrooke Down and Kings Tarrant. In the end they caught him, but he set fire to quite a few things. So difficult to catch these people.

A chap who lived over the green, bit lightfingered he was, pinched the odd chicken. One night it was snowing and apparently he walked down here, took a chicken, walked back, and these people found in the morning that a chicken had gone. The local copper followed the footprints right back to this bloke's door, and he still denied it! He got fined five shillings in the magistrate's court.

The ghost of Mrs Gardiner-Clarke is supposed to walk around the rose-walk at Mumford Hall, but I've never seen her. Sam Gapes reckoned he saw her once, but I think he'd been on the mead. He was walking down Blind Man's walk, and suddenly his dog stopped in its tracks with all its hair standing on end, and refused to go any further. There's supposed to be a ghost in the doctor's cottage, but we don't mention that because his wife gets a bit upset. One woman got the vicar in to exorcise her house. I've never seen a ghost myself. My mother claims to have seen one, in Scotland, but I've never had any psychic feelings, although I know one or two who have. I do like to read about ghosts. It can't be all trickery, I'm convinced of that.

The pub's better than it used to be – it was very quiet in my younger days. Friday was the only night worth going, because it was club night. We paid a few shillings, and they played darts and dominoes and whist. You'd go down with ten shillings and have a game; two or three halves of light ale and a packet of cigarettes and you still came back with one and ninepence! But were they the good old days? Not really, I don't think, you just *think* they were.

We had to work much harder, and we didn't have the comforts we have now. We didn't have central heating, but we weren't worried; you get used to that at boarding school! On a frosty night the dormitory windows were always open, and we would hang a towel in front of the window and pick it up by the bottom in the morning and it was stiff! People were tougher. Now somebody sneezes in the pub and the whole village gets it. Somebody's always got a cold or a cough. I don't remember people having colds like that when I was young – maybe I've forgotten, but I can't remember ever having a cold.

I should think it was quite interesting living in a place like Swanbrooke Down at the turn of the century. It would have been a different life from what I can remember, and pretty hard. The old boys told me that sometimes when there wasn't work they got sent home. The cottages leaked, the plaster fell off the walls. But Mr Stockbridge wasn't a bad lord of the manor; he built houses, pulled old places down, he developed Swanbrooke Down quite a bit. His buildings weren't that brilliant, but they weren't too bad either.

MATTHEW AND EILEEN CHALLIS

Architect and wife

Walking along the Little Bendysh road on a bright blue day in June, I passed half-a-dozen cottage gardens on my way to see the Challises: flower borders tumbling with the first peonies; lupins and foxgloves scattered amongst dense herbaceous plants. Baskets under the eaves cascaded trailing geraniums, scarlet and pink, against a mist of blue lobelia and white alyssum. The fragrance of roses hung on the air. In the quiet of mid-morning the only sound was of bees buzzing in sage and thyme. Grasses rippled in the shade of elder trees; clusters of muscatel-scented elderflowers hung like lace.

We sat around the Challises' dining table which commands a view of cornfields across to Keeper's Wood. An ancient apple tree, the full glory of its blossom just fading, drifted petals across this blue-green vista. A wheelbarrow stood underneath it, full of freshly-pulled weeds, and the hedge behind was almost obscured by cow-parsley. Dark purple irises lined the driveway which climbs steeply to their front door, for the Challises' house is built into the slope of the valley.

Matthew is an architect, a tall, slim, bespectacled man in his early sixties, with a distinguished head of grey hair. His gentleness of manner and breadth of vision are immediately appealing, his intensity and enthusiasm for his subject infectious. Over the years he has become involved in the conservation movement. His views, softly expressed, came over with profound intelligence and passionate concern about the balance of rural communities, indeed their very survival.

Eileen spoke first, pouring coffee and tempting us with delicious home-made biscuits. She is very much a home-person, and likes to design her life quietly around her family. Her dog Cinnamon is her constant companion. The Challises have two daughters, now in their thirties, who both have jobs connected with conservation and the environment. The large garden in which they grew up is a semi-wild paradise designed as a haven for native species. To walk their 'green lane' in high summer is pure delight.

A planner's dream

Eileen We've been here for ten years. We were looking for a house for five years before that, because where we were living was becoming too suburban. We wanted land, to make a little nature reserve, and it took five years to find what we wanted. The builder of these houses showed us round the area. We came along the Haverley road and stopped at the top of the hill. He said, 'I'm going to put two houses on that piece of land.' Matthew and I looked at one another and said, 'We'll have one of them.' We didn't know anything about the house, or the village. The builder was going to start straight away, but there was a lot of trouble about the houses in the village, and it took him a year longer than he expected. He got planning permission eventually, after an appeal, and we sold our house near Brentwood, where we had lived for twenty years.
Matthew I was working in London, and we thought I should be near the train-line. This was a rural area, and we were living in what was becoming suburbs – it was attracting yuppies.
Eileen I liked the idea of a village. If I had known how easy it is to live and bring up children in a village I would have moved here much earlier. We had been drawn to Brentwood because of its good schools, but both children have said, 'Gosh, I wish you'd moved to Swanbrooke Down earlier.' I felt we should live where the children could walk to school – I didn't like the idea of bussing, but it's obviously quite easy. There are good schools in the district and I could have done it. If I had my life over again I'd bring my children up in a village like this, because I like the mix

of population. I wouldn't want to live in a little terrace house in a mining village, because that is not a mixed community. Nor do I like the conformity of 'good houses' and 'good people' in pearls and twin-sets that you find in 'nicer' areas of towns. I like a mixed population.

Matthew In a suburban area you tend to get a lot of people about the same age who move house quite rapidly. Although this village is changing, in Brentwood they moved every two or three years, so you never got a feeling of community. The town itself had quite a good social life, but in the outlying areas you didn't belong to any place – it was just a suburb. So one of our expectations was that this would be a community to which we could belong.

Eileen We did join in very much; we came with that intention. We went to church, we went to the local history society, which met in people's houses, and that was *very* nice. I tried the WI, but I'm not WI material. We got involved, and we enjoyed it. But after some years the population started to change. People left, and the generation coming in was younger. Whereas when we first came, life seemed to be run from the church, I would say now it's run from the pub. I've nothing against pubby people, but we are not pubby people! We tend to keep ourselves to ourselves. But the age of the population has changed too.

Matthew When we first came the typical village people seemed to be older residents who had an interest in and affection for the countryside and were in close touch with it. There was Miss Dalliday, a great botanist, who looked after two nature reserves. There was Miss Braybrooke who was very keen on birds, and there was Percy and Lilian Drayton. Len Cakebread was here. We felt the place had its roots in the countryside, had values which were not suburban, not totally to do with money. Today there are a lot more young people. I've nothing against young people – it's just that the ambiance seems to have gone. The church was very much the social focus. The week had a different pattern; Sunday was going to church, picking up people on the way and chatting, walking back and meeting like-minded people in the street. It gave an ordered pattern to a Sunday after a week in the City. That doesn't happen now.

Eileen Maurice Mansfield came just after we arrived, and he is very high church. He thought Swanbrooke Down was going to be very high church and it isn't. The vicars before him had been high church, but they fitted in with the village. Maurice wasn't really prepared to. He's more or less written Swanbrooke Down off. I used to belong to the PCC and you could tell that he was getting fed up with this village. He just does his duty and then goes.

Matthew I think he found Swanbrooke Down difficult. He came from a London parish where he did social welfare work with the unemployed and youth clubs, and he was terribly busy. He found it difficult to adjust. Thursday used to be his day for visiting in the village, but he doesn't do that now. The crunch came when this parish was rolled into one living of three villages.

Eileen It's hard for a vicar to see the needs in a village like Swanbrooke Down. It's hard to do good works, especially if you don't live here. People's problems may not be that obvious on the surface, so you've really got to get to know them. You don't do that over a cup of tea every six months.

Matthew It's difficult, because the village is too small to have its own vicar.

Eileen The visiting he *did* was to people who went to church. I thought he should be visiting the people who *didn't* go, so we didn't have a very good relationship! I like him as a man, but I'm disappointed in him as a vicar. I would love a vicar like the one in the village where my daughter lives; he's on a voluntary fire service so whenever the hooter goes he has to leave whatever he is doing, get on his bike and go along to the fire! He cycles through the village waving hello to everyone!

Matthew We once had a series of meetings with people who were interested in talking about the place of the church in their lives, and in the village, and what they thought of things like faith. Maurice came along to most of them, and the idea was that instead of just having the church as the centre of social life and religious faith, we should meet in people's houses. That was the same as saying that the church doesn't just mean the building, it means the community. We had some very interesting talks. Maurice was very good – he's quite an intellectual, and was quite prepared to discuss and argue about these things. But he just isn't an outgoing, warm person, not the pastoral type, which is a pity. We used to talk about what beauty meant to us, and love, and faith. It was fascinating. To start with everybody just sat there, because it was embarrassing to talk about things you felt deeply about, but after a while it really took off.

Our first serious problem was that the village strongly objected to development on this site. We felt rather concerned about it, so we kept a very low profile, not wanting to upset people. The site was covered in brambles and blackthorn, and the village people remembered it as a place to play. They gathered blackberries here. Even after the house had been built we found Jack Jacobs in the garden picking blackberries! They had all come here, and we felt it was very important to try to preserve it. In any case, we didn't want to tear up the trees and shrubs, and we told the builders not to take anything down at the back, we kept it all wild. We also thought it would be nice to allow people who had lost their country walks, because of the intensive farming, to walk up there. So I wrote a letter to the *Village News* about keeping the garden as it was, really to give people the feeling that we weren't going to be vandals, but were going to leave it, and maintain the wildlife. The letter had a very good reception.

At the end of our interview Matthew looked out a copy of the letter.

> 'Wild garden' is, I know, a contradiction – wild means a state of nature; a garden is a cultivated place. Yet wild garden expresses well what we had in mind. We have no assurance that this image will be realised but hope to follow where experience will lead and create a garden by selective adaptation of the existing landscape.
>
> Blackthorn and bramble have re-erupted . . . round the old apple and pear trees behind Sparrows Farm cottage, and outlining a series of grassy spaces descending the hill from the hedge at the top. Butterflies and moths were plentiful and have yet to be studied. One clump of soapwort (*Saponaria officinalis*) was in bloom near the house.
>
> A rich and varied landscape then, except where the excavated chalk and clay had been spread over the original sward in front of the house and where naked clay faces, crumbling in the frost, stand exposed at the back revealing flints and one George III silver bank token of 1812.
>
> We feel duty-bound to preserve this rich inheritance and will attempt to manage it as a natural landscape and shelter but to reinforce and enrich it with additional trees and plants which

can survive and intermingle. These will be chosen, particularly, to provide nest sites and food for birds and insects, and to perpetuate endangered wild flowers and plants.

We are aware, too, that the plot extends into arable land to the east and provides the first cover in that direction for a great distance. It is a refuge and we hope to keep it as such, although we foresee possible conflict with the interests of the farmer and the gardeners who may consider the rabbits, bullfinches and sparrows to be pests.

Two or three ponds are necessary and the roof drainage has been piped to serve one of these at the front of the house. Nest boxes for bluetits, owls and spotted flycatchers are to be considered and bird tables and bird baths are in hand.

The artificial knoll at the top of the site is to be left with its circlet of blackthorn and planted this winter with a group of hornbeams to be seen from the Haverley road.

A group of hawthorns are to be planted lower down to break the arbitrary line of the new fence, together with two or three crab-apples for the birds. Perhaps the wild Japanese *rosa rugosa* can be introduced to cover the bare clay and to grow into the existing thorn and bramble, together with honeysuckle and wild clematis.

I suppose it will take about twenty years to see our image realised – meanwhile the ground hardens under the frost.

Matthew Challis

Eileen A brigadier who lived over the road didn't speak to us for two years. People felt *very* strongly – and over only two houses!
Matthew The village must have been much closer-knit then. They went to extreme lengths. The plans went to appeal. We heard afterwards that there were all kinds of pressures to move the house this way or that to keep people's views clear! People are more resigned now, they feel things are bound to change. But it indicates a lack of togetherness. With the plan for twenty-two houses behind the church, I was aware that if one took sides it would split the village. People have strange ideas about other people's motives, you get two camps, and it strains relationships. Eleven years ago, though, the village had a feeling of togetherness, and strong country values.

The countryside hasn't changed that much in that time. One or two hedges have gone; one of the oldest hedges near Mumford Hall was massacred. Part of a double hedge was taken out. It was lovely, full of spindle and brambles and briar roses, a wildlife reserve in miniature. We were shattered. I wrote a letter of protest in the *Village News* and the farmer concerned was extremely upset. He rang up to say that he had very strong interests in the countryside and conservation, and was in fact managing it very well. But I was partly upset because he was using a flail, and if you use a flail on an old hedge you get chewed rubbish. Pieces of timber are split and macerated so it's a horrible sight compared with a laid hedge or a properly managed hedge. That protest went quite far – a couple of MPs got involved, and the farmer obviously felt very hard done by.

Eileen Both our daughters have taken up this theme of wildlife and conservation in their careers. The wild garden has been their background. We had a cottage in Norfolk, too, for about twenty years, all the time they were growing up. We went there for holidays and weekends, to get away from suburbia. But it's a worry; when we come to sell this house, how will we find someone who will keep it in the same way? You can't put a preservation order on this sort of garden, only on trees.

Matthew The back of the garden is virtually wild; it joins a wild strip at the top which goes across to the meadow alongside the Gap. It is all untouched – a wildlife corridor – one of the few strips left. Wilf and Dora Middleditch have walked up the garden quite a lot. They once said to us, 'There's nowhere to walk in Swanbrooke Down any more. We used to walk along the country lanes.' Dora particularly likes wild flowers, and all those country walks and green lanes and hedges have gone. She said wasn't it lovely to come up here – in the spring we have primroses and cowslips, and it looks like a country lane.

Swanbrooke Down looks like a very pretty rural village, but there are no country walks. There are marked-out footpaths which are more or less walkable, but it's not countryside as it was. New methods of farming have taken the pastures and green lanes away. It's better further west, where you still have mixed farming, and where they're not so rich! You get little farms with cows and sheep, a lot of hedges, lots of trees, lots of wet patches, and the downland. But this is Essex. It's been over-ploughed, and all the land is very thin now. The soil here is on top of chalk and you can see patches of white in the field down there. The land only survives with fertilizer, it's been so intensively farmed.

The village as a place is very nice, it has a stream and its old houses, a nice setting in a hollow, but when you look at the fields there's not much of interest. There are very few wild flowers now; there used to be lots – chalk downland is rich in flora.

Eileen Even the chalk pit has been devastated. They've tidied up, and there are very few interesting wild flowers left. They use it for motorbike scrambling and clay-pigeon shooting. Mind you, so long as they're not shooting the real thing I'll keep quiet about that!

As we mentioned there's young blood in the village, and we've got seventy children now, but they haven't anywhere to play, and they can't run in the countryside. There's more recreation space in London.

Matthew When I was a youngster we lived in the suburbs of East London, and although it was very urban, I grew up with ponds and trees all round. In holiday times we were out in the fields all day, out with jam-jars to get sticklebacks from the ponds, out climbing trees – and that was virtually a built-up area. It was before the building boom of the late thirties, and the land later became housing. It was wasteland, but it was a great adventure playground. In the villages now they've used every scrap of land. It's rather like Holland, although there they make much more provision for recreation. There the land is highly utilised – you don't get hedgerows or grassy verges because they plough right up to the road. The Dutch are very conscious of the value of land, and they have a wholesale recreation and conservation plan. But in farming areas there is no spare space, so they don't have country walks – just roads with a ditch and a dyke leading to the next farmhouse.

I'm rather pessimistic about the future of farmland now that they are looking at alternatives for land-use. Farming is essentially a business, it has to make money, and housing is the most profitable thing to do. There's no money in recreation unless you make a golf course, or create something lots of people will pay a lot of money to visit. If you just give land over for recreation space, there's no money in it at all, so I don't feel hopeful. The local authority has to be persuaded to help.

I'm talking generally about villages now. In this part of the country, in the light of present change in agriculture and government policy, the community ought really to look at itself as a village and make its own plans. It needs to decide very clearly what it would like to have, and stick to that in the face of all changes. Because there are going to be enormous changes. The government are virtually saying, 'We are not going to be very strong in this area of housing development, because housing is badly needed and the cost of land is so high.' There is not much hope for official support when it comes to other issues – the village has to do it on its own, and to persuade the local authority that its plan is good. The local authority and the village have then got to get together against the government.

Eileen One of the problems here is that the population has become younger. That is fine, but it makes planning difficult. The play-group is having problems now, yet at one time it was full. Things go in cycles.

Matthew That's always the problem.

Eileen But not with a larger village like Haverley.

Matthew No, not so much. But you get a similar problem on housing estates, where everybody moves in at the same time, and are usually in the same age-group. You get a series of crises: first, play-group is needed, then primary school, then secondary school. They call them 'cohorts' in demographic terms – that cohort goes through the whole system. That's why it's ill-advised to have a large housing estate here, like the proposed development behind the church. You get a very unbalanced community. The only way to balance a village community is to have slow spasmodic development, with small groups coming in over a long period. The population could get just as big in the end.

The question of size is quite interesting: we have 298 people in Swanbrooke Down, and it is special. Perhaps because it's small and compact, it is possible for people to interrelate. It has disadvantages too. A village this size hasn't got a strong enough demand for a recreation area, for schools, or shops or buses. At the same time, you know everybody, you go down the street and you see every house in the village, whereas if you live in Haverley you never really see the whole place, and almost everybody is a stranger.

I don't know whether you can plan this. Some people have a *laissez faire* approach – things happen and that's life; others think you should try and order things to be better. I'm probably somewhere in between, but to me *laissez faire* causes tremendous problems; you've always got a crisis because you never have seen what's going to happen.

There is a need to plan, particularly now when some farm land is going to come out of use. But it's no good making plans on paper – you've got to get people to agree. Then you've got to deal with money, the profit angle. If I was in a position to do it I would like to invite the farmers and landowners in this village simply to have a discussion, to explore possibilities: 'What do you think you're going to do with your land?' 'Have you got any ideas?' 'Do you think you're going to farm less, or that you'll be more intensive in some areas?' I'd like to go through all the problems; water with the water board, drainage with the local authority, and see if one could achieve an optimisation of facilities. We could have a much better controlled water supply, we could have lovely woods and green areas. You could do something fantastic with the village! All you've got to do is unleash people's better feelings. While they're all in little camps, each wanting to protect himself, it won't happen.

Eileen That's just a planner's dream!

Matthew There are villages where the people have got together and done enormously inspiring things.

Some people can be too pro-farmer. But you can't get anywhere by being bloody-minded, either. You have to co-operate, try to influence people by seeing where their best interests lie. Some people condemn all farmers, saying they are unreliable and avaricious, that they should be controlled by the local authority, that the land ought to be bought for the state. It's an interesting view, but it doesn't necessarily produce the answers. It puts the farmers' backs up. With a more co-operative, constructive attitude you can probably bring them around to your point of view. You can't get rid of the farmers. You've got to come to a collaborative arrangement. So if something benefits the farmer and is nice for the community, that's great. But you've got to work out what is possible. That's not planning, it's being able to see possibilities, and allowing people to decide for themselves.

There is a possibility, however slight, that the village could get together over these matters. To get all the landowners together would be very interesting. This problem is common to all villages of this size and type in the area, so one would want to look at what other people are doing and see if one could get help and feedback from other experiments. At the same time it may be important to take a lead and create an example, to be an inspiration. But you've got to be very careful; if you start throwing these ideas about they could think it's a lot of rubbish, and impractical, and then you lose out altogether. You've got to move slowly, take the time when it comes, and be ready for that time. It's difficult to know whether, in Swanbrooke Down, to try and get the co-operation and interest of the parish council.

Some parish councils are good, but this is rather a weak one; it doesn't have positive views. Another point worth thinking about is that you can get people to take an interest in the village and the countryside through the children. You can see how interested schools are in nature trails, and in children's contact with the countryside and with farms. All parents of young children could be interested in that aspect, and farmers could possibly be interested in having some contact between children and the countryside.

Eileen The trouble is not having a school here. There's a centrifugal force which operates to take them out of the village.

Matthew Our elder daughter ran a very successful project along those lines, in Suffolk. She found that although the children lived in the country, some had no contact at all with the land. This project tried to bridge the gap. Farmers took them on countryside trails, and they were given projects. They had a big exhibition at the Suffolk Show, which Princess Diana opened.

This village is going to change radically in the next ten years, and it's very difficult to know what to do about it. If it just goes its own course, there'll be a series of applications for new properties and there could be a series of battles, and you won't have any coherent pattern of change. If you get a number of 'starter homes', they aren't big enough and people move on very quickly.

In one village the other side of Haverley, these starter homes created a sort of suburb where people came and went. It's a nasty little village now. It could quite easily happen here. I don't know what the local authority's feelings are; they sit on the fence a bit. However, so long as the village gives an impression that it will resist, and has positive views, I think they will take that into account.

So it is up to us. If the village doesn't care, and its voice is not heard at an appeal, the planners may not take such a strong line. It's a democratic process; you have a chance to comment on planning, built into the legislation. People don't use the chance so things go by default. But if you use it properly and the parish council have meetings about it, it will work in our favour. There should be somebody, on the parish council or a working party, who reviews all planning applications as a regular thing.

Eileen Our parish council would be dead against that. They are not going to be easy to deal with. I don't think they've got any goodwill towards people who don't agree with them.

Matthew It's unfortunate that the property developer has moved into Mumford Hall. That's not going to be helpful. He basically is a successful developer, it's his game. He can farm a bit and play around in his helicopter but essentially he's into development. Probably he'll end up a great tycoon. It's a great pity there isn't a lord of the manor type at the Hall, who has the interests of the village at heart, who would hold an annual fête, and provide land for children to play on.

He does, however, reflect the new social mix in the village. New blood can be a good thing, because it's energy, although there is a lot of the yuppie contingent. But there is also the element of conserving the rural idyll. Some of the more progressive younger people think other people only want to stop development because they're 'all right Jack: I've got my little paradise and I don't want anybody else in here.' Some may feel like that, but I don't think we do – it's not the point.

There was a village in Cambridgeshire where they interviewed the old villagers and the yuppie newcomers. There was very unpleasant feeling, because the new people with all the money were totally against development in the village, whereas the village people wanted more development. Swanbrooke Down is split in different ways. Here quite a lot of old village people don't want development; they like the countryside and the village, and there's been enough anyway.

We used to stop and talk to Len every time we walked down to the village – he was always somewhere in the garden. He made you feel you had a connection with the old village.

Eileen My younger daughter and I must have been the last people to speak to him. We used to go to the chapel on Sunday evenings and so did Len, so we gave him a lift back. The next morning he was found dying; he'd had a stroke. He never actually said he was a Methodist – he sang in the church choir when he was a boy, but I don't think he was happy in the church under Maurice. He preferred the simplicity of the Methodist service to the high church feeling of the Anglicans.
Matthew He had a seat of his own in the corner just inside the door – a large one!
Eileen Everybody liked him, and he was full of things to say. He used to do odd bits of building work, and he told a story about Sparrows Farm where he had done some restoration work. The new owner was talking about the part that had been restored, and said, 'Of course, it's not genuine.' Len said, 'What do you mean, not genuine? I did it myself!'
Matthew Len knew he was the Village Character, and he played it with tremendous panache. He was the last of a line.
Eileen He came to the local history meetings, and always had some sort of comment.
Matthew The people we met at the history society, and through the church, were different from most people in the village now. The community was centred around the Middleditches, the Draytons – about twenty people who knew each other and were comfortable together – there was no edginess, and that was very

nice indeed. That's what we thought villages were like! But of course they aren't really, all villages change.
Eileen Everybody who lives here for a reasonable time sees change, and you have to accept it. You've heard your parents say the same thing, and your grandparents. It's just that it's happening that much more quickly. The price of housing has changed enormously. We couldn't afford to buy this house now.
Matthew The only people who can afford to live in villages now are those who can afford to pay £200,000 for a cottage, and that has a tremendous effect on village life. You could say that because people are paying over the top they are going to be very protective of their patch. But people used to see their house first as a home, and secondly as an investment. Now they see it primarily as an investment, perhaps even a short-term one, because their jobs are likely to move them and they've got to be on the ladder.

There are two layers in this area of social change and planning. If you look at a village as a self-contained place, it's somewhere you can recognise, with people you know. But the influences changing it are nothing to do with the village particularly. Nationwide social changes and housing policies affect Swanbrooke Down, they affect everything, so your village is immersed in uncontrolled and widespread change. Whatever you do in the village you can't change all that. The village is almost a victim.

There is a lot of current interest in providing low-cost housing in the countryside. No young person, or local person, or old person, or persons on low incomes, can afford to live in the country. The rented housing has been sold off and done up, so it goes up in price. It's down to economic forces. Firstly there are far fewer people in farming, so there are no jobs. Secondly at one time when a couple wanted to get married they'd probably find a little house near their home. It isn't like that any more. So you get the dispersion of families and the break-up of communities. Young people have to go where they can afford the housing – usually to estates outside the towns or villages. This is awful. You could say it's a symptom as well as a cause of family break-up.
Eileen I think our generation is the last who lived in the same place as their parents. It's a change of life-style – people spend half their time travelling!
Matthew No doubt younger people in the village don't feel the same way. They've been used to that kind of life, whereas we

were used to a calmer existence with simple pleasures. We didn't want jacuzzis and helicopters! But you can't turn the clock back to those Saturdays spent walking across the fields with a bottle of pop and a sandwich, and getting home hours later tired and hot and happy.

TIMOTHY GOODWIN

Agriculturalist

Timothy Goodwin and his young wife live in the last house along the Elmshaw road leading out of Swanbrooke Down. It is a modern bungalow in a meadow beside Winter Water, looking across to harvest fields on every side. Poppies splash the verges, barley is turning gold under the July skies. It is the middle of the month, and the dreaded St Swithin's day approaches; will it rain on July 15th and then for forty days without a break? The racing thunderclouds presage an ominous answer. For several days the village has been subjected to bad-tempered rainstorms which have smashed patches of ripened wheat, the ditches have been racing with water, and the ford at Grinchell's Manor is impassable.

Timothy knows this pattern of English weather well. He was born at Grinchell's Manor, a lovely, romantic house half a mile outside the village, where his father was a tenant-farmer. The name Goodwin goes back to Domesday in Swanbrooke Down, for Goduin Sech is named in the Survey as owning Bledstowes, a great estate now obliterated from the map. Timothy is the sole remaining male Goodwin, so unless he produces a son the name will die out in the village.

There is a beautiful garden at Grinchells, part walled, part screened by high hedges. Old-fashioned roses scramble over fences and outbuildings; a white clematis clambers over a pergola. Winter Water, a slender stream at this point, winds through the garden. It has an air of other-worldliness, breathing a tranquillity and loveliness scarce in the busyness of the late twentieth century.

This is a secret garden, the place where Timothy played as a child. He had to leave it in his early teens when his father gave up farming and moved into the village.

Timothy now works as an adviser to young farmers and agricultural students, and writes the farming report for the *Village News.* At harvest time he is up at Cold Spring Farm for the gathering-in of the crops. He married a local girl, Rose, when they were in their early twenties, and they have a three-year-old daughter. I came to know Tim through his egg-round; he keeps free-range chickens and provides villagers with eggs. So once a week there is a knock at the door and there stands Tim; a sturdy, ample figure with round red face and heavy boots, he pauses to chat, quite shyly, before going quietly on with his round.

The last of a line

Timothy There's only one person surviving from my father's family. He was one of ten children, and my mother was one of three. Just one aunt is still alive, and her memory's not all that good, so when I want to find out something about the family she can't help. My father's mother was a Lagden. I've got the Goodwin family tree, but not the Lagden side so far; you've got to get four family trees to study the family history thoroughly.

I've lived here all my life, and although there's not a great number of actual family left, I've never had any great desire to move away. You've got to have a purpose to move away. My Aunt Florrie died about two years ago – she had lived next door for all the time I've been alive. She used to help in the dairy on the farm. I remember seeing her skimming cream off the shallow cream pans – those old-fashioned wooden ones – and patiently turning the handle of the wooden churn until the cream turned to butter. Then she would pat it into patterned blocks. She was a marvellous cook, and she gave us special teas sometimes as a treat – home-made scones with real butter, home-made jam, and cream from the dairy! She used to complain that we didn't eat very much, but we tucked in like anything!

She seemed to ask very little of life; she never married – she looked after her father and, after he died, her brother. That was my father, she was housekeeper to him until he married. I never heard her speak ill of anyone. She played the organ in the church for countless years. Another aunt married one of the Cooks at the farm on the hill, so she lived there. Two other aunts lived at Haverley, so they were all around.

Grinchell's Manor was the family home, and I lived there until about 1966. The house had 150 acres of farmland which my father and his family had farmed for two or three generations. It was a tenanted farm and the people who owned it wanted to sell up. I was only nine or ten and my father was quite elderly. He was over sixty, and in the early part of the sixties, farming wasn't that good, so forking out a lot of money was quite a commitment. He didn't see much point in buying it then, so the farm got sold.

It's a lovely house – it's nice to talk about it, although it's much nicer to visit than to live in! It's nice, but it's old and draughty and there are leaks, and it needs a *lot* of money spending on it. It's been slightly modernised and the rooms turned round a bit. There's a lovely oak-panelled room, and a magical garden. The garden's been kept in better order than the house – there's a lovely shrubbery. But I've only been into the house once since we moved out.

I was an only child. My father and mother married quite late in life – my father was about fifty and my mother must have been in her mid-thirties, so there wasn't a great deal of time to start a family. They had me and probably thought, 'Oh God, this is enough! Don't want any more!'

My father was one of six brothers. One nobody knows anything about. One died at birth or very soon after – no one talks much about that. The eldest worked on the farm all his life until he died. The second became a butcher in Didbrooke and in Swanbrooke Down; the third went to Australia for a while and became a sheep farmer. He died soon after he came back. The fourth was my father, and then there was the youngest, who also helped Dad on the farm. He died six weeks after he got married, to a schoolteacher from Haverley. He went out after breakfast and slipped, crossing a little stream up here. I heard that he choked on his own vomit and died.

On the girls' side there was Jane who married Charlie Cook. His first wife died soon after giving birth to their first son, so he married my aunt and she brought up the little boy, and they had a son of their own. Another aunt married a chap from Haverley; she was a midwife, and brought many babies into the world although she didn't have any herself. The fourth sister married a taxi-driver from Lillingford. He died last year – he was nearly ninety-eight and she's either eighty-nine or ninety but she's like a fifty-year-old, or younger. She runs around everywhere! She has a birthday on Christmas day.

There were only four children from those ten people, and the only boy was killed in the Second World War. Myself and my daughter are the only surviving Goodwins. There were some in Australia who were related somehow to Father. There was a Charlie Goodwin who must be dead now, and he had a son who must be about seventy, who's still alive in Australia – his name's Timothy too. I shall try to have a son, I suppose – it would be nice to keep the family name going, but it's not the end of the world if I don't.

I was brought up on the farm, and you probably learn more about it that way and are keener to follow it than if your father was an accountant or whatever. Farming doesn't start at nine and end at five o'clock; it even carries on through the weekend. It's never dull. It was a mixed farm, with an old-fashioned rotation growing hay and potatoes and cereals. Just a few animals – cattle, pigs and chickens. It wouldn't be a living now. It wasn't a very good living then, but it was just about adequate. I helped as much as I could but I was very young when my father gave up. I did drive the tractor occasionally which is totally against the law! We had a binder to make sheaves before the combine. My father only had a combine for the last two or three years. I remember carting the sheaves in, and getting the threshing tackle ready. Things were much more leisurely, there wasn't, 'We've got to get this done by a certain date'. If you didn't get it done it didn't seem to matter all that much.

I'm still connected with farming. My main job is as training officer for the Kings Tarrant training group, a group of seventy or eighty local farmers. They pay a subscription, and I arrange training for the farmers and their staff. That takes up eight or nine months of the year, and then for a couple of months during harvest and drilling time I help out at Cold Spring Farm. When I left school, before I went to college, I worked there for about six years until the farm was sold, just after I got married. Then this job came along.

There used to be seven or eight farms around the village, with probably twenty or thirty people working on them. Now you can count the people in farming on one hand. The countryside has changed too, in those twenty-five years, but then nature changes the whole time, whether for the better or not. For example the October hurricane last year completely changed the landscape. Old trees, young trees – gone. People learn from their mistakes too, but I think things always seem better in the past. Things were slower, we had better weather, everything is always better in the past! You remember the good things and forget some of the bad things. The main problem has been that farming in the past ten or fifteen years has changed because of outside interests coming in. You've had big insurance companies and pension funds buying up land and wanting a bigger return off it. If some people try to do that then the rest try to keep up. They have probably tried to get too much out of a scarce resource, and you can't do that. But those type of companies are leaving agriculture at the moment and perhaps it's not a bad thing. Everybody makes mistakes and I think there have been some mistakes made, ecologically speaking. The farmers who are going to stay in the job can see that; they've got to live in it, they've got to work there, and they may be passing the land down to their sons and daughters, so they feel they can't ruin it for them.

Recently we've seen how 'conservation' can be detrimental to the countryside. I'm certain that a lot of the trees blown down in the hurricane had conservation orders on them, and a lot of them shouldn't have been standing. People want the countryside to change overnight. If you plant a good oak tree it's going to take forty or fifty years before you even notice it. People are very anti cutting a tree down if it's still alive. But unless you plant more around it, by the time that tree dies its natural death, you've got nothing. Conservation has to look further ahead. If you want to see trees coming up quickly that's the wrong way to go about it. We've got to plant the right sort of trees and it will be years before they come up. It's worth waiting for them rather than putting quick-growing things in.

A lot of the people giving advice on conservation – FWAG [Farming and Wildlife Advisory Group] and Nature Conservancy – are doing a good thing, but you've got to be careful about conservation. Sometimes you have to be cruel to be kind, and just planting up trees willy-nilly and not cutting down trees before they die or keel over is the wrong approach. We've got to look after the countryside, we've got to have something that's worth looking at. It's no good pulling the curtains back in the morning and seeing a wilderness. You want to see trees out there.

Unfortunately it costs money to look after woods. One of the biggest problems of the last twenty years is that the woods have got out of condition, people haven't spent the time in them. It's very expensive to do the cutting out. People sell some of the wood for wood-burners now, but even so it hardly covers costs. We've got to make money available so that the woods are worth looking at and we can perhaps let people into them. You can't let people into woods at the moment because you wouldn't be able to get through.

Shooting is a help – people are prepared to pay to go shooting, and that money can be reinvested into looking after the woods. I'm not particularly pro-shooting, I don't get any fun out of it, but if it's done properly it's good for the countryside, because farmers will spend time and money making the cover acceptable.

A lot of hedgerows were taken out unnecessarily. Some people complain if *any* hedgerow comes out. A lot came out that weren't doing much good anyway. But the real, big hedgerows with the wide bottoms, if you take them out you ruin the whole ecology – the food chain with all the insects and so on. But a lot of hedges are being planted up now, it's quite surprising, and so is the number of trees being planted. If you've got shares in tree nurseries in the next few years you'll do well! They are working all hours to get things planted up. Obviously you're never going to have the number of hedgerows there were, but if you have a smaller mileage, looked after properly, you keep the ecological balance. We can see the error of our ways; when hedges are dug up and you see what happens, you go back and make good what you did wrong. Soil erosion on the Fens, for example, was considerable – sometimes they have to redrill after the winds of March and April time.

Farming now is almost totally reliant on pesticides and fertilisers. It's a big problem. Some farmers are going over to organic farming and organic-type fertilisers. Once we can see what happens on a reasonably big scale, rather than looking at smallholdings of ten acres, if people can see that it works they may well go over to organic methods. With pesticides, farmers are getting more choosy, purely because of the financial implications. Unfortunately it's not entirely up to them; the chemical companies have such wide margins on their pesticides that when farming margins come down they make the sprays that much cheaper. While the sprays are still reasonable one tends to use them. But farmers are very reluctant to use more than is absolutely necessary. A bill was passed by parliament two years ago, the Environmental Protection Act, which was partly to do with spray regulations. Now any farmer under twenty-five has to pass a test before they can apply any pesticide, so soon anybody who applies pesticides will have had to take this test. That's one example of conservationists exerting pressure on government. FWAG's money comes from farmers who want advice on how best to use their land for maximum conservation, and in Essex it's very successful.

Swanbrooke Down school was closed in the early fifties, and when I was ready to go to school in September 1958, I was two or three weeks under five. Everybody from Swanbrooke Down went to Haverley School. We trotted up there, and they said, 'How old are you?' and we said four and eleven months and two weeks or whatever it was, and they said, 'Sorry, I'm not taking anybody from Swanbrooke Down who is under five until I have to.' So we tried Didbrooke, but the schoolmistress there was about to retire, so in the end I went to Lillingford Primary, and spent my first six years there. It was run by two elderly ladies who were fairly strict, and held very much to the old-fashioned way of teaching; timestables and so on. I enjoyed it. They retired my last-but-one year there, and the new headmaster was more up-to-date. Although his teaching was more suitable for my secondary education I did prefer the old-fashioned way. I had some great times there.

There were only two or three children in Swanbrooke Down of my age, and they went to Haverley School, so there weren't many pals in the village to play with – meeting time was Sunday school in the chapel. I went from when I was about seven, until I was eleven or twelve. We used to sing a few hymns then divide into four groups – the little boys and the little girls and the big boys and the big girls. We'd chat about the text of the day, collect your stamp and off you go! The vicar wasn't very pro-children, so Sunday school was a nice alternative to church. Every week there must have been fifteen or sixteen at the minimum – most of the children in the village. That was the only time I really met the others – there was the occasional birthday party. I suppose I was rather lonely, being an only child, and the first ten years being up at Grinchell's. I couldn't just pop down the road to play – we were half a mile away so Mother or Father had to drive you.

Although I'm on the PCC, we're not every-Sunday people; we go to church once a month or so. I'm not over-religious but I do like the church, it's a lovely place. I help to cut the churchyard and things like that. It's a bit sad that we haven't a resident vicar but it's a case of economics. The way things are going, unless attendances do go up, we may well share our vicar between five villages instead of three. Things are very tight in the church at the moment, and although people are prepared to give money for the fabric of the building, when it comes to church attendance the average is 12½! You can't afford a vicar on 12½ people. The chapel's got problems as well. Nobody young comes to chapel now and they have a job getting the numbers. Whether we'll have a boom in attendances like the American style, we shall see – we tend to get things from America, good or bad. Perhaps we'll become Bible-bashers!

I'm a pub man, although not so much so since our daughter was born. I very seldom go on my own – I don't enjoy that much – I go with a friend or with Rose. I enjoy it without feeling deprived if I don't get down there! The Dog and Duck is a nice little pub; Derek is just the right person for it, and Toby is part of the furniture. He's part of the atmosphere – some pubs don't have that at all.

We try to go to functions in the village hall, if it's something we're interested in. Knowing what these things take to arrange, if people have taken the trouble we try to support them. We meet people in the pub, in church, at these activities, and we've got friends around the village. I see about twenty or thirty people on my egg-round. I've been doing that for six years – I've got about three-dozen laying hens. I don't do it purely to make money; I do make a few pennies out of it, but it is a nice thing to go round and see people and catch up on the gossip. I keep my finger on the pulse!

One or two good people in the village do a lot but don't want thanks for it. Nobody knows about it until they move away, and then they realise. There are lots of things going on – one or two for the bad, but it would be unreal if that wasn't so.

Every time an older person dies or moves out they are replaced by a person from a different way of life, and a different level of income too! To buy a house in Swanbrooke Down now you have to be very rich to start with, or on a very high salary to pay the mortgage. One would like to think that all these people coming in would mean there's more money for the village itself – but I'm not sure. But there's nobody moving in that I feel, 'I don't like them and I wish they weren't here.' You might think we are becoming part of the stockbroker belt. There's not a lot one can do about it, whether you like it or not.

There are some people you never see at any social thing, and others who move in and want to join in. I don't think too many people are using Swanbrooke Down purely as a weekend place – there *are* one or two who have two or three houses, but I think most people join in in some form; there is something for everybody here.

Perhaps there's not so much for the younger people – although we've got the Tuesday evening darts and table-tennis going now. That has survived because instead of it being run by adults thinking 'the children need something', it started off with children saying, 'We want this'.

A lot of Hawthorn Hill houses are privately owned now, so I don't see why anybody down here should feel superior to people up there. So long as they don't feel inferior I don't think there's much of a social divide – people are people as far as I'm concerned. Once, when we were carol-singing, we decided to go up to Hawthorn Hill. Someone who hadn't been here more than six months and had probably paid about £120,000 for their house, said, 'I don't see any point. You won't get any money up there!' We went straightaway of course. That was someone who had just moved in and that was their perception of the village. The fund-raising wasn't the point of the carol-singing, it was an aside to going around singing.

I hope they're not going to sell off all the Hawthorn Hill houses, because all first-time buyers can do now is to live in a council house or rented accommodation. But the planning authority doesn't seem to give a damn. There are very few homeless people in the area, it's reasonably rich. But I don't see why young people should *have* to move away. We've had the issue about starter-homes being built by our new lord of the manor, but it's only OK for the first person. When they sell it's a free market and up goes the price. But I can't see any more council houses being built in Swanbrooke Down.

We thought that with Stansted Airport coming, a lot of houses would be built in the villages but the district council seem to have got their way of putting major development in the towns, and restricting development in the villages. I feel ambivalent about that; I don't want Swanbrooke Down to become a massive village, but there are always going to be houses built here. The odd one or two.

Whether you like or loathe the property developer, helicopter and all, he's obviously in it to make money. But you can't stand still – we've got to keep numbers up in the village, you don't want them to drop much below three hundred. The real problem is that we're not on mains drainage and I can't see us getting on it in the foreseeable future.

There's always a little bit of a divide in the voice of the village. In the old days anybody who didn't work either on the land, or locally, was the exception; now anybody who does is an oddity! There always will be a bit of a divide, but it depends on how you take it; if you're on one side you don't need to feel inferior and if you're on the other you don't have to feel superior. Everybody's got to do something different. Is the dividing line the size of your house, and if so what's the market price? I think there's such a mixture here you can't have a clear dividing line. In the old days you had slight divisions, and perhaps Hawthorn Hill might have been looked down on more than it is now. There might be a divide between those who have lived here all their lives and those who hadn't. If they get together perhaps the feeling of 'we're the original types' tends to come out, but it's nothing serious. It's a very friendly village. Most people are willing to help if you have a problem; there'll be a phone call or a knock on the door. If anyone moves in near us we'll always go and see them the next day and introduce ourselves. In towns, even where you've got adjacent flats, people seem not to bother – you can live next door to a person and not know who they are. Not many things happen in the village that most people don't know about fairly soon – it gets round by way of the post or the church or the pub! Whether it's the same story when it gets right round is a different matter!

PADDY AND BRENDA WALSH

Schoolteacher and wife

Apple Tree House is Swanbrooke Down's most adventurous piece of architecture. Probably, if plans for it were submitted today, they would not be approved by the council. But this extraordinary building went up twelve years ago, when controls were more relaxed. It is open-plan, with a huge picture-window roof-high, so you can see into the house in cross-section. Not at all a typical village house.

Paddy and Brenda built Apple Tree House themselves, and have settled into the village with their two young sons and Paddy's widowed father. Much creative activity goes on within its walls. Paddy is restoring a massive organ which was rescued from a derelict church and now dominates the main room. Brenda practises her singing and studies for an Open University degree in between tending to her family and milking the goat. Grandpa Walsh spends hours at the piano, for he was a professional pianist in his day, and still teaches students. The boys have painted a striking mural on the inside wall, and invented and constructed a Heath-Robinson contraption as an intercom to their bedrooms.

Paddy is a teacher in a comprehensive school some twenty miles across-country. He has a humorous turn of phrase and an infectious laugh. Brenda, a gentle and sincere woman, a Quaker, insists on a close and cohesive family life. Their contribution to the community has been considerable. Having run the playgroup and the Sunday school, she now organises a children's concert every Christmas. The Walshes are as unusual and interesting as their house.

The back garden used to be an orchard, and has been left more or less wild, with little corners for favourite flowers and shrubs, and a small vegetable plot. Through the leaves of the apple trees the ripe corn shimmered in the heat of a late July afternoon. A large goat stood tethered in the corner of the orchard, patient-eyed, shaking its bearded head to flick flies off.

It's not a rustic corner any more

Brenda One day, about fifteen years ago, the lady who lived next door knocked on my door with half an enormous fruit cake and said would I like it as a present from a lady up the road. I didn't know about Mrs Rush then, but my neighbour told me that she liked children. My elder son Tom was very young, and she said would I take him down to see her – she must have been about eight-eight then. So I started taking Tom, and he really liked it. She sat him on her lap and sang him little songs. Her kitchen was amazing – she was a laundress and did fancy ironing. She didn't have electric irons, she had lethal paraffin stoves with different weights of irons on top of them. She used to heat her irons up and iron these tucks and pleats just like she always had. I never saw Fred, her husband, because as soon as visitors came, Fred was out in the outhouse until they went! But Mrs Rush used to make enormous cakes almost as a business – she didn't just make one or two, and she had the biggest cake tins I've ever seen.
Grandpa Walsh Everybody in the village had to have a cake!
Brenda She got a friend in London to buy her the fruit and she taught me how to make fruit cake. When she died I had her cake tins; nobody else wanted them. During the power-cuts one winter she was without electricity and she tripped over a mat trying to make her feather-bed in the dark. Fred came up to us for help – it was quite late – but she wouldn't have the doctor. We were very worried, and tried to get a doctor, but she kept saying she'd be all right and would we help her into bed, so we did. But it was dark and nobody could see what she had done to herself. The next day she wasn't very well, and had obviously done some damage, so she went to hospital and she never really recovered. She had shattered a bone in her leg, and she died of the shock.
Paddy We went to Cambridge to the hospital to see her, and

took Fred with us. We went in to this enormous foyer and he said, 'They must need a lot of paraffin stoves to heat this place!' The best thing was when we took the lift; we stood there, like you do in lifts, and went up to the next floor. When we came out it looked just the same as where we'd gone in. Fred said, 'What did we go in that little room for?' It must have seemed extremely mysterious, just standing in this little room with other people and pressing buttons, then coming out again! It was a real treat to find somebody so innocent!

The following excerpt is a tribute to Fred Rush, written by a friend and published in the *Village News.*

'Hello, Fred!'

'Lovely day,' he would reply. Even when rain was promised (so long as it didn't stop him working) it would, to Fred, be a lovely day. Often I have met him coming from his regular job, to start on another as soon as he reached home; Hollyhock Cottage, so aptly named and as real in its rustic simplicity as Fred was a real person – indeed a gentleman in the true meaning of the term.

He had nothing but contempt for sluggards, for whom he reckoned a good spell on the farm would 'larn 'em'. To Fred activity was life, until – nearing his ninetieth year – a fall from a ladder put a stop to anything more active than a hobble across a lane where, when warm and sunny, he would sit on the railings opposite his door. Here he would answer the waves from the passing motorists who knew him (and many did) and enjoy the neighbours who would stop for a chat. He seldom grumbled; nor did he lose his sense of humour though often in great pain; nor forget to thank the many who helped him.

'What will be, will be,' was his attitude, and he accepted his fate with little question, like the true countryman he was. The only thing that seemed to upset him when first in hospital was the non-stop television: 'I'd like,' he said, 'to put me boot through it!'

I shall remember the warmth in his voice as Fred spoke of the crops: the ploughing, the sowing, the harvest, the lifting of potatoes – all that was important in the life that had been his.

As his health deteriorated he would sit, day after day, in his favourite little room, in the same chair, listening to the wireless with his cat stretched on the table beside him, holding forth about the changes he had seen in his long life, or what he considered wrong with the world today. 'I reckon ...' he would begin. And how often it seemed his reckoning was right.

Grandpa Walsh When we were first trying to get the garden organised, Jo Hutchinson was village handyman. He was in his eighties, and he dug the holes for the fence-posts. He could dig them faster than Paddy could put them in! I was trying to encourage a lawn in the front, from seed, and it was beginning to grow a little; one day I got the mower out, and Mr Hutchinson said, 'Excuse me, Mr Walsh, you shouldn't mow new grass, you should *swunge* it!' I'd never heard that before – it was the first word I learned of the local language. I said, 'Have you always lived in this village, Mr Hutchinson?' He said, 'There are just two places I've lived: Swanbrooke Down and Egypt.' He did his war service there, and after the war he stayed on as a batman to the forces and obviously loved it there.
Brenda He was gardener to our neighbours. It was beautiful too, really immaculate. He would come round and get the ground elder out from our side of the hedge so that it didn't go round his side! Quite a responsibility living next door to a gardener like that.

We moved from a flat in Harlow and we hadn't had a garden before. As leaving presents from Harlow Hospital I'd been given garden tools, and they were still wrapped up. Paddy went out to do some gardening, and the gardens down the lane where we lived first are all open-plan, so it was like an allotment. Paddy got going with a spade, but Arthur Spooner said, 'That wants forking.' Paddy had just peeled all the wrapping off the spade, but he went in and got his fork and unwrapped that. Then the wheelbarrow had to be unpeeled! 'That wants raking,' he said.
Paddy So after about four of these ceremonial unwrappings – they were all standing there watching – he said, 'I don't suppose you've done much gardening before ...'
Brenda Us newcomers from Harlow! But it was really nice because they were always giving me advice about the garden – my onions were as big as Arthur's one year, so I was really chuffed. Arthur's were always perfect; mine were always very weedy, espe-

cially after Tom was born because I couldn't do much gardening then. And I didn't get much help from you, did I?
Paddy I gave up gardening after the unwrapping, and after an episode of searching for brussels sprouts, which I didn't realise grew up the stalk of the plant. I was looking for them in rows of individual sprouts, like little cabbages. Brenda kept sending me out to get them – 'I know there are some out there,' she said. Finally I thought, perhaps they're growing up these stalk things – pulled up the leaves and there they were!
Brenda He'd never lived in the country.
Paddy The darkness was what amazed me at first; I'd only ever lived in places with street lights. I used to go outside a lot when I first came because it was so incredibly *dark*! The silence too – then. The motorway wasn't here.

Coming here was a random accident – we just wanted to live somewhere out of Harlow, but there wasn't anything.
Brenda Then the estate agent in Kings Tarrant offered us one of the Vickerys' cottages. We rented it for a year. It said in the blurb 'large garden at rear': but it was snowy and you couldn't see which was field and which was garden – it stretched to the horizon. So we didn't know where we had come to really, except that it was a nice big house, and we hadn't anybody on top of us or underneath us. We were a bit worried about being noisy, what with the piano and that, so we knocked on next door's to say, do you mind noisy neighbours? She came to the door; her children were quite small then, and they stood there around her like a lot of chickens – under her arms and legs and skirts, and kittens were coming out from between their legs I seem to remember! And she said, '*You* were worried about the noise? *we* were going to say the same to you!' We got on very well after that – we even had an intercom between our two houses. We didn't mind the boys playing on our garden, and it was really good.
Grandpa Walsh The village is still a pleasant place.
Paddy I'm not here enough to know, really. I don't know anybody here.
Brenda I didn't get to know anybody until I had Tom, apart from my neighbours. After Tom was born we gradually got to know people with children the same age. It was the children that broke the ice.

Because we rented our house, we got to know people up

Hawthorn Hill, and all the other people renting. After we bought the land from our neighbours here, we were invited to an At Home and our hosts said, 'When do you hope to come and live in the village?' and we said, 'Actually we've been living here for three years.' They didn't know anything about us because we were renters! Talk about a social divide. We got to know them all – if we hadn't been renters first we'd never have got to know the Hawthorn Hill people, not on Christian-name terms.

After we bought the land, Jo Hutchinson started calling us Mr and Mrs Walsh; before that he'd always called us Paddy and Brenda. We'd gone on to the next level, as far as he was concerned. Yet it wasn't as if we'd stopped calling him Jo! We noticed it very much.

Paddy We live in a class-ridden country. I'd be off like a shot to another country if I could.

Brenda You never saw the Hawthorn Hill lot at the cheese and wine party, for example – they had their own little world, weren't interested in the higher society lot.

Paddy I think it works both ways. It's self-perpetuating.

Brenda After all, the renters go and clean for the owners, that's the other thing, and you've got your divide again. Where would the owners be without the renters? Mind you they're getting fewer and fewer – a lot of renters must be getting rather elderly for these things.

Paddy Education is the next divide: those who send their kids to private schools, and those of us whose kids go to state schools. The children don't get to know each other – even the ones who go to different private schools.

Brenda Before we started our concerts, a lot of the older children in the village had never even met each other. Now they know each other. Everybody who was interested in music could get involved, so it broke down barriers. We've done Christmas concerts for three years now. I had stopped doing Sunday school and I wondered what to do next. The concert idea worked. Tom's taken it over now. We felt we were privileged to live in such a nice house, which is meant to have music made in it, and Grandpa Walsh's musical friends were only too pleased to come and play, so we held concerts. They are free but people can give donations to charity if they wish. We arranged that after the first few times. People felt better about coming.

Paddy We're lucky to be able to do it.

Brenda Not many village people come: just a nucleus of eight or nine.
Paddy The music we're promoting isn't for everybody – it's classical, and in any population you wouldn't get many interested.
Brenda But there are people in the village who would go to the Festival Hall, or Covent Garden, but they wouldn't come to a little concert in our house.
Paddy People go to hear music for lots of reasons; it's a social occasion and they like going to London, or whatever.
Brenda I was on the village hall committee which is how I came to start the playgroup, because we wanted to use the village hall. When the Sunday school was on I helped with that. I was quite involved. You weren't.
Paddy No, I tend to be a recluse.
Brenda You've got your own world at school; it's such hard work, and you see so many people. You need to be able to get away.
Paddy In the evenings I'm still involved with school work, and in the holidays we go away quite a bit, so I don't really know anybody here.
Brenda Every time you do meet them you think, 'Aren't they nice! I wish we had time to get to know them.'
Paddy It's my fault that I don't. But it's changed a lot, this place. You change in yourself, too, so I can't really judge to what extent it's me or it. But it doesn't feel to me like the rustic corner it was. Sixteen years ago we were down an unknown lane behind a hedge; now I feel like part of north London.
Brenda It's partly because there have been so many new houses, and people coming in, and we haven't had a chance to get to know them. Some years nobody would move, then there'd be a 'moving year'; but people didn't move away – they just used to move houses – they did the rounds!
Paddy It's partly communications as well: the first time I drove down the new M11, I thought, 'I'm really living somewhere else now.' Instead of that long trundle through Epping Forest and Harlow and down these tiny lanes – which seemed to me the ultimate mystery, having grown up in London – I was thinking, now I can whizz down the motorway, twenty-five minutes from Redbridge, speed along to Lillingford and you're here in no time.
Brenda Although if we'd travelled by train it would have stayed the same.

Grandpa Walsh Traffic in the village has increased a hundredfold. When we first came I used to open the window to have a look if a car went by!
Paddy I wouldn't choose to live here any more, if I was looking around. If I was looking under the same criteria, for somewhere quiet and out of the way, I'd need to start another hundred miles further north.
Brenda Perhaps we've got more discriminating.
Paddy Yes, as I say, it may be the way I see it! But fifteen years ago people weren't affluent like they are now – just look at house prices. We built this house for about £20,000.
Brenda I think it's much better that there are a lot more children, it's much healthier. Except there's nowhere for them to play. But at least there's table-tennis on Tuesdays – Johnny loves going. But it's the only regular thing for the kids. The church doesn't offer anything and there isn't a Sunday school.
Paddy I regard the established church as dying its proper death. It's written itself off by remaining so medieval.
Brenda The children are still *there* for Sunday school, but nobody is willing to run it. It used to be a free-church and Anglican venture, but in the end none of the Anglicans felt they could help, so it was a bit one-sided. They expected us to take our children down to *their* services as well! Not that we minded. I didn't know what an Anglican service was like. I felt awful standing at the front with no idea what to do and all these children looking at me to see what to do!
Grandpa Walsh Some churches in London are becoming community centres, and catering for people's needs during the week.
Brenda We have wondered why they didn't close the church and just use the chapel? Or update the church? You could put a kitchen in, heat it and make it cosy – you could put a false ceiling in part of it. You could have used part of the church as a community centre, keeping the altar part good. People used to use the church as their social centre. It seems foolish just to have it standing there and somebody having to walk up every day to unlock it for no one to go in. It's always cold. If the village could have clubbed together with the church, and modernised the back of it, they could have used it for functions. Then the church would have become a living place. The reaction is What a suggestion! Couldn't possibly do that!

Paddy The church's days must be numbered. Yet it doesn't take many people to keep it going. I once suggested in a meeting that religion could become like ice-cream vending; vicars should go around with a ding-dong van with an inflatable spire and set up wherever they happened to stop or whenever somebody came out of their house. It wasn't quite serious as a suggestion, but it met with fairly intense silence . . .

Brenda The village has been a very caring place, and I hope it keeps on being like that. They once tried to run a good neighbour scheme, and there wasn't any need for it. All the old people were being looked after by their neighbours anyway. They'd already *got* a good neighbour scheme without having to organise one.

Grandpa Walsh I think I'm very fortunate to be here, although I don't know a lot of people intimately. I spend most of my time here, and I get out for walks a lot. I find it very friendly. It's a very pretty village, it *smells* good. Even the animal smells are better than the cars and smoke of London.

Paddy You don't half notice it when you go down there now!

Brenda There are all types here, and they all seem to get on well. The social mix has changed but people still seem to know each other. People waiting for the bus all talk together, or after playgroup they go to each other's houses.

Paddy Is there any work in the village as such?

Brenda Rex Vickery has ten making their living off his land. Then there are people in domestic work. People who work at the pub. Ros, who writes books . . .

Grandpa Walsh The decent thing is the gentle tempo – in London you're rushing everywhere. When you're retired you like to do other things, and you think, 'What are they doing all that for?' Extraordinary. Even driving down the street you're under pressure! I don't know how people go up and down to London every day.

Paddy My journey to school takes about forty minutes – it's a quiet, pleasant drive along country lanes. So I'm a commuter too – with a difference.

At this point we were joined by the younger son, Johnny, arriving breathless and bright-eyed from the Tuesday night youth club. He was full of glee because he had won a doubles table-tennis match. An extrovert nine-year-old, he settled in and added his views about Swanbrooke Down.

Johnny I like it here. Compared to what though? I've lived here all my life.
Paddy Suppose you could live in a town though?
Johnny You could go down to the shops, but you haven't got the fields and trees. We've got big gardens, and I've got friends here. I don't get *bored*!
Paddy Think of all the driving every time we want to go somewhere.
Johnny We go to school in Stevenage because *you* do. If we hadn't a car we'd have to use the bus or the train, or walk. I'd rather live here than in a town by a long shot. I like towns when we're on holiday, but I wouldn't like to live in one for a long time. Didn't like London at all. I like the countryside around here, but I was talking to Tom the other day about us not having any meadows left. There's one up by the Gap, there's one up Mouse Hill, and there's one up towards Didbrooke, and that's it. There's no empty space left. No woods that you can go in. A few footpaths. But it's still good.
Grandpa Walsh We've got a fine new crop of footpath-indicators with no footpaths to walk on.
Brenda What I noticed most after Mumford Hall was sold was that they put up notices about private property. Although it wasn't really allowed, we used to walk right round one of the fields, up a little path and down round the edge of Mumford Hall grounds. They stop you walking there now: 'This isn't a footpath.'
Johnny We used to do another walk and even though it wasn't a footpath they didn't mind. But now it's 'Sorry, this isn't a footpath, can you get off now please.'
Brenda I feel a bit more trapped here than I used to. I was brought up on a farm and we had two or three grass fields which were lovely. But when I went to London I was stunned; the people I was staying with took me to Richmond Park which I'd never heard of. It was wonderful in the autumn with all the deer. When I went to college in Bayswater I could get down to Kensington Gardens, to the Round Pond and back, so easily. I couldn't get over how beautiful the trees were. Our farm had

marvellous Suffolk hedges, but not these big trees and places where you could walk for miles. People in London are very lucky with their big parks.

AUDREY LONG

Wife and mother

One of Swanbrooke Down's more incongruous weekend sights is a glimpse of Harry Long walking his dogs. You never see Harry during the week; he is managing director of a giant international company, very busy and important. His chauffeur collects him in the morning and returns him at sundown to the Old Vicarage which he bought seventeen years ago for his family – Audrey and the four boys. Their daughter was born there, and is now a keen horsewoman, much to her mother's consternation since she doesn't much like horses and has to help feed them and muck them out every day.

The sight of Harry walking the dogs is vaguely comical only because one is an Irish wolfhound the size of a small pony and the other a Yorkshire terrier the size of a dust-brush. Harry himself, gently rotund with beaming benevolent countenance, moves at a leisurely pace to exercise these sublime and ridiculous dogs.

Audrey is Swanbrooke Down's most unfearingly outspoken person, much loved for her ability to upset apple-carts and call a spade a spade. There are no flies on Audrey. Dressed usually in jeans, parka and wellingtons she tears around looking after animals and offspring and by her own admission never gets around to housework. She loathes cooking, so if you have a smart meal with Audrey it is provided by caterers. Although she bemoans the loss of the old characters in Swanbrooke Down, she is undoubtedly one of them – it is just that she is nearer fifty than ninety.

Audrey debunks the rural idyll as we sit in her kitchen by the Aga. A beautiful white cat lies on a cluttered table, there is an air of permanent friendly chaos in this large, solid Victorian house. A late March wind gusts the trees in a garden that is mainly grass and surrendered to the needs of chickens, goats and geese.

The idyll is unfounded

Audrey I was born in Rhodesia, now Zimbabwe, in 1937, and it was fairly primitive then. I left when I was twelve or thirteen, so my background is proper rural! Everything on the farm was done by oxen – the pace was as fast as a small boy walked, because the oxen were led by a piccaninny. My only regret is that I didn't realise it was passing, and how fascinating it was. We milked a hundred head of cattle twice a day *by hand*. We grew maize too, and of course the labour force was enormous. We were ten miles from the nearest town, and three miles from the nearest road. We had no telephone; an emergency was a boy on a bicycle, with a note.

The farm manager, who lived with his wife Bessie on the other farm my father owned, had one of these emergencies one Christmas Eve; the ubiquitous African on a bicycle arrived, saying, 'Please come quickly: Bessie's had a baby.' Bessie thought the prunes she had had for supper had upset her, she didn't even realise she was pregnant. He was marvellous with cows, but *he* didn't notice either!

My parents separated when the war ended. When father came back from the army, mother left, and we came back to England and I went to boarding school. We lived in Lingfield in Surrey first, then Torquay. At seventeen I moved to London, so I lived in Wimbledon between the ages of seventeen and thirty-three.

We moved here because of Harry's job – he's always worked

for the same firm. It had just amalgamated and his office was moved to Harlow. He came back one day and said, 'We've got to move.' I said, 'What do we do about the boys' school?' and he said, 'That's all right. I play golf with someone who teaches at a school near Ware, which is somewhere near Harlow.' So we got the boys into that school, then had to find a house you could get to the school from, and then on to Harlow, because I am bitterly opposed to boarding school, and we couldn't afford it anyway!

We looked and looked, and it was very difficult. There were houses with twenty-two bedrooms, and houses with three bedrooms, but no houses with five bedrooms, which was what we needed. Then we saw an ad for an old vicarage in a place I had never heard of. Neither the M11 and nor the Ware by-pass had been built, and it was the most appalling slog out east, so nobody came out this way. It took three hours from the edge of London, never mind from Wimbledon! Anyway, one Easter weekend we trailed out here, saw the house, thought 'smashing' and bought it.

That's seventeen years ago. I'm not particularly fussed where I live, but Harry would go, 'We can't move there, you can see a house from the windows.' But I don't ever look out of the window! I just get on with it. I can't even say I had any impressions of the village, except that the people were a bit sticky-fingered. The first day here I made a call from the telephone box and left my purse on the shelf. Harry had just given me the housekeeping money, so there was quite a lot in it. I went into Lillingford to shop, realised I'd left it, came back – I had been gone all of twenty minutes – and it had gone. So I thought, 'So much for the rural idyll.' You're told that in the country people are so honest.

This is part of the myth. I once dropped my purse off the back of a motorbike in London, and got it back from the police station. I dropped it in the snake pit at the zoo once, and got it back! Untouched, with my silver watch in it. I never had a cat run over in London; I've had one run over here, and one hit outside the gate.

People try to make out that it's Utopia; but it's rather like marrying a man and making him out to be Prince Charming on a white horse. They try to make Swanbrooke Down into their idea of what a country village should be.

Anyway, I needed a house with five bedrooms. It was a particularly traumatic move because I was very busy. I had four small children, and we had horrendous school runs. But moving here didn't make all that much difference to me. I don't think I've ever taken *any* notice of the community. I do like people, and I'm interested in them and I think they're fun. I like to see what makes them tick. But I get very irritable when they won't do what I want. It's just that I don't take any notice of what is around me. If Harry walked in now and said, 'We're going to go to Australia tomorrow', the only thing that would slightly appall me is the thought of shifting all the animals there!

I have always like animals around me, and we have quite a menagerie. We had pigeons until my bloody neighbours shot the lot. I'm not wild about my neighbours. Now our menagerie consists of two goats, four geese, I don't know how many chickens, two dogs, two cats and a lot of house birds. And two ponies and a horse. It keeps me busy – that's why the house is in the state it is!

I can't honestly say I notice *any* difference in the village, except that there are no characters left. I miss old Len, he was great. He used to tell the most scandalous tales, so rude they are quite unprintable. You'd be sued for libel if you published them. He was so funny about one of the farmers' wives – I can say this because they don't live here any more. Julie – bless her heart – gave herself marvellous airs and graces. She became chairperson of the local arts group; she used to queen it with the most beautiful enunciation and she was wonderful at her job. But she had the misfortune to have been born in the area, and what Len had to say about her and her past was – talk about scandalous . . . I have no idea how true these stories were, but she's moved to Warwickshire now, where I'm sure she can get away with it!

There's no Sam Gapes to set your watch by as he goes to the pub every lunchtime. Other things have changed; there was a fishmonger who delivered, there was a butcher, we had bread delivered – and we did have a village shop even though everything was very old. The flour was always damp, but at least the shop was there.

Len was lovely, I loved Len. We used to have him to Sunday lunch and my only regret is that we didn't put a tape-recorder on. Len was like the characters in *Akenfield.* I'm not sure he had even been to London.

Len's boss took him to the Essex Show the year the Queen

came and he was sitting under a tree eating his bread and cheese when a policeman came along and said, 'I'm afraid you must leave, sir.' So Len looked around and said, 'Why?' The policeman said, 'Her Majesty's coming by.' So Len looked around again and said, 'Well there's plenty of room for she and I,' and sat and ate his bread and cheese!

Old Daniel Nottage was wonderful – he was mahogany-coloured with dirt; used to wash his feet once a year whether they needed it or not. My old labrador used to go up and go '*poh*!' The smell that emanated from his place . . .

I don't honestly know whether it's a nice or a nasty village – it's just a place to live. I don't know that it's any different from Wimbledon. I had trouble with my Wimbledon neighbours – they didn't shoot my pigeons, but they complained because the children made a noise. They were elderly, and the boys did make an awful din. I didn't let them play in the road so they brought their friends into the garden, and my dog was always getting out. To me, this village is *no* different to Wimbledon. In fact there were more places to walk the dog. You could walk where you liked. Here there is nowhere: 'Dogs on leads', ploughed fields or ploughed-up footpaths – and your dog isn't allowed to stray off the footpaths if you follow the letter of the law.

It's much the same sort of social mix too. They had endless coffee mornings; you could sit on twenty-two committees in Wimbledon if you felt like it. I used to get very cross when one of the WI ladies here, queen of the village in those days – I just caught the end of her reign – she had moved down from London and said how frightfully difficult it was living in Westminster. I did not agree.

It's nice or nasty according to how you get on with people. Fortunately in those days I got on with all my neighbours – we had a saintly vicar at the bottom of the garden. The boys drove a go-cart and made a dust-storm and the noise was horrendous. He never murmured. I'm very fond of my neighbours at the top of the garden – we used to have steaming rows because I had to wade through their sewage, but I am very fond of them. But my neighbours at the bottom now, who shot all my pigeons, are a pain. They complain every time you sneeze. The awful thing is that right is on their side! One can't blame them – it's just irritating. The fact that my forty-two pigeons kept alighting on their roof must have been rather galling.

We are Roman Catholics, so we seldom go to church here – we go regularly to Mass in a chapel the other side of Haverley. I did occasionally go to evensong across the road, and we still go to all the big festivals: Stations of the Cross on Good Friday, the carol service, and if we're still living here when our daughter gets married I shall move heaven and earth to get her married there, because it's handy.

I wonder if having a resident vicar makes a difference? I don't think so. People are so hypocritical. When we first came it was standing-room only at harvest festival. Now only part of the nave is full. I was very shocked. That *is* a difference. I don't know why people don't go to church any longer. When we came here there was *the* most fabulous man, Canon Williams, and he was a saint; he was like Sir Thomas More, all things to all men. He didn't mind in the slightest what you were, who you were, what your religion was.

That caused the most frightful dissension. The abrasive brigadier, who fought with everybody, had been married twice so he had slight sympathy with the vicar. But some people said that the vicar must be above reproach and must go, whereupon the brigadier called them prudes to their faces, which I thought was frightfully funny.

Now we've got this nice, well-meaning little man, nothing wrong with him, does funerals beautifully, it's his speciality. Even children's funerals – he does them magnificently. I don't quite know what he lacks but he's not comfortable in his skin. He tries terribly hard and I think it's pathetic that people don't meet him halfway.

In the Roman Catholic church you just go to church and that is that – even if you hated the clergyman it wouldn't affect you. In the Church of England people go only if they like the vicar, as far as I can see. Has Maurice Mansfield really emptied the church? I don't think the young lot would have gone anyway – they weren't brought up to go. We *were.* Maurice has not got the light touch and all he has succeeded in doing is putting them off.

We used to go down the pub on Sundays and have a drink with friends in the saloon bar, but children weren't allowed in so I didn't really know what went on in the pub. It was in the days of old Doug Duff, who was a good publican. I go down there now if I'm too lazy to prepare a meal – I will go down with my daughter for a ploughman's. Otherwise no, I don't drink very much, and I'm not very community-minded. I don't know anything about the community here, or the so-called 'community spirit'. The Hawthorn Hill lot mope and moan about how there's no community spirit, but I don't know quite what they're looking for. I mean they never jolly well come to the Christmas do so how do they know there's no community spirit? And when they do they complain that nobody talks to them. It's their attitude, not ours. Unfortunately relationships are a two-way thing: you've got to be prepared to make an effort. I can't be bothered to make the effort so . . . If they want to come and see me, I'm delighted to see them; but I'm not going out of my way to see them!

I'm not anti village activities, it's just that the village activities don't appeal to me – although I did run in the pancake race once! I *hate* cocktail parties. You very rarely find me at one. We have one every year only because Harry makes me; he insists we have half the village to a New Year's Day celebration. I think parties like that are an insult – I almost think I should give people a present for coming! Or that *I* should write thank-you letters to *them* for coming. I think they are *horrible.*

There is this preconceived idea about village life. You read *Akenfield* and *Cider with Rosie*, and think, 'That's lovely'; but they both make the point that village life died with the motor car. And it did. I mean, what *is* village life? I remember being coerced into running the cake stall at the parish thing in Wimbledon; now I'm coerced into helping with the bottle stall at the handicapped children's thing. There is no difference, except in Wimbledon we could walk right through to Richmond Park. Nowadays of course you'd probably get mugged – but you never know round here either. I promise you this happened last week in a town near Harlow. Our chauffeur's son was walking down the main street with his girlfriend, at half-past ten at night, and he was set upon by four youths, and had to go into hospital!

People in Swanbrooke Down have a middle-class 'idyll' attitude. They forget that the countryside is the equivalent of an industrial estate. People who live in the country make their living in the country; not everybody is involved in folksy arts and crafts. It's very unpleasant, farming; my mother gave it up because she had to take the calves to slaughter. If you analyse farming, it's estate management, and that means a certain amount of killing. Nature is red in tooth and claw, and this is what city people will not accept. As it happens I don't kill the animals I keep, but if you farm you have to. It is actually very nasty.

Grain farming has turned East Anglia into an industrial estate. During the war everyone was desperate to produce food, now we're producing too much. It *has* ruined the look of the countryside, but you can't argue with progress. People get so nasty about farmers because they are successful businessmen; I get very cross about this.

Development is going to come, and if you don't like it you ought to sell up. The South-East has opened up. Instead of taking four hours to get to London, as it did seventeen years ago, Harry gets to his office in an hour and ten minutes. It's convenient now. Stansted is going to grow whether you like it or not – I think it's horrid, but it's going to happen.

It may not be *nice*, but animal husbandry isn't nice either. Nature's very cruel; the weak don't survive. I remember the lions in Africa – the number of cubs that died of malnutrition was horrendous, and that's if they weren't killed by their parents. Places like Longleat produce far more lions, because the cubs survive – they give them vitamins and things.

Mother became a vegetarian after she took the calves to slaughter – she only did it once. I sympathise. Have we any rights over animals? Probably not, in which case we mustn't muck about with them. I'm prepared to accept that to a lot of people hunting is offensive, but you've got to be logical; unfortunately we do use animals. Are animals put here for our use or not? I don't know. I hate shooting, but it's very illogical of me, because I'm not anti-hunting.

It is mankind, after all, who has mucked up the beauty of the world. If we left nature alone it would be perfectly all right: the weak die, and the carnivores keep the herbivores down. Townfolk haven't lived on a working farm. Dad was the nearest thing to a rural farmer I've ever known – nothing intensive, he farmed for fun. Yes, he killed his chickens, sent his calves to the slaughter-house, and when his cows looked sick he shot them. There's never any sentiment in farming.

There are just too many people. Even up in the dales it's wall-to-wall people. That overpopulation means we have lost our green lanes and our meadows. But at least babies aren't dying any more. The parish registers are very sobering – one baby in four survived, if you were lucky.You hanker back to the 'good old days' because you forget the bad bits. Yes, there were lovely green lanes, you probably could wander through the meadows, but my mother-in-law says there was just as much rape and child-molesting, you just didn't talk about it.

I think the stocks were a good idea; shame is proper punishment. I'd rather have shame than blood. If you flog people you brutalise them. You brutalise them by sending them to prison. I'm quite sure it's a waste of time. Once you've gone to prison you've had it. Flogging might have done the trick for the Victorians, but I should think the stocks, to be ridiculed, is much more effective.

People move into a village and they forget that country people are different. Slow-spoken, gentle, nice people. One of the smart set called one of our farmers a 'bloody peasant'. I blew up. I said, 'I'm sick to death of your sanctimonious attitude. Who the bloody hell do you think you are to speak about people like that!'

Being a small village is neither here not there – people divide into factions wherever they are. Wherever you are you build up a community, it's just that people have preconceived ideas which are wrong. Like the people who fled to London because they thought the streets were paved with gold. Rather a shock when they got there!

'The fault, dear Brutus, lies not in our stars but in ourselves'

... It's what *you* make out of where you live. If you want to have a community life in Swanbrooke Down you can – you just get yourself involved. I don't honestly mind what other people do; leave me alone and I'll leave you alone! I'm very unpopular in the village – I'm always causing offence. I float through causing one sort of discomfort or another. There was this protest about dog excreta on the footpaths, and I bought a plastic one and put it on the chief protester's lawn! It's so silly – where do you expect the poor animals to go?

MAURICE MANSFIELD

Vicar

The vicar of Swanbrooke Down is a small, neat man with an earnest expression and a soft voice. A roundish face, bespectacled, he emanates an air of an intellectual, and speaks with a particular beauty of expression. Words appear to be the tools of his faith; whether in conversation, as here, or in church as he recites the litanies, his voice falls into instinctive cadences which caress the ear. His funeral services are masterly.

But Maurice Mansfield is not often seen in Swanbrooke Down. His job extends over three parishes and he visits the village only for Sunday services and to comfort the sick and bereaved. His gentleness of manner belies an austerity of attitude, which generally speaking is not popular amongst the inhabitants. They crave a more sociable, pastoral clergyman, more lightweight and extrovert. They are frequently to be heard comparing Maurice with Canon Williams, a genial man of the people who could down a whisky with the best of them. Yet 'to know him is to like him', as many of the villagers have said. The pity is that not many folk *do* know him except by sight; and then only because he is seldom to be seen out of his black cassock.

Maurice's interview was in striking contrast to the others. Although we were discussing the same issues, it could almost be said that he was responding in a different language. This stood out in some relief, in both senses of the word, touching another dimension. To some extent it vindicated his not altogether happy position. His thinking is on a different plane, making a fascinating finale to 'the way we live now'. A voice in the wilderness, perhaps.

I cycled to the vicarage in Haverley on a perfect August day – high blue sky, light wind, hot afternoon sun. The harvest fields were teeming with activity: combine-harvesters made their heavy, noisy, dusty way over the wheatfields, leaving neat stubble behind. Tractors with trailers laden with harvested seed trundled down the lanes. Men prepared to burn the stubble; straw-balers were at work.

August has its own particular colours: the leaves on trees and hedges are dark dark green by now, old green. The stubble-fields are pale straw-gold, edged with stately hogweed, creamy white. Lavender comes into flower in gardens, attracting clouds of white butterflies. The sky has lost the intense blueness of June and July. In the sultry evenings a huge low sun casts elongated shadows as it sinks behind the hedge-lined horizon, and twilight lingers until the moon rises. Nocturnal moths, multi-dun-coloured, flutter softly around my lamp late into the evening.

Priesthood and the faith-life

Maurice Primarily I'm a parish priest. I'm not a social worker, nor a do-gooder, nor an administrator: I'm first of all a parish priest.

That does of course incorporate a pastoral role. A priest takes his priesthood from Christ, and one of the fundamental qualities Jesus portrayed was his pastoral care and interest in people. I suppose you could say that the setting in which my priesthood operates is people. Part of my priestly work therefore is pastoral; another is to assist in the formation of the faith-life of the church community, in order that Christians, at whatever stage of development in their faith-life, may see that development as a journey.

Some of my parishioners are at the heart of the church's life, others are on the edges, others aren't involved at all. There are some who are actively against. It is inherent in my work to be open to all of them. For example one part of my job is to conduct services like marriages or funerals. Not everybody who gets married in church is at the heart of the life of the church. I give the same care – or I think I do! – I show the same interest in the happiness they are hoping for, to people on the fringe as to people at the heart of it. It may mean different things to those groups, but I am interested in people at whatever point they might be on their journey. That's part of how I try to respond to whoever I meet.

Listening is fundamental to being a priest. It's a fundamental part of counselling, and that comes into my work a great deal; listening to things which are not immediately very significant but have a habit of turning out to be very important. Every meeting can be a moment of grace, not just a casual encounter. The immediate meeting may not seem important, but it may be laying the foundation for something. Perhaps, later, somebody will want to tell you something that has been on their heart for years. So absolute confidentiality is another fundamental part of my work. I lose my integrity immediately if that is not understood. All those things are part of my life and work.

Part of my priesthood is to try to tease out what is fundamentally important to people in their lives, to see if they have any religious awareness at all. I try to ask the kind of questions that might lead them to say, 'Yes, well that's not all there is to it.' Sometimes that leads on to people saying, 'I'd really like to know more about this.' I am also involved with small groups of people in their formation of the Christian faith-life. I keep talking about 'faith-life' because it makes religion an active, dynamic thing, not a static thing that you have *done* to you. It's about growth and depth and maturity and awareness.

I have to be there, not just as a resource person, but as someone who is himself involved in this process of journeying and trying to understand what I mean by trying inadequately to be a Christian. That can involve trying to learn how to pray better, trying to understand the meaning of worship, trying to understand what my response to living humanly in the world as a Christian *is* at, say, seven years old, fifteen years old, mid-life and towards death. A lot of my work brings me in touch with people close to death, and who die when I am involved with them. Which brings me to the area of bereavement and the grief process, which is quite a large part of my work. It's central to what I do.

The experience of death affects people in different ways, but it's still *death*, and it's happening to *people* whoever and wherever they are. In a country parish like this I have probably had more contact with them than in a very large parish. But the expression of emotions that go with the experience of death, that's not different. Different cultures express it differently. The culture here is perhaps a little reserved – unfortunately, I think. I believe that grief is not something about which you should say, 'I ought to hold tight'. You ought to let go as part of the grief process. I've been to burials where the whole service is a kind of wailing. It never bothered me. If the feelings hadn't been expressed they might well have caused great trouble later on. The bottling up of things is not normally helpful.

People approach death differently, and not all of them in ways which confirm faith. Certainly some people have told me their feeling of being at peace with themselves; I have been with some people as they died who have had a great sense of restfulness. Where people have died violently or in great pain – less common now, with drugs to help – it has not been quite the same. Often relatives who were present have experienced a closeness at those later moments. One thing that can bring together people who love each other very much and are to be separated by death, is for them to be as honest and open about what is happening as possible. I realise that some people have to be careful about that; but all through one's life one hopes to be honest and open with the person one is closest to; I find it sad when people at this crucial moment say, 'I don't want them to know.'

I first wanted to be a priest in my early teens; I'm the only member of my family who is a priest. I don't think I had a very mature approach at first. I was attracted to the historical people I had seen being priests, particularly in East London. I was brought up within the church, although like most teenagers I went off everything! Then I did my national service in the RAF and went off the whole idea. I didn't stop going to church, but the idea of ordination just went away. I decided I wanted to be a teacher; I would have been the world's worst! I was accepted at teacher training college, but all through my training I kept in contact with the life of the church. Towards the end of that it suddenly became clear that teaching was not what I was meant to be doing. I asked to have my vocation tested by the church, and was accepted for training. I believed and still do that there was a definite invitation from God for me to do this job, which was tested by the church. I was ordained at about twenty-four, so I've been ordained twenty-five years.

I was vicar of North Woolwich before I came here, – in fact it was the Royal Docks, now famous for quite another reason than shipping! It was a downtown parish, but with the marvellous sense of community East London has always had. Many people would say that this is breaking down now, but I lived and worked in Bethnal Green and Stepney, and places like that have always had a great sense of family identity. My parish was a mixture of high-rise flats and terrace houses. As people now realise you can't set a terrace on its side and expect the same kind of community. But the community sense in East London is very powerful, compared with the countryside. I had a brand-new church with a community centre attached. About two thousand people used it. I had three staff, two paid and one voluntary, with a lot of local voluntary help. It just wasn't true that because it was the inner city, nobody knew each other!

When I came here ten years ago there was still a residual sense of family, but almost as soon as I came people who had been here a long time were beginning to say, 'It's not like it used to be.' But it's a much looser-knit community now; the things that hold people together are more tenuous. Perhaps that's true of every community, bearing in mind how our lives have changed with the motor car, television and so on. Those things connect us more with the global village than with our own community.

I did get a sense of community consciousness, and it is still there, up to a point. Village people at the heart of organisation in the community say it is the same faithful few who run things, and that there is real difficulty in carrying on what may have started *so* long ago. I feel it in the church, too, certainly in Swanbrooke Down. There are two reasons why the church community here is very small. One is that many elder members have simply died, the other is that several members have left the area and not been replaced. Why? is the question I am working with! I would be a bold man if I could say I knew the answer. There are indications, and I am trying to reflect on them. People who move in may not have had church connections anywhere else, therefore they are not immediately going to say, 'The church is where I want to belong, whatever else I belong to.'

Perhaps the Christian faith does not have the hold on people that it had in the past. But what did people mean by Christian faith? Whenever that golden age was when it had a hold on them, was it simply that there was nothing else to do? At one time the church was pretty good at providing social activities. But was the faith-life, the heart of Christian faith, never sufficiently part of one's normal living responses; so that, like many things, it was set adrift once you found something else interesting to do?

At one time the village *had* to go to church because of the 'lord of the manor' approach; the servants and so on *had* to go. As soon as they were free from that compulsion, if it hadn't got a hold on them they were naturally happy to be free. Another possibility is that faith is not so important to people today. They are not quite sure what faith means. I am sure that the church has some responsibility for people not knowing what faith is.

Our modern age has seen a general secularisation. New idols are replacing the old, and materialism has a very strong hold on people's lives. 'Getting on' is the bottom line. I've never quite understood what that means. Creature comforts are our points of reference; one other reason, perhaps, why religion and the Christian faith are at a low ebb. But Christianity doesn't deny the importance of matter – this is a central part of the Christian incarnational thinking. It does however challenge people's putting these things first, especially when so many people in the world are without basic necessities.

The image of the church can often have been off-putting too – I'm trying to be generous! So there are many reasons for the low profile of the church at the moment. But people will always find an excuse for not wanting to be involved. There are many proper reasons which ought to be reflected on – that's what I mean by trying to be generous – but there's also an 'I can't be bothered' approach from people, which is not a worthy route for any of us.

I don't think I would find my job easier, or do it better, if I were vicar of only one village. In today's world villages are too small to have one priest in one place. I realise that many people would disagree, but I spend some afternoons knocking on doors, and there's nobody there. The man's at work, the woman is often out doing some hobby, or she's at work too, because almost everybody has a car, except for the elderly. A lot of elderly people will say, 'I really am stuck nowadays unless somebody will take me to the shops.'

I have always tried to see my job not in an individualistic sense. I may be a significant part, but I'm *only* part of a team of people, whose talents, abilities, interest and enthusiasm are often far greater than mine. I have a significant contribution to make, but it's *not* to be a jack-of-all-trades! Sadly, many clergy have been looked upon as jacks-of-all-trades. Some have been happy so to be. The initiative has concentrated round one man. Sometimes he is very talented and can make all kinds of things go on. Others cannot do everything – quite rightly; why should one man be expected to do everything? But the concept of a working team-partnership has not been a normal part of church life. We need re-education, to see that everybody, certainly in the church, has a contribution to make, not just people like me. It's very difficult to get that over, and much more difficult in the countryside, because of the legend of the local vicar personifying the community life, let alone the church life. People have this myth that this is the heritage.

In the city and the town things change quickly and have to be accepted quickly. More happened in a week, in London – changes would occur which take *years* in the country, shifts of attitude included. Someone could have been murdered one day, and there were all the things to deal with around that. The next day the vicarage door-window might be broken – it happened once or twice a month. A factory could have been closed down. So seeing the local vicar as the one man who coped with it all was just a nonsense. But things are beginning to change in the countryside.

Do country people feel they *need* a vicar today? It depends who you mean by 'country people'. There aren't all that many *country* people left. The people who live here? A lot of people here have never had much contact with the church or the clergy. I think you had better ask them whether they want or need a vicar! It's unfair of me to assume what they may say. Certainly this village – and I don't think it's alone – doesn't seem to be attracted to what the church *is*. Apart from certain events in the building, there is no great interest in the life and work of the church.

Many people here have extremely responsible jobs. Their work brings them considerable conflicts in certain areas of decision-making. I get the feeling – acknowledging the exceptions – that a Christian response, and what the Christian faith might have to say about those matters, is seen as irrelevant. Are they reflecting in a Christian way upon these dilemmas?

So where will the next generation learn from? What concerns me is the way people have to make decisions nowadays. People in responsible positions, in politics and everything else, almost seem to have to make decisions on television! It is the media approach to everything; you need the right word at the right moment when millions are looking at you. There seems to be no time for reflecting. You are watching an aircraft being hijacked and having to think what is going to happen in four or five countries if you do or say this or that. What is happening to the human beings involved? Where are the processes of reflection taking place?

You can take it, writ small, right down to the family level. The family that has a meal together nowadays is an exception. Either the television does the talking, or they're not there – they're on the 7.45 train that's three hours late, or they've got to get out to this or that function. When do they actually meet? That's a central part of Christian faith-life, and a very important part of what I do, and encourage people to think about.

People need to be *taught* about stillness and silence – it doesn't come naturally to sit still and be quiet. I have a contemplative prayer group, that meets once a month for an hour, and being still is a significant part of it. It saddens me that it's difficult to do it alone, but it can be done, if you give the time. People are willing to do other things, but they neglect some things that would really be beneficial! They will have trivial reasons for not doing them. People are out of touch with their feelings, their thinking and their imagination – with their bodies even. Silence is a way of getting in touch with ourselves again.

The spiritual direction I am involved in is in accompanying someone on their journey in their faith-life. This means sharing how one views God, how one's prayer is seen, how it affects one's development, how it affects worship, and how it affects everyday decisions. The framework of your life develops as you move towards God. I am involved a great deal in this kind of work, including retreat work, which includes a deepening understanding of stillness and silence. I think the absence of these in so many people's lives is detrimental. It's quite worrying how people cannot be without blaring noise in the background. My children find it difficult to do their homework without music; a whole new culture is obliterating the positive aspects of stillness and silence. It's deforming to the soul. I have always been interested in stillness and I have never been afraid of silence. I have never wanted to run away from it.

I am sad that more people don't feel able to cross the bridge into seeing other people as sharers in this journey. Some people feel they have to have a 'right answer', or that they're not really competent. If people are on a journey, every little thing on that journey has a significance. I spend hours listening to people's faith stories, from childhood on. That is what people are about. I can be myself in this work, as well. I don't have to be this figurehead in robes that performs – although I realise that's not unimportant.

A village community reflects society at large – or at least that of south-east England. I'm uncertain how typical you can say this is of the 'countryside' – which countryside? The mixture of people in this village is fairly monochrome in its class structure, and getting more so, because the people who were born and bred here are dying out. What happens when a community becomes more monochrome? It can lose vitality perhaps.

I try to say that people all have their shutters up. Those shutters come away quicker on some people in some communities, sometimes they take longer. I do see part of my job as visiting people who *aren't* churchgoers – and I don't have to go looking for work! A lot of the contacts I have are from people who don't go to church. It isn't true that I spend my time solely with people who go into the building. If it's appropriate to invite non-attenders to join in, then I do; if I'm listening to them and there's a spark of contact, something in their past perhaps, and it seems right to say, 'Can we talk about that?', or let them tell me a bit more, I take the opportunity. I don't go barging in saying, 'Why don't you go to church!' Some people can get away with that, but it's not me, and I wouldn't work like that.

A YOUNGER GENERATION

As summer waned, the chestnut by my thatch turned red-gold, and purple clumps of Michaelmas daisies stood tall in cottage gardens. Spiders' webs glistened in the light morning frosts; a chill dampness crept into the evening air. I spent these weeks of early autumn talking with the young wives of the village, walking around Swanbrooke Down in the dank stillness of late September and early October. Limp leaves dripping, yellowing, over the bramble which was heavy with ripe blackberries. Behind the leaded window pane of Grace's cottage stood her autumnal vase of nerines, dramatic pink lilies which defied the subdued, dying tones of the aging year.

I approached a dozen young women, from mid-twenties to late thirties, all of them married, with a list of structured questions, to elicit an 'average' response to aspects of living in a village.

Of the twelve, one had lived in Swanbrooke Down for only seven months, while one spanned nineteen years. Most had lived in the village for between two and six years. Half of them hoped to remain there 'for ever', the others expected to stay for between two and ten years. They came from all over the country, although a fair number were from East Anglia and the Midlands. Three had never lived in a village before.

They were a predominantly middle-class sample, their

husbands being scientists, businessmen, money-dealers, a doctor, publisher, quantity surveyor, chemical engineer, merchandise manager, art-studio director, environmental health officer and builder. Only two did not go out to work, the others having part-time jobs including librarian, lab technician, youth worker, secretary, personal assistant, beauty therapist and teacher. One, a book-keeper, worked full-time, but she was the youngest, and the only one who did not have children. Half had had full-time careers before starting a family; two had been nurses, the others in occupations including clothes technologist, book-designer, buyer and bank-clerk.

The principal reason for moving to Swanbrooke Down was its proximity to the train line to London, where their husbands worked, or because the men had moved to jobs in nearby towns. Most of them had found the village 'by accident'. They had all chosen a village in preference to a town, although their reasons varied. Some had 'always lived in a small community', some felt it would be 'easier and better for bringing up children'. Others wanted to escape the pressures of town-life, and the response 'for peace and quiet' was universal. Some had a romantic notion of 'thatch and roses', and 'always wanted to live in a village'.

All of these women had their own cars; two families had three or more cars. They all shopped in the supermarket in Kings Tarrant, apart from three who went further afield. Only two used the shop in Haverley.

Their social life was relatively unadventurous: two couples went out only at weekends, while most of the others went out once during the week as well. Only one couple was out as much as four nights in the week, usually in the pub. When they did go out it was to have supper with friends, or in a restaurant. Only three mentioned the theatre or cinema, one played bridge, and some mentioned school- or work-related functions.

When it came to leisure time, more than half listed gardening as a priority, and other activities included tennis, walking, cooking, bellringing, riding, working in the house – and sleeping. All families, except one which watched none at all, watched television for an average of two hours per night, and all claimed that their watching was carefully rationed. Only one listened to the radio 'all the time', others tuned in for a couple of hours every day. Four listened to no radio at all, but most who did chose

Radio 4 as their favourite programme, with Radio 2 a close second. Two tuned in to Radio 1; Radio 3 didn't get a mention.

At weekends they visited friends, took the children swimming or on an outing, went shopping, tended the garden, did DIY around the house, went sailing, riding, walking or played tennis, read the *Sunday Times*, and slept. Most went out regularly on a Saturday evening. Holidays were spent in the Lake District, France, the West Country, Bournemouth, Australia, Isle of Man, Northumberland, Greece, Wales, Ireland, Majorca, Portugal and Crete.

The general feeling was that social and recreational opportunities for children were limited, but that they had expected this. There was enough for children to do up to the age of about twelve, with the youth club and the Haverley Cub Scouts; but after that age, unless they were into horse-riding, there was nothing. It was 'perfect' for tiny children.

They rated Swanbrooke Down very highly for prettiness, but low on 'convenience'. Although they had all found it easy to enlist help for work in the house, gardeners were described as 'gold dust'. On a scale of 1 to 10, the village scored an average of 7 for character and 8 for friendliness. Some felt that in spite of surface charm it was pretentious and suburban, and that the younger people had snobbish attitudes. Although they found the older people friendly, they had thought it would be friendlier than it had turned out. They all felt that it was 'just the right size'.

In spite of rating low for convenience, the young women did not avail themselves of everything on offer. They used the post office once or twice a week, but half did not use the mobile library. Only one used the grocery van; the pub was frequented by some three times a week, by others just once a month or 'occasionally'. Half never went to church, a few went to the major festivals, and only one went as regularly as once a month. None used the bus service, and only one bought fish from the van. Two used the delivery service from Haverley's mini-supermarket regularly, and two used it at Christmas. When asked what facilities they would like to see in Swanbrooke Down, they mentioned a Sunday school, a village shop, and a recreation area. Only one said she would like street lighting.

The question 'How many people in Swanbrooke Down do you visit regularly?' elicited a varied response. The three who had lived longest in the village claimed ten or twelve; four others said four to six, two said three, one said she visited only one, and two said none. Most got on reasonably well with their immediate neighbours, although they made comments like 'never see them', 'they are nosy', 'she doesn't know who I am after seven years'. Only one person was not on speaking terms with one of her neighbours; otherwise a tolerant and co-operative attitude prevailed.

Only one woman belonged to the WI. Two-thirds of them used the playgroup, and ten went regularly to village events. Two had served on the parish council but the others had nothing to do with village politics or the church. Five were bellringers, and a few sent their children to the youth club. One was involved in editing the *Village News.* They all felt that these activities were a valuable part of community life, and gave them a sense of belonging. They did however feel that the same people invariably organised and attended these functions. They all felt there were enough community activities, but suggested that more could be organised for the children and that people tended to 'lead their own little lives'. When asked whether Swanbrooke Down should have its own school, they all said how nice that would be but that the village was too small. None of them was interested in local history, but most said they would prefer to settle in one place rather than move around.

The row about the developer's offer of a recreation field in return for his housing development was still reverberating, so when asked about expansion in the village the women had their thoughts well-marshalled. Most said that a gradual 'in-filling' was inevitable, but they didn't necessarily want it. None wanted large-scale development, or even a small estate, feeling that it would be difficult for the community to absorb. But it was generally felt that a little building here and there would be healthy for village life.

ADVANTAGES OF VILLAGE LIFE

Getting to know people better than in a town; being out of the city bustle – and the fact that you are supposed to have nice walks on your doorstep. The general quality of life.

Laura

I can relax and unwind, because village life is what I am used to. I would be out of my depth in a town – I'm not used to umpteen locks on the door. I couldn't tell you where the back door key is – I don't believe we still have it.

Stephanie

Being away from town traffic and able to live in your own home as you wish, not slap-bang up against a neighbour. The children are safe playing outside. To be in the fresh air, to be able to walk my dog and look at the trees.

Felicity

You feel on your own without being on your own. You get to know faces to wave to.

Clare

The quiet; the friendliness. I enjoy being in the country and feel secure there. I like the community life, and feel strongly about the children being brought up in a village because I was. It's a very rich way of life. They learn to be friends with people of all ages. And it looks pleasant – it's nice to come home to!

Helen

We wanted to bring our children up without bars on the windows and security alarms. Some people say, 'You're not preparing them for the real world' – but the 'real world' isn't that wonderful to be prepared for. We can live a quiet family life.

I'm on my own all day, and the village gives you a secure feeling; there are people next door and round the corner and over the road. Some people think you might feel isolated in winter, but I think city life is far more isolated than a village.

Elaine

When I lived in a town I knew hardly anybody. Since I've lived here I've made so many friends. If I was in trouble, or wanted someone to talk to, there's half-a-dozen people I could pop round and see.

Elizabeth

I like the peace and quiet of the countryside, and I like to have a distance between me and my neighbours. The kids have been brought up to be happy doing their own thing – they make their own amusements, and don't have to have hordes of people around, so I am not on the hoof all the time taking them to this and that.

Henrietta

If it wasn't a happy place I wouldn't stay. You tend to think it is a backwater, but it reflects national preoccupations on a small scale. Everybody watches everybody else so some of the major problems – vandalism and violence and drugs – don't affect us. There's more private entertainment here and children don't have those opportunities to get into trouble. Discipline of the children is good, because everybody is helping everybody else. Kids can't get away with things, because they are not anonymous.

It's very easy to get to know people, and for older people, or if you have problems, the village is a very good place to be.

Teresa

Village life incorporates all the things you have to search for in London, above all friendliness. In a big city you've got to work hard to find it.

It's lovely to have a view, but you're not entitled to it: as long as you appreciate that, that's good. Also, you tend to get a cross-section of people in a village, whereas in London you choose your area and the area dictates the sort of person who comes in.

Belinda

DISADVANTAGES OF VILLAGE LIFE

The place, to live in, is so dead. To come home to it is fantastic – I can see my husband's point of view – but not to live in 24 hours a day!

You think you'll be living in the country, with fields and fresh air; but there are no pastures, nothing the children can enjoy. You step off the footpaths and the farmers are after you. They must have binoculars fixed to their noses. The air is so polluted by the farmers that it's certainly not fresh – you can't even go for picnics. They must improve the facilities – you can't just keep putting people in here without facilities.

Your life is spent carting kids to and fro. You cannot let the children go on their bikes – they drive like loony bins round here, and the roads are so narrow.

Janet

There's nowhere to take the children for a picnic or a ramble. It's a great disappointment that while you're living in the countryside you haven't got access to it. It's inconvenient too; no shops, and having to go everywhere in the car.

Elizabeth

People come in just for their quarter-acre of picturesque beauty; they don't particularly want to be involved in the community. They see a pretty village, a pretty house, and think, 'I'll invest in this, and in two years we'll go on to something bigger and better and just as pretty.' Having said that, some come with that idea and *do* get involved and don't move.

You have to be prepared to go everywhere for whatever you want. Nothing gets delivered like it used to.

It's very bad for the kids constantly to get into Mum and Dad's car to go everywhere. It would be better if they could take a bus sometimes.

Helen

What surprises me is that when you go through the village in the middle of the day, during the week, you see hardly a soul. There don't seem to be many folk walking about. I met somebody one morning opening up the church, and they had driven from one end of the village to the other!

Stephanie

I expected there to be country people here – or at least country-loving. But a lot don't care about the country, they just want to use it – or to say that's where they live because it sounds good. People who fancy living in the country and try to become the gentry.

Henrietta

One of the things that disappoints me is that a number of people don't stay long enough. The houses aren't big enough for growing families, and aren't near enough to the secondary schools. There aren't any local shops. Also, if neighbours don't get on it's more obvious in a smaller community.

Being forty miles from London, it is becoming an area just for those who can afford high property prices, which might give it an air of artificiality, suburbia even. It's all very well having a beautiful place to live in, but it's nothing if it hasn't got anything under the surface, no character. If we incorporate people who go elsewhere for entertainment then village life isn't of particular value. It's a shame that a lot of new people don't join in; they *could* enjoy going to Cambridge or London *and* having our own entertainment here.

Belinda

THE RURAL IDYLL

It's not a rural idyll. I thought that there would be more fields for the children to play in, but I can't even let the dog off the lead because there's no pasture land.

Janet

It is very much a 'yuppie' village. It is a false society because you have much the same class of person throughout, whereas in an ordinary village there is more of a social structure. People here are much more sophisticated. After living in a town they decide they rather like the 'rural idyll' associated with living in a village. But jeans and sloppy jumpers are frowned upon here – it is much more the Porsche-belt!

Laura

I don't think of it as an 'idyll' – it is my way of life. I find it amusing when people tear their hair because it is raining, or because they can't get to school when the ford is flooded. To me, that is what living in the country is all about. It is mud on my wellies, soaking-wet dogs, children covered in mud from head to foot and having to be hosed down in the backyard before they come in. It is being able to leave the door open, and let the children out in safety. Generally it is a much slower pace of life.

Felicity

It is a picturesque, chocolate-box village. I'm sure everyone who drives through thinks, 'I would love to live here; this is just what I imagine village life to be like.' Some people are trying to make it like that, but they can't re-create what village life was like in the past.

Clare

We felt it was quite a 'find' when we arrived here. We thought we'd arrived in Paradise. We drove down the lane, saw this house, and decided within three minutes that we were going to live here. I thought it was just lovely. Before we moved, I would drive here to show friends the house. It was shrouded in trees and shrubs and I think they wondered why I was so excited! But sometimes you know what is right for you. I suppose it was for me a fulfilment of the 'rural idyll'.

It is a pretty village and people will pay right over the top to live here. But it is also very phoney. My husband is used to living in a village and he would never go out and buy himself a Barbour, green wellies and a Range-Rover to pose as a country chap!

Elaine

When we first saw this sweet little cottage it was like a dream. Seven years later I still like it here. It's even better than I expected because of the friends I have made. The only thing is that although we are surrounded by open space and fields, we can't use any of them. There's no open space for the children to play in, let alone discover the countryside.

Elizabeth

The 'rural idyll' does perhaps exist somewhere: not here though! What with tractors trundling past from morning till night, cars tearing down the road, farm machinery, bird-scarers, planes going overhead – hardly the sounds of the country!

Teresa

Unfortunately a lot of people are in search of the 'rural idyll' because they think it is the 'thing to do'. They reach a certain level in their career, and then they want to become one of the landed gentry, and so try to become something that they're not. That sort of person doesn't fit in. They haven't got the basic attitudes to country life. The only way you could really have true country life is to live in a house all by yourself, miles from anywhere, surrounded by countryside and away from everything.

Henrietta

The 'rural idyll' is a myth. I've always lived in villages and I know what village life is like. I simply prefer the country: I'd rather have the sound of the birds and the odd tractor than heavy traffic thumping past. But I had no illusions that it would be an idyllic life-style.

Laura

The 'rural idyll' is one of those pictures that has been painted in pretty colours. It's a hard thing to find – and I'm not sure if it still exists at all. Swanbrooke Down is perhaps close to it: it's very pretty and it doesn't have the constant roar of traffic. 'Rural life' goes on, but it's no longer that old rustic thing that is untouched by the outside world – now big lorries come in and out of the farmyard, not just the tractor and the haycart! That's a thing of the past.

Julie

The 'rural idyll' exists in the imagination. The more you worry about having it the more neurotic you become, so much so that in the end you don't appreciate what is actually *there* before you. You become so obsessed by what is happening at the back of your garden – noise, building or whatever – that you worry constantly. You shouldn't look for the cracks or think about what *might* happen, otherwise whenever you sit in your garden and hear a noise, you will think, 'Where did that come from?' 'Who is doing what?' 'Do they have planning permission?' 'Is it going to affect us?' You are more likely to put up with that in London, because it is happening all the time, and you expect it to happen.

The 'rural idyll' is based on false expectations: the bucolic image of rustics with straws hanging out of the corner of their mouths, herding sheep along the village street. If that's what you want then you're forty years out-of-date and you might as well do away with your washing machine and your dishwasher and the rest!

Belinda

I don't think the 'rural idyll' exists. It's a lovely idea, but it makes me cross when I look back. I was brought up in this area when apart from farmers and farm-workers, nobody wanted to live here. People were very poor and London was the fashionable place to live.

Our village was a tremendous place for kids. I could name everybody who lived there – that was one of the games we used to play. I remember the first commuters moving in, and the trouble and mistrust they caused trying to change things. It wasn't a bad thing really – the villages needed their affluence to survive – but now only affluent people can live in the villages, and young folk who are brought up in them can't afford to stay.

I do get cross when people who have moved here think that other people shouldn't be allowed to move in. You don't buy an environment with your home – it's not something that any of us *owns.* If jobs are going to be brought into the area, people have got to live somewhere. I don't want a housing development here any more than anyone else, but it is inevitable.

Swanbrooke Down will be all right because it is 'idyllic' – it has the charm of the Cotswolds, and will be kept as a place to visit and admire. It is the villages that aren't so pretty that will become developed.

Swanbrooke Down has an idyllic 'toytown' image, but this isn't true to life. We all shout at our children, have naughty dogs and aren't all rich. However, everybody is very friendly, and there's always somebody there to help you if anything goes wrong. That's wonderful and it's perhaps unique. But I don't know how much longer it will last because of the way that house prices are going up. From now on only certain types of people will be coming in. You only get the kind of community spirit we have here with a mixed community.

I feel sorry for our children today – they don't have the freedom that we did. I used to go out of the door at nine in the morning, come home for lunch, go out again and come home for tea. We used to just roam around: there wasn't the traffic there is today and we had no reason to fear strangers as hardly anyone came here. There were lots of meadows and we spent much of our time picking flowers, mushrooms and apples.

The 'rural idyll' that people have in their heads when they buy cottages here, is false. It's very suburban now. During my childhood it was still very rural – that was before commuters moved in. It was very interesting to notice the difference between them and us: we didn't have any fences and people's dogs strayed all over the place, but it didn't bother anyone very much. However, when commuters arrived, their attitude was: 'I don't want your dog on my garden!' 'This isn't tidy enough,' 'We won't win the best-kept-village-competition.' The local people weren't bothered by such things. It was the people coming in who were particular about how everything must look. They were importing their suburban values.

Helen

VILLAGE GOSSIP

There's an awful lot of back-biting; it's really quite bitchy. But there's also an active interest in people – who's gone into hospital or who's dropped dead – and you would be hurt if nobody told you.

Stephanie

I'm always the last to hear anything, but I prefer it that way. The nice gossip is fine – who is having a baby, who has a new car – but there is also a lot of perverted gossip. Apparently Ian and I were wife-swapping the other evening! It is just screwed-up people living in each other's pockets. It's best to keep your head down and not get too close to these people. It's the same in any village – there are a few who enjoy stirring things up.

Laura

I certainly don't gossip. I don't hear as much now as I did before my neighbour moved away; I used to rely on her for my in-fill.

Felicity

Although we don't have much contact with the village, when we *do* meet people there is a tremendous amount of gossip. It's nice gossip – it's part of their idea of social life, getting to know people and telling everyone about you!

Clare

There's not as much gossip as I would expect. In the old days, if somebody moved in you'd have known all about them before they came! People aren't as interested in each other – or pretend not to be! I'm really nosy. I love to know what's going on.

Helen

I tend to hear what gossip there is in the post office. Anything else is usually secondhand from the pub. There's enough flying around – probably too much. But that's just village life, and if you don't like something you hear it's best to forget it.

Elaine

In a way it's nice; when my mother died, everybody knew within a day or two, and they were all so kind. It's not nosy gossip; in a small community you have to expect that people know when you are doing things. If you get too involved, though, things become difficult.

Elizabeth

I'm simply not in the right places to hear malicious gossip – most of it goes on in the pub or at social events I'm not at. Doing the postal round I do hear things about what is happening to people in the village, as did Pauline before me when she was on the round – but by no means everything.

Teresa

I'm not interested in gossip. I hear enough news of what is going on. There is a lot of back-biting – possibly not as much as there was.

Henrietta

I hear a fair bit of village talk up this end, but if somebody dropped dead in the pub I might not hear for weeks. I'm not heavily into gossip. There's enough flying around to keep the village aware of what is going on, if that's what entertains you. But it only gets around if you let it out in the first place.

Julie

If there is back-biting I don't hear it. I don't especially want to know what's going on. Some news travels fast, but on the whole people are pretty good about *not* being nasty behind people's backs. There's a lot of concern, and tittle-tattle, but I rarely hear anything malicious. There's not too much trivial gossip or back-biting. I always say I never hear it – I wait for somebody from Haverley to tell it to me!

Belinda

COMMUNITY SPIRIT AND THE SOCIAL MIX

I've had to go out and look for the original village people in order to find friends. The people who have bought their way into Swanbrooke Down are particularly unfriendly; they are basically not villagers, they are town people. We haven't found much community spirit; in many respects it seems to be every man for himself.

We have not had so much as a knock on the door to say hello since we moved in. We use the pub a fair amount in order to meet people and make friends. We made a conscious switch from the saloon to the public bar. Prior to that, if we had moved out we wouldn't have missed anyone nor they us. The vicar hasn't spoken to us once, and here we are next to the church!

If you push your way in they push you out. I didn't expect it to be open house; I expected to have to bide my time if I was going to be accepted. But there is a 'them and us' situation: you have the sons and daughters of people who have lived here over the years, and the people who have moved in. One lot gets together in the pub, the others have dinner parties, and there's no link between the two.

Stephanie

The snobs spoil this village. It's very cliquey, very snobbish, and people who come here react to that. They are always on their guard, they're not themselves.

Janet

There's not a proper social mix here; you haven't the structured ranks of a proper village. In Devon you still have the farm labourers, and everyone lives in the one village. Here the cost of housing prices a lot of people out of it. As the older people die off it's going to become a much younger mix, and perhaps a more mobile society.

But generally the community spirit is very good. If you have a problem, people rally round, and they are very nice.

Laura

The indigenous population has gone to Hawthorn Hill, and the people who have come in are commuters, young, educated up to a level, the new consumer generation. They know what is what and they can afford it. They are Mr Conran's bread-and-butter, buying style, copying, trying to achieve a degree of social prestige. They follow trends; they madly resent the upper classes because they think they have got everything. They are creating their own dreadful level which must be ghastly for them because there are no guidelines.

I don't know about the community spirit because I don't take part in it, but it is probably very good. The conversations I have had have in no way made me want to join in. I have moved a lot and had to establish my own network at least six times, so I can't be bothered with trivial friendship. When you move in it is very appealing when everybody rushes up and says, 'Do come for a drink'. But in the first quarter of an hour comments were made which made my heart sink. I pitched my association with people I had more in common with.

It has everything to do with 'class'. I keep away from all village activities because they are run for and by people I consider completely out of place. Having been brought up in a much higher stratum I don't wish to have anything to do with them. They all earn quite a lot of money, and need to show it. There must be a name for this new class. They are welcome to their new-found social freedom but I resent them encroaching on me.

Some people term it a cliquey community, but if it is it doesn't affect me and I am not conscious of it. Cliques are to do with social alignment and I am not involved in that. With my background and home-life, my social life has developed through what I do and the people I know – working the old-boy network perhaps. You meet through school, you are selective along the way, you find your level and the quicker you learn to discard what you don't like, and pitch yourself within a fairly narrow band, the easier for you. It's the English way.

Felicity

We've got a set of commuters, we've got one or two of the poor people who they put up with, and we've got the nice old people. But I don't call that a good mix. There's a Hawthorn Hill divide; and the younger ones who move into the little cottages in Elmshaw Lane, they feel it too.

I don't think there's much community spirit. People are far too busy trying to make money. It changes too fast – you haven't got the stable core of people. You've got a lot of talkers, a lot of moaners, but you haven't got the doers.

There's a lot of jealousy, and there are a lot of bored women who want the rural life, but belittle the rural activities. It is not good enough to be seen knitting or gardening or playing with your children, yet they want to live in Swanbrooke Down.

Janet

The society is monochrome, and becoming more so. There's no changing that – it's due to economic forces. But although everybody is on the same material level, we all come from different backgrounds; if you peel off the top layer you'll find a lot of differences underneath. They've come from all parts of the country, they've had a different education, so it's probably more of a social mix than it appears.

I like all the old people here. Some of them have lived in quite a few of the houses and can tell you about them – all sorts of things that happened many moons ago.

A bit of in-fighting goes on which is much the same as most villages. It's a pretentious sort of village, because it attracts people setting themselves up as country people. It doesn't seem able to help itself. But it doesn't worry me what people do for a living, or where they come from.

Elaine

The older people, the genuine country people, have real community spirit. They actually care about other people in the village.

The social divisions are not just to do with money; it depends how people achieved their money – *nouveaux riches* want to make out they are somebody when they are not.

The Hawthorn Hill people are very nice; they have far more of a community up there, and seem to know each other better than we do down here.

There are lots of different social classes, but I don't think you would ever get them all mixing. You have one clique of those who socialise in the pub – and I don't mean the old boys. The amount they drink is beyond belief.

Henrietta

The community is a mixed bunch. They may not mix much, but there is variety. The Hawthorn Hill divide is certainly there – I haven't met a soul from up there yet. The established ladies make themselves known to you. I welcome that – they've done their bit for the village and they deserve credit.

It's a very cliquey village. The village we lived in before was much more of a unit. Here you've got the bellringing group, the pub group, the churchgoers and so on. If they were all in one room it would be very hard to break down these groups. Even if you put them all together and shook them, they'd fall into their little sections!

Julie

It is quickly sliding away to a very middle-class village. There's been so much movement in the past three years and the same people are getting fed up with doing everything. The new people don't seem to be as involved as the older ones were. But there is still a hard core of community spirit, though it may fold up if it doesn't get more support. Above all there's a good spirit of helpfulness. People like us who have been born and bred in the country both offer and accept help, because they had to; it was the only way they could survive when life was hard. There is a tremendous openness between country people.

Grace next door gets so many visitors in the winter to check that she's all right that she gets fed up with it! If her milk doesn't go in by nine o'clock they're all on her doorstep! But that's wonderful, because you hear of old people lying dead in their homes for days. The English are too reserved in coming forward to help each other – and we're not good at asking for help, either.

Helen

When we moved in seven years ago we had the recreation field, a cricket club, and a village obstacle race through the stream. Nobody would do that now.

Newcomers don't want to join in straight away – they take a while to settle in. You don't make friends overnight. With so many people coming and going it's difficult for the activities to be genuine. The minute it becomes forced, it's phoney, and people don't like it.

The people coming in tend to be more up-market. Their children hardly ever go to the local school, so they don't mix much. They don't make friends so easily because they don't have things in common. The only mixing is done at toddler-stage.

If you go into the pub you can talk to a farmer, to somebody who works in the City, somebody in marketing, a solicitor and, so on. Take the bellringers; there's a complete cross-section there. But it's a shame the older people are disappearing; when they go their houses will be bought by affluent families and renovated.

Elizabeth

The social mix is a bit heavier on the rich side, but they are all very genuine people. The people who haven't got money think there is more of a divide than the ones with money. Many of the latter couldn't care less what you've got. Some of the very young people have quite a bit – their houses are worth God knows what. But once you start comparing yourself with other people it all starts getting a bit negative. The 'them and us' situation between us on Hawthorn Hill and the village is more in people's minds up here, because they feel, 'Oh, those young things . . . ', and I can understand that.

People aren't too pushy, they are just interested enough; the rest is up to me. It's not over the top, but as soon as you move in people welcome you. I've never had that in a village before and it is fantastic. But I'm the sort of person who says, 'Hang on a minute; I've only just moved in!' It's a good job there are people like that about, though, or everybody would go their own way. People could become very distant. You need village activities to bring together all these different people.

Up here it's very friendly. I know many of the people up this end, and the Pilgrims are such good neighbours; we come home from work and find lettuces on the doorstep. You don't get that in many places.

Clare

NOVEMBER IN SWANBROOKE DOWN: ENDPIECE

A grey mist hangs over the valley as twilight descends. The village street is subdued and people go quietly about their business inside their houses. The stream, swollen with winter rain, gurgles under the bridges into the dormant fields. A pale sun struggles thinly through the ghostly trees. No birds sing.

The circling year closes around Swanbrooke Down; the reality and purpose of its existence are clarified – past and future seem contained in its present. The restless surge of human life, the complexities and strivings, passions and emotions, thoughts and dreams of men and women through the centuries come into focus. Nothing changes, yet everything changes. Everything is important, yet nothing is important.

A gentle wind shakes drips from the misty twigs, and a weak shaft of light illumines shapes of walls and gates and houses and chimneys. The daily domestic round continues in its banality and significance. As time and the seasons roll on, the people we have met here will move away or die or have more children or get married or paint the front fence or walk the dog or mourn somebody they love. They all will ultimately be forgotten; perhaps stone memorials in the churchyard will record a few of them; but who will remember them? The funeral monument of Sir Francis Gilbert and his wife in St Michael's reminds us; a voice from three centuries back speaks the one certain truth:

As ye nowe are so were we
As we nowe are so shall ye be
When ye remember us forget not your selves

As the afternoon light fades into evening Dora and Wilf sit by the fireside, reading; Grace writes a letter at her desk by the window, and the Colbrookes watch a TV programme. The pub lights come on, and Toby Wagstaff prepares the bar for another busy evening; Clarice draws a shawl around her thin shoulders and hugs her little dog to her for warmth; young mothers bath their children and cajole them to bed. Up on Hawthorn Hill coal fires are lit, curtains are drawn, and twists of smoke curl upwards into the darkening mist. A muffled silence descends on hill and valley as the village draws to the end of another day.

Scribners Scribners Scribners Scr
ners Scribners Scribners Scribner
Scribners Scribners Scribners Scr
ners Scribners Scribners Scribner
Scribners Scribners Scribners Scr
ners Scribners Scribners Scribner
Scribners Scribners Scribners Scr
ners Scribners Scribners Scribner
Scribners Scribners Scribners Scr
ners Scribners Scribners Scribner
Scribners Scribners Scribners Scr
ners Scribners Scribners Scribner
Scribners Scribners Scribners Scr
ners Scribners Scribners Scribner
Scribners Scribners Scribners Scr
ners Scribners Scribners Scribner
Scribners Scribners Scribners Scr
ners Scribners Scribners Scribner
Scribners Scribners Scribners Scr
ners Scribners Scribners Scribner
Scribners Scribners Scribners Scr
ners Scribners Scribners Scribner
Scribners Scribners Scribners Scr
ners Scribners Scribners Scribner
Scribners Scribners Scribners Scr